Surviving
The Age
of Fear

BY
WILLIAM D.
LANGLOIS
&
JOHN
O'CONNOR

PUBLISHING

A Division of WRS Group, Inc.
Waco, Texas

First published in the United States of America in 1993 by WRS Publishing, A Division of WRS Group, Inc., 701 N. New Road, Waco, Texas 76710
Front jacket photo source—Paul Bannister, Fleet Street West
Back jacket photo from Bill Langlois Collection
Book design by Kenneth Turbeville
Jacket design and photo manipulation by Joe James

10 9 8 7 6 5 4 3 2 1

Library of Congress Cataloging-in-Publication Data

Langlois, William D., 1934–
    Surviving the age of fear / by William D. Langlois & John O'Connor.
        p.   cm.
    ISBN 1-56796-013-8 : $12.95
    1. Langlois, William D., 1934–   . 2. Police—California—San Francisco—Biography. 3. Undercover operations—California—San Francisco. 4. Aged—California—San Francisco—Crimes against—Prevention. I. O'Connor, John, 1954 June 8– II. Title.
HV7911.L327A3 1993
363.2' 092—dc20
[B]
                                                        93-8927
                                                            CIP

To my family and friends
and all law enforcement officers.
Those that stand tall and those who had to fall.
Herein is the witness of my heart and of how it was.

—Bill Langlois

For Madeline

—John D. O'Connor

Chapter 1

CROSSROADS

The day after I had been robbed for the two hundred and fifty-sixth time, I was summoned to the Hall of Justice by Chief of Police Frank Jordan for a morning press conference, and what should have been the proudest moment of my twenty-eight years in law enforcement.

Instead, it turned out to be one of the most embarrassing.

To be absolutely correct, I guess I shouldn't say I was "robbed" all those times exactly. "Having a felony perpetrated upon my person" would be more precise. Over the ten-year period I was attached as victim officer to the San Francisco Police Department's Street Crime Unit and later its Robbery Abatement Team—known affectionately to those of us who served in it as "The Rat Unit"—I was beaten too often to count, kicked, thrown down a flight of stairs, and nearly stabbed by a transvestite who left a ten-inch butcher knife embedded in my belt.

In the course of a routine day, I could count on being assaulted at least once, maybe having my pocket picked, and more often than not, finding myself the object of the malevolent intentions of small squads of criminals who stalked me through the streets like lions trailing a wounded gazelle. During the unit's early incarnations I posed as an inebriate or derelict, slumped over in a doorway and waiting for a street tough to come along and take advantage of my seemingly unconscious state. And while I was successfully "robbed" over two hundred times while serving as decoy during those assignments, it was not until 1986 and later, 1987, that our strategy changed and I found myself in one of the most challenging, and potentially dangerous, roles of my career.

It was during those years that I took to the street not as Officer William Langlois, fifty-six years old and a still relatively fit and feisty ex-marine, but rather as a character I soon found myself calling "the Old Man." This was a character I patterned after the many older people I'd known or encountered while walking my normal beat assignment in the city's Taraval District. This character was to become more and more a part of me as time wore on.

The Old Man was born of a very special need. In 1986, when the crack cocaine epidemic was in full flood in our city, robbery investigators began to chart a string of violent, at times fatal, attacks on elderly citizens in the Tenderloin and Western Addition areas of town. Groups of young men and women, most of them ex-felons driven by the need to secure money for the instantly addictive drug, had keyed on the most vulnerable element of society, the elderly. These jackals were systematically following, beating, and robbing people—often in their own homes—in the belief that these brittle victims were less likely to resist or ultimately identify them in court.

At the height of this shameful epidemic, we were seeing as many as a dozen of these robberies each week. At least four ended in death for the victims. Most other victims were beaten so severely they had to be hospitalized. Their persecutors often lingered for hours, we learned, torturing these people in the most horrible of ways or killing their pets in an attempt to extract information about hidden valuables. Through it all, word began to filter down about a particularly evil robber. Our investigators began calling him "Whispers" because of the way he murmured assurances to his victims as he confronted them on the thresholds of their homes or apartments.

"It's okay," this creature would tell his terrified captives, his lips pressed close against their ears while one arm snaked around their throats. "Everything's going to be all right." And then he would push them inside, out of sight, and beat them unmercifully until they told him where whatever money they had was hidden. He would then leave the scene cleaner than he had found it, carefully obliterating any physical evidence of his presence.

When the robbery rate jumped twenty-five percent in the Tenderloin area alone, it was decided to reform the Robbery Abatement Team and send them out to target Whispers and the criminals like him who made a living from preying on the elderly. Working with a carefully selected crew of backup officers, I took to the streets to serve, essentially, as bait, walking the streets as the Old Man while my backup team monitored my every move.

With the aid of a little hair dye, spirit gum, and a few carefully selected props, I found myself settling into the role of a retired Russian merchant mariner, a World War II veteran, a disabled pensioner—a seventy-six-year-old man caught in the relentless grip of old age. Walking with a cane or hobbled by the orthopedic shoe I had purchased at a local hospital supply store, it was my job as victim officer to appear more defenseless, more vulnerable, than anyone else on the street that day.

I managed to accomplish this in a variety of ways. Falling down occasionally—all too aware that eyes were narrowing and heads were snapping around up and down the street as I hit the pavement—proved to be effective. I also drooled or carried on lengthy but disconnected conversations with myself. Everything I did during those long hours on the street was carefully tailored to give the impression that I was nothing more than a defenseless old man, easy picking for a thief out to score money for what more often than not turned out to be a raging drug habit.

Things went well. Maybe too well.

In the course of the Rat unit's latest incarnation in 1987, I actually walked the streets of the Tenderloin in my Old Man persona a total of thirty-three hours and forty-five minutes. In that time I was assaulted on nine separate occasions—once every 3.75 hours—by a grand total of seventeen people, many of them working in teams of two or more. One of them turned out to be the brother of a mugger who had assaulted me the year before. Just minutes after each assault, all of these people were scooped up by my ever-watchful backup officers, who from their vantage points were able to observe these crimes unfold from inception to culmination and who warned me of imminent danger through a one-way radio receiver I wore in one ear like a hearing aid. In 1986, my team netted twenty-six suspects who attacked me and a woman colleague in seventeen separate "hits." This after just two months on the street.

There was, as one might expect of undercover officers on a difficult assignment, a certain esprit de corps among the members of the RAT unit. Out of the peculiar black humor common to police officers, but also because our normal radio code names proved too long to use over the air, we soon began calling each other names which best described our roles within the team. Lt. John Brunner, the robbery detail commander assigned to coordinate our efforts in 1987, quickly became known as "Super Rat." Officer Tony Rockett, a street-smart officer normally assigned to Southern Station, was dubbed "Curb Rat" because it was his job to parallel my movements from the opposite side of whatever street I happened to be on at the time. There was "Cab Rat" and "Hooker Rat," a male and a female officer who played the undercover roles of a male cab driver—complete with borrowed taxicab—and his lady-of-the-evening passenger.

To these and other members of my team I quickly became known as "Rug Rat." This name caught on in 1986 soon after the first time a pair of would-be strong-arm robbers pushed my face into the carpet of the decoy apartment building we used as a sort of safe house for the Old Man. The experience was the first of many which would be repeated again and again in the months to come.

The day before the 1987 operation was finally closed and the unit disbanded for the last time, I set out on my normal route down Eddy Street in the heart of the Tenderloin. This is a densely inhabited area slightly less than a mile square—an area known for its hard-working, multi-ethnic community as well as for its appalling crime rate. Teeming with newly arrived immigrants from the then Soviet Union, Southeast Asia, and South America, the Tenderloin was a true melting pot, with well-patronized Vietnamese noodle houses doing business right alongside porn emporiums and crack cocaine dens.

The area had been my home for the last two weeks. I had no way of knowing that this day would be the last time I would walk its streets in character.

I had removed my dental plate as usual that day to help muffle my speech as well as to prevent further damage should someone punch me in the face. I was still sore from the day before—when I had been attacked and beaten by two separate packs who had stalked, assaulted, and robbed me within an hour and fifteen minutes of each other—and I didn't have to work too hard to affect a limp. On my last day as a decoy I was informed by Tony Rockett, watching from his usual position on the other side of Eddy Street, that three people had suddenly fallen in behind me.

"Careful, Bill," Curb Rat whispered over my radio receiver. "You got three of them behind you now. A male and two females, and they look anxious. They may try to take you down on the street."

I used a hand signal to show Tony I had gotten the message, as I moved on, mumbling and dragging my bum leg, careful to let the trio behind me see the hospital bracelet I wore on my right wrist. Come and get it, boys and girls, I thought to myself. Come and get it.

They followed me a total of four blocks, hanging back just far enough to keep out of sight and waiting until I entered the safe house apartment building at 400 Hyde Street. The last thing I heard over the radio was Tony calling out to the troops: "They're moving on him, people. It's sphincter-tightening time!" And then the three of them were on me, pushing me into the decoy apartment we were using, knocking me to the floor, and getting their licks in before "Closet Rat," Officer Ed Dullea, and "Room Rat," Officer Reno Rapagnani, rushed in as planned, shouting for them to freeze.

When the operation was first started, the decision had been made not to use service revolvers during arrests, our people fearing that any gunfire in cramped quarters would almost certainly endanger other officers as well as suspects. So Dullea, Rapagnani, and eventually others—armed only with their short batons and their brawn—pounced on the suspects. But the three would-be hunters, realizing that the situation had reversed itself and they were now the hunted, bolted from the building and ran outside— straight into the arms of "Hooker Rat" and others who had been alerted by radio.

Rockett signaled, "Code four, subjects in custody," as I pulled myself up from the floor, rubbed my face where one of them had hit me, and realized they had stolen my glasses. "I gotta get into another line of work," I muttered, earning a big grin from Dullea. As damaging as they had been, the blows I had taken during the course of the operation were better spent on me, I rationalized, than on someone whose bones were less likely to withstand the onslaught.

And in a way I figured all the abuse I suffered at the hands of thieves and robbers half my age was actually almost complimentary, a sort of bad guys' tribute to my fledgling acting ability.

The entire process, from the time the latest pack of thieves first began stalking me until the moment they were led away in handcuffs, had taken just ten minutes, the fastest recorded assault that anyone on the team could remember. But we had been compromised. While I was standing there licking my wounds, the decision was made to end the operation. All the activity of the past two weeks had not gone entirely unnoticed. Other undercover officers whose job it was to mingle with the street people had overheard the locals pointing to me on the outside and saying, "See that old man over there? He's a cop."

Offering me up as bait to those looking for an old person to rob was one thing. But once it was known on Eddy Street that I was a police officer, chances were that I would be running into a different breed of cat someday—someone bent on killing a police officer and not just on getting my wallet. Sadly, it had happened to others before, so we decided to shut it down.

On the way back to the Hall of Justice, I ran through some quick mental computations and realized that, if every miscreant who had tailed me "home" over the last two weeks had carried out their attack, there would have been seventeen hits instead of nine, and thirty-two suspects languishing in City Prison instead of seventeen. All those people after little more than a day of actual decoy time on the street! I couldn't help but wonder what it was like for the truly elderly people, the ones I've come to regard as living history books, who are forced to live out their lives day after day on the same street I had walked in an Old Man's shoes for only thirty-three hours.

Still, I was pleased and more than a little proud of what we had been able to accomplish. As far as I was concerned, we had taken seventeen people who had demonstrated a proclivity for beating and robbing elderly people and put them behind bars where they belonged. Every one of them was eventually sentenced to a long prison term and the RAT unit was able to boast a one-hundred percent conviction rate.

But perhaps the most satisfying—and most frightening—moment of my career came the day we turned the tables on a man I believe to this day was "Whispers." It happened just moments after he had thrown one arm around my neck and leaned close to my ear to tell me: "Don't worry. Everything is going to be all right."

I still get a chill whenever I hear that phrase.

Those thoughts were within me when I arrived at the Hall of Justice at Chief Jordan's request that morning in July 1987. It was hot, unseasonably so for San Francisco, and I arrived at the Hall as I normally did, parking in the back lot and entering the building through the rear door of the tactical division office. Most of the RAT unit were already there, laughing and kidding around in the squad room. Many of the eighteen team members were wearing their specially designed blue "RAT" T-shirts for the occasion. We were told we would be going before the cameras at nine.

I wasn't looking forward to the press conference, mainly because they always asked such stupid questions. It was all a little too much for me. I mean, how do you capsulize what you have been doing, thinking, feeling, all those long hours and days? The reporters wanted it packaged so neatly, and I always had a hard time answering because there was nothing neat about what we had just done.

I wanted to get dressed in my Old Man stuff, not so much to present myself to the media that way, but to cover the fact that I was going out on yet another undercover sting operation for the burglary detail that very afternoon. So I sat down and started putting on my makeup, slipping into the character again for what I knew would be the last time, adopting his mannerisms—the lolling tongue, the facial tic, the limp—as easily as another person would slip into a comfortable old shoe.

I was dressed by nine, choosing to wear my favorite beret and picking up the cane I had used several times on the street. Then word came down that the press conference had been postponed until ten, then eleven, and the tension began to build. In the interim I attended a small retirement party for my friend and colleague, Jimmy Meyers, who coincidentally had announced his retirement that same day. I had been with Jimmy for years in the department's canine unit, and the party was a very emotional thing even though everyone who attended did their level best to keep smiling and keep the old war stories coming. It got even hotter in the little room and my makeup started to run.

They had the cake in the squad office. When things got a little quiet, Jimmy and I talked briefly. Seeing him on his last day provided the real essence of something I had been feeling lately, a sense of finality, of a good thing coming to an end. It really touched me. My wife Kitty had been trying to get me to retire since the preceding year, especially after seeing me come home battered and bruised from my tour of duty with the team. "It's just not worth it," she would say. And while I argued the point at first, after a while I had to admit that the bruises and old bones just weren't healing quite as fast as they had at one time.

Seeing Jimmy off got to me more than I had expected. Whenever this kind of thing happens, people gather around saying goodbye, having cake and all, and you can't help but think that some day it will also happen to you. Some day you will also get a cake and a small party with people shaking your hand and slapping you on the back—and then you're out and eventually forgotten.

A little after eleven we got the word that the chief and the television crews were ready. We made our way upstairs to the police commission's hearing room, waited in a little anteroom until the press had set up their cameras, and then were ushered out to face them. Chief Jordan, sitting at a table with what looked like a forest of microphones on it, was talking as we filed out, the team stringing out in a line behind him. The glare from the camera lights was horrific, and I tucked my chin down low to help further disguise my face.

"Many of you know we have been having difficulties with strong-arm robberies and street robberies in the Tenderloin area," Jordan was saying. "We have had an increase there in the number of assaults on elderly victims.

"We reinstated the Robbery Abatement Team you see behind me to work in the Tenderloin area, particularly during the last fifteen days. Offering up a decoy officer as a target for prospective criminals, the team was involved in ten cases, the end result being seventeen arrests in about fourteen days. Many of these assaults occurred in broad daylight with as many as three people attacking a decoy officer made up to look like an elderly male who had just gone to the grocery store to pick up some groceries and was walking down the street to get to his apartment. Once the assault was started and the suspects began tearing at the clothes of our officer or punching him, then the backup officers moved in to effect the arrest."

It was a good show. The press was attentive and seemed to like what they were hearing. Several were peering at the surveillance pictures that "Photo Rat"—District Attorney's Investigator, Vanetta Pollett—had taken of me during the street robberies, the Old Man cowering and trying to protect his face from the blows.

I stood a little behind Lee Tyler, better known as "Cab Rat." Lee was a big, strapping guy, and I stared out at the battery of television camera lights from over his shoulder. Karen Hibbitt, another district attorney's investigator who rode in Lee's cab dressed as the team's resident *femme du pave*, was off to my left.

Jordan was still talking. "We initiated this program because of a twenty-one percent increase in robberies in the Tenderloin area, and from my point of view that's way too high. We have found that we have curbed that activity as a result of this program. Unfortunately, when you make this many arrests, word does begin to get out among the community, and we were forced to end this operation out of concern for our undercover officers.

"The average number of hours spent on the street before each arrest was about three, so it didn't take long. We wanted to make it known that we are not going to tolerate assaults on the street, particularly ones against those who are the most helpless, those who are senior citizens and who are not able to fight back."

I was sort of half-listening to what the chief was saying, my mind wandering back to Jimmy Meyers, the inevitability of my own retirement, and then, suddenly, for some strange reason, to an old man who had been beaten and robbed in his Tenderloin apartment many weeks earlier. An image pushed its way inside my head and stayed there. From that moment on all I could think about was the chalk outline the homicide investigators had drawn around the spot where this old man—whose name I couldn't remember—had fallen and later died.

We had used the apartment as a base for the Old Man during the RAT operation and I was once very nearly stabbed there. The mental picture of that little room, the outline on the floor, and the fear that its original inhabitant must have felt in those last lonely hours was suddenly so overpowering that I almost didn't hear the chief call my name.

"Bill," he said, motioning for me to come sit at the table laden with all the microphones. "Why don't you come up here."

I felt awkward, almost as if lost in some dream state. I tried to make a joke, which is my usual manner, and people laughed. But something was wrong. I just couldn't force the images of the man's apartment out of my mind. The television lights were hot and the reporter's faces were a blur. I reached the table, sat down, and started talking.

"What I wanted to say is that it is a sad thing in our society, really, that police officers have to resort to this sort of trickery in order to catch those people who are preying on our citizens," I said, improvising and starting out relatively well.

"And I suggest that the legislative bodies of this state and this country enact a law to the effect that anyone attacking a person over sixty years of age with any violence whatsoever, that these people be incarcerated for twice the length of time that is normal, that they don't consider these normal crimes and that they realize that the depredations upon these elderly people cause all sorts of trauma to them which never go away and which shorten their life spans."

I took a breath. Someone tossed me a question. I answered it, trying to concentrate. For some reason, my breathing had accelerated. I fought to clear my head and went on to the next thought in my mind.

"You, as members of the media, have given a lot of attention lately to a breed of dog known as a pit bull. These people, the ones who are exacting these depredations on the older people of this country, are the pit bulls of our society. They are as vicious, as heinous, as tenacious as any animal you can find.

"And I don't understand as an American, as an ex-marine, and as a twenty-four-year veteran of this department why the young men of our country for two hundred years have gone to fight in wars to preserve our way of life, and in the end the old people..."

The dead man had been a veteran. World War I. I saw the room again, the chalk outline, the stain on the carpet where he had fallen, the pale patch on the wall where the thieves who had beaten and robbed him and left him for dead found the picture where he had stashed his money and took it down, the bare patch behind where it had once hung so glaringly different from the rest of the wall.

The first sob was out of me before I could snatch it back.

"...the old people are set upon and their lives ruined." That was it. The memories were just too vivid, and they were coming much too fast for me. I used to sit in the dead man's apartment between hits. It hadn't been repaired since the murder, and I used to go there to recover. And I remember thinking at the time about who he was and who he had been, safely distanced by the callous protective barrier most police officers use to separate themselves from the potentially haunting sights they see every day.

At that time it didn't bother me; it was just something I did. But at the conference it entered my head; it was more or less a personal mental emphasis to me about what I was trying to say. That here was a soldier who had gone through a war in the service of his country and this was how he ended up, alone and forgotten, murdered in this despicable manner.

"I'm sorry," I said, crying openly and feeling every inch the fool. "That's all I have to say..."

There was an awkward minute of silence punctuated only by my sobs before Chief Jordan stepped up next to me to divert attention from me and onto him, an act of charity for which I will forever be grateful. He began talking about how stressful the last two weeks had been for his officers, about how they had sacrificed so much and about how it was plainly evident that it had been a dangerous undertaking. The rest of the team shifted uneasily around me for the first time in the long weeks we had been together, unsure of exactly what they could do to help.

It was a sorry end to what should have been a glorious

day. They turned the cameras off, and I went to the back of the room to collect myself. My breakdown had not been a "cop" thing to do, I realized painfully, but my emotions were honest. I decided to live with the consequences.

I found out later that the problem of crimes against the elderly is actually part of a disturbing new trend sweeping this country, that it is not just something people in a few tough areas of San Francisco have had to live with. It's everywhere, and frankly I think of it as nothing less than a national disgrace.

Thankfully, I had little chance to deal with the emotional aftermath of my on-camera breakdown. An hour after the last light blinked off, I had changed clothes once again and was driving into the Mission District to assume a new role—my last undercover role—as a larcenous pawnbroker and part-time fence named Bill "Tiger" Taggart. I was privately grateful for the assignment, not wanting to be left alone again with my thoughts.

I saw myself on the evening news that night. I tried not to acknowledge the worried look Kitty gave me when she saw my performance, and I called to discuss the whole affair with my dad, whose opinions I respect very much.

Dad said not to worry about it; that if my emotional state was taken as anything other than an honest reaction to gross injustice, then so be it. I hung up feeling much better about the whole thing.

Then the mail started to arrive. Bags of it. I got about 450 letters from the general public in the days just after the press conference and I kept them all, grateful for the contact. The response was mind-boggling, especially for a beat cop and part-time undercover man used to toiling in anonymity. The letter that really took me apart was from a thirty-five-year-old woman; she said she was already thinking about getting old and about how these crimes could happen to her and how she was glad someone was out there trying to stop them. I found her response gratifying and terrifying at the same time. When people start getting indoctrinated to being victimized, something has gone terribly wrong.

A law student from a local law school chose not to sign his letter, saying it wouldn't be politically correct for it to be known he had written a cop, but going on about how he approved of what we were doing. One letter came from Atlanta, Georgia, from a woman who had happened to be visiting San Francisco and who had seen the press conference on television. She wrote me after she got back home. I saved all the letters and look at them from time to time.

There was some question in my mind about whether or not I should respond to these people—again, it wasn't the normal thing for a cop to do. My own father said the letters didn't elicit replies, that these people were just trying to tell me something. But I just thought it was a time when not many police officers would get this kind of feedback, and although these people didn't expect a reply, I thought it would be good to respond. For me, it was therapy; writing about these things gave me a chance to "talk" it out, get it out of my system. It helped me a great deal in the weeks and months to come. With each response, I sent a picture of the Old Man along with my thanks.

A lot of cops called me, too. More than ten called to say my on-camera collapse was the best acting job they had ever seen. They were just bowled over that I could control my emotions to such an extent. I just let those clowns think what they wanted to think, taking comfort in the knowledge that for seven months after the RAT unit and the Old Man had packed up and left the Tenderloin for the last time, not a single assault on an elderly person was reported anywhere in the city. Not one.

To this day, I am perhaps proudest of that simple fact more than anything else I have ever done in my life.

My affinity for older people might be traced to my earliest—and most pleasant—memories of the days I spent with my grandmother.

I was born in San Francisco in 1934 and found myself

shuffled off to live with Grandma Alice in her third-floor flat at Fourth Avenue and Lake Street—just across from the Little Sisters of the Poor, in the city's Richmond District—at an early age. Too young to realize my parents' marriage was in disarray, I fought the early nightmares and sense of abandonment and lost myself in the attentions of this diminutive but regimented woman who seemed to care for me above all else.

"Don't worry, William," Grandma Alice would say with a soothing hint of her ancestral French, as she rubbed me down with glycerin and rose water after a particularly bad night. "Grandma will take care of you."

During those early years Alice was everything to me. Both mother and father, she took my young life and shaped it. She was a wonderful woman, slight but strong and full of charm. Born on the Isle of Mann, she had emigrated to Canada and moved to Vancouver Island. She met and married my grandfather—a character who liked to imbibe with some degree of regularity, I'm told—in 1888. They had four children. My dad was the youngest. After Grandpa died, my dad immigrated to San Francisco and took Grandma with him. As my father's marriage deteriorated, I began spending more and more time with Alice.

Often, when the afternoons were long and warm, she would give me two nickels and send me down to the Larabarrou Bakery at Third Avenue and Geary to buy some bread. One nickel was for the bread, she would tell me, the other was for my pocket.

But charitable and kind as she was, my grandmother was also not entirely without ulterior motives. She knew that it would take an eight-year-old quite a while to walk the distance from her flat to the bakery and that she could count on at least an hour of uninterrupted gossip with her friends while I was away. The neighbor ladies—often arriving as I skipped out the door—chatted about the latest war news as more and more local men went off to fight the island battles in the Pacific. Alice, it was said, had a gift. She read tea leaves, and the neighbor women were anxious to have her divine their futures and the futures of their loved ones.

But at that age my thoughts did not revolve around talk of war or even my future. Rather, they were centered on the loaves of fresh bread I would get with the nickel Alice had given me, the shell of the bread hard and cooked to a golden brown, still warm in the paper the baker had wrapped them in.

I would crack the bread open and eat the fresh middle on the way home, just as Grandmother expected. It gave her even more time with her friends.

"My, William," she would say with mock severity when I finally returned, the women looking my way and making the obligatory comments about my growth as I stood there shifting from foot to foot.

"You were away an awfully long while. Was the bread good today?"

Even then I thought Alice was remarkable. She led a very orderly life, getting up early every morning to dust and fold. She was exceptionally neat. After cooking breakfast for us and cleaning up the flat, she would go downstairs to check the mail. There were fifty-seven steps down to the lobby, and I can still hear every one of her footsteps on those creaking stairs. About eleven every morning she would go into the front bedroom and take a short nap, lying down on the made-up bed fully clothed, very carefully pulling her dress out flat from under her so as not to wrinkle it. She would nap until noon, when the chimes sounded at the Little Sisters of the Poor, and she would get up to start our evening meal.

During these afternoon naps it was very common for her cat, Gingembre, which is French for Ginger, to climb up onto the bed and fall asleep beside her. He was about sixteen or seventeen and had had rickets when he was a baby so his hind legs weren't in the best of shape. Alice spoiled him. The day he died, his paws were the same pink as they had been the day my dad had brought him home for her. He walked on nothing but carpets his entire life.

Gingembre liked to take his naps with Alice, but he

couldn't leap up onto the bed because of his legs. So he would come into the room, reach up as far as he could, and then sort of drag himself and those worthless legs up onto the bed, curl up, and nap alongside my grandmother until the chimes rang.

We found them both dead on the bed together one day in 1962. I was twenty-eight years old. We don't know who went first, Gingembre or Alice, but I suspect that, when the cat got up on her chest, he realized that she was no longer breathing and he just gave up. We thought at first there had been a gas leak or something, since they had both gone so peacefully. But as it turned out, it was just two old souls who were lucky enough to pass from this world quietly and in their sleep.

Alice was ninety-six when she died. Years before she had taken me aside, and, talking to me in an uncharacteristically earnest fashion to drive the point home, she had informed me of a special request she wanted fulfilled when the time came for her to pass on. She pointed to an old crucifix, the cross made from wood blessed at Lourdes, and some remnants of palm fronds handed out at Palm Sunday services a century earlier, and she told me my sole duty on the day of her funeral was to make sure those things ended up on top of her casket.

Her second son, my uncle George, had won an Irish Sweepstakes ticket a couple of years earlier, and with typical Langlois pragmatism had purchased two crypts, one for him and one for Grandma Alice. On the day of her funeral, I climbed a small ladder, put the crucifix on top of her casket the way she had told me to, and said my goodbye.

While in my teens, bouncing around from boarding school to boarding school and dodging the iron-fisted discipline of the nuns who meted out punishment with enthusiasm, I made the decision to join the Marine Corps. And it was during the nine years I ultimately spent in the military that I began to realize someone up there was constantly singling me out to do strange things.

It seemed I was always being handed the most bizarre

assignments. Time and time again, through no apparent
fault of my own and usually through some quirky twist
of fate, I found myself out in the middle of nowhere
doing something I had never dreamed of doing. Whether
there was any reason or sense behind the mission was
always open to debate, but there it was and I seemed
stuck with it.

It started in October 1951, when I graduated from a
platoon of forty-three Marines and prepared myself for
duty in Korea, something I looked on with the normal
mix of fear and excitement expected of a cocky, newly
graduated seventeen-year-old infantryman. But any
thought of serving my country in Korea soon went out
the window.

It seemed that the war had claimed an undue number
of soldiers under the age of eighteen. People were
screaming and Congress was listening. The Uniform Code
of Military Justice (Mother's Justice to us) was introduced,
and those of us who happened to be seventeen or under
at the time—and there were quite a few—suddenly found
ourselves placed on thirty-day mess duty at the Marine
Corps Recruiting Depot in San Diego.

Our superiors didn't know what to do with us, so we
were given a lot of busywork while the rest of the platoon
went off to war. About a week or ten days went by, and
half our group received orders to report to Kodiak, Alaska,
in the Thirteenth Naval District. Well, they were destroyed.
The rest of us were laughing our tails off. I mean, who
had ever heard of Marines in Alaska? They were apparently
meant to provide security for naval barracks there.

Shortly after this, a couple of other guys turned eighteen
and they were gone, shipped off for parts unknown. The
rest of us were left looking at one another, wondering
what was to come. Then my orders came along to report
to Kodiak, too, and now the laugh was on the other side
of my face.

When I finally reached Kodiak, I walked up to the first
gunnery sergeant I saw and said, "Sarge, I didn't join the
Marine Corps to guard a bunch of swabbies. I really resent

being in a barracks surrounded by all these gobs. I mean, they gave me a can of Brasso and it's going to be up to me to keep these guys in line and that ain't for me. Isn't there a place around here where there are other Marines?"

He looked me up and down like I was some kind of bug he had never seen before and he finally said: "Yeah, over on Adak they got a 137-man detachment. All Marines and all by themselves out there on their own little hill. How's that sound?"

It sounded great and I told him so. What he didn't tell me was that this particular area was set aside for the corps enigmas, walking legends crazed from either the rigors of too much combat or homemade liquor in foreign ports. These guys needed to be kept away from people. They used to send them to Wake or Midway, way out in the middle of the Pacific where they couldn't hurt anyone. Now the corps' "Elephant Graveyard" was on Adak, but Gunny neglected to tell me that part.

It was then that one of the little twists of fate that would continue to haunt me throughout my life came into play. The clerk who cut my orders for transfer to Adak misread my serial number while typing and gave me another, one that transformed me instantly from a recently shorn "boot" into a twenty-two-year veteran in one swift stroke.

When my DC3 finally landed on Adak, I couldn't believe what I had done. It was foggy and miserably cold, my winter parka like tissue paper against that awful chill. Even worse, there had to be 125 Marines standing there, almost the entire detachment, all of them turned out to see who this latest malcontent was going to be. I mean, anyone in for twenty-two years and still a rank private had to be cut from the same cloth in their eyes, and they had all come down to meet the plane and see this legendary screw-up, the Marine who stormed Tarawa single-handed and ate officers for breakfast.

When they caught a glimpse of me, a pimply seventeen-year-old so skinny he was practically swimming in his cold-weather gear, each and every one of them turned away in disgust. And when they found out that I had actually asked to go there, they immediately assumed that I really was crazy and avoided me like the plague from that moment on.

They put me on guard duty one night to punish me for my naiveté, planting me outside what was left of a giant Navy warehouse on the island. It was only six years after the war and there was still a lot of *matériel* around up there, but this thing had burned to the ground long before I got there. It was typical Marine Corps' logic: guard something that isn't there. All that was left was the original entry shed which was still at the front of the building and in which the poor soul assigned to guard duty tried to take shelter against the bone-numbing cold.

There was talk going around that a werewolf was menacing anyone caught out alone at night. I figured they were just trying to scare the new kid, but I kept my eyes peeled anyway. It was pitch black and cold, and I was nervous to begin with. Pretty soon I heard the tick, tick, tick, of nails on rock coming my way. Dogs. An army of dogs. In true Marine fashion I challenged the closest beast, even though I couldn't see it, and I got a low, guttural growl in response. Gunfire ensued and I lit up the area with my .45 until I heard splashing in the mud puddles on the roadway and the tick, tick, tick, sound of animals running away at speed.

I was shaking, standing there in complete darkness with my gun jammed.

Occasionally the beacon from the airfield light a couple of miles away would swing around and illuminate the scene briefly, but I still couldn't make out a thing. All I could hear was my own heart and the pounding of the surf on the beach behind me. After a century or two, the sergeant of the guard came barreling up in a jeep, mad that I had pulled him away from the comforts of the guardroom and wondering what all the shooting was about. I stammered out a story about being attacked by a platoon of werewolves, but I could tell by the way he looked at me he wasn't buying it. Everyone else on Adak was a mental case and he figured he was looking at another one.

He had just finished threatening to put me on ten days' bread and water for firing my weapon, when his driver, a good old boy from the Kentucky hills and something of a tracker, strolled over to a spot not far away and shone his light on a dark shape in the middle of the road.

"Uh, Sahgeant," he said, nudging the thing with his toe. "I think our boy hit sumthin' out heah."

It was a real beast, part wolf, and with two of my bullets in him. They recognized him as one of the dogs which hung around the Navy compound, waiting to be fed during the day and prowling with his pack at night. Then the driver said, "Gawd, Sahge, there are tracks from eight or nine animals heah."

Things finally swung my way and I felt a little bit better, daring to think for the first time that I wouldn't be going to jail after all. My sergeant was happy because the Navy had been made to look bad once again and I had proven that there were, in fact, werewolves out on the tundra. But I'd committed the cardinal sin in the military; I'd attracted attention. After a couple of days dragged by, my superior, Lieutenant MacNussen, called me in to his office and said, "You know, you really don't belong out here. We have an eight-man detachment in Dutch Harbor. How's that sound?"

"Where's Dutch Harbor?" I asked.

"It's halfway back to Kodiak," the officer we called "Black Mac" said, already initialing the transfer order. "And it's away from here."

So they put me on a PBY and flew me out to Dutch Harbor. Immediately upon my arrival, a corpsman named Marcou approached me, looked me in the eye, and said, "I am the leader of this family and there will be no fighting or bickering in this family; you won't even slur another man. If I hear of any of this, you're going back to Adak. We'll get along great, period. Got it?"

And that was the way it was. Eight Marines out in the middle of the Aleutians. After Marcou, the guy in charge of the detachment, such as it was, was a guy named Carlos Ballou, a Korean War vet who had apparently done something bad in his past life, too. He drank constantly. The men found out I didn't drink beer and naturally put me in charge of the beer locker. I was the only man who ever saw Carlos Ballou regularly, because it was my job to deliver his beer ration. I would fetch a case of beer and go to his room and knock. The door would creak open and out would come this gnarled, bony hand like one of Howard Hughes'. He'd give me his money and his empties, and back in he would go. It was that kind of place.

Our assignment was to patrol the thirteen-mile circumference of Dutch Harbor and keep all the supplies still stored there, safe. Only they didn't tell us who would be crazy enough to want to take things from such a desolate place. There were no inspections, no parades. No one came to see us for months. We were the Lost Squad of the Aleutians. Once, we loaded up our boat with beer and set out for the Pribilof Islands to watch the sea lions breed. We were halfway across the Bering Sea before someone realized that all eight of us were in the boat, including Carlos Ballou, who was firing his pistol off the bow like some demented Horatio Hornblower, already into the beer locker and having a grand old time. I wondered how we would explain it if we got lost up there or the engine quit on us. "Eight Marines Lost at Dutch Harbor," the headlines would read. "Jarheads Disappear While Watching Sea Lions Mate."

It was a desolate place, but beautiful at the same time. I befriended a bald eagle who nested in the rocky crags of the island and who would fly to me once he learned I would split my steak ration with him. I used to hold him and launch him into the wind. He would glide a bit and then come back for me to do it again. Nothing unusual, I suppose. Doesn't every seventeen-year-old have his very own eagle to play with? I called him "Deuce."

My tour of duty on Dutch Harbor came to an abrupt end one day when the signal light blinked on in our shack, indicating an incoming message for the Marine detachment. I headed for the Air Force signal station four miles away to pick it up. It turned out the message was for me, although no one had thought I would be the one to see it first. The words hit me like a hammer blow: "Please inform Pfc William D. Langlois that his mother has passed away..."

The PBY crew who had brought me to Dutch Harbor chipped in their own money and bought the aviation fuel for the hardship flight back to Adak. Within hours I was winging my way back to the lower forty-eight and the funeral in San Francisco.

I was home, but not for the reason I wanted.

A year later I was transferred to Seattle, where I was assigned to a transient barracks and courier duty to keep me out from underfoot. Being a courier sounded much more glamorous than it actually was. I could go anywhere I wanted in the Greater Seattle area as long as I was within an hour's driving time from the barracks and was always near a pay phone. It was probably the greatest job in the Marine Corps at that time, but it bored me to tears. I would go to the movies, check in by phone, and be sent off somewhere to pick up a briefcase full of payroll money for one of the nearby naval stations.

Guys would have killed to have had my job, but I was tired of it. I wanted to get away from the Navy and water and be a real Marine. So I was shipped back to Camp Pendleton, where they immediately sent me to school to learn how to operate an ANPDR Geiger counter—the only one in the outfit. I was floored. When the nuclear war everyone expected back then actually happened, I was supposed to be the one to walk into the cloud with my little Geiger counter to confirm everyone's worst fears!

Finally, in 1953 I actually got my wish for overseas duty with a regiment of fighting Marines. I was on my way up the gangplank of a troop transport bound for Japan when a weapons carrier pulled up on the wharf and a clerk jumped out. He went straight to the officer of the deck and said, "I need these three Marines." He gave the names and I was one of them, standing there slack-jawed in full field pack, wondering what I'd done this time. It turned out that the first Marine should actually have been discharged eight months earlier. He had kept telling everyone he should have been mustered out, but no one had believed him. The second was wanted for some petty offense committed while on shore leave. In my case, I learned they were looking for truck drivers to take a battery of howitzers to Twenty-nine Palms, and some clerk somewhere had seen that I could drive a truck. Lightning had struck me once again. Before I knew it I was off with the artillery.

I made corporal in 1953 and sergeant in 1954. Still trying to get overseas, I put in for embassy duty at one of the ninety-six American embassies and legations around the world. I wanted to go to the Orient, but found myself assigned to Moscow, which I had heard was really tough duty. They had given another guy Taipei, Formosa, and that sounded better than Moscow to me, so we swapped assignments and off I went.

Taipei was very austere. Again I was in a detachment of just eight Marines. It was a world of dirt and dust, bicycles and khaki pants and white shirts, and a tropical climate. I could spend three or four days on liberty and never see another Caucasian face. Every time I sat down in a restaurant to eat, fifty people were sitting around watching my every move. We were just so strange to them that the people would look in my pockets, touch my watch, and my shoes. Old women would snip locks of my hair and run away.

I was there two and a half years and loved it. I loved the people. But one day a Marine working at the American legation in Kuala Lumpur went to his commanding officer and said, "I gotta get out of here. I shoulda been discharged a year and a half ago." No one believed him, of course, because everybody wanted out of there. But eventually they checked, and found out he was right. They owed him something like twenty thousand dollars in back pay, which really made the paymaster angry, so word went out to send in a list of names of Marines who had been on consular duty for more than two years. They sent in my name and after a couple of days a communiqué came back from Washington asking, "Who is Sgt. William Langlois?"

They had lost me. Again! I could have been standing guard in Taipei for another twenty years! Eventually, they asked me where I wanted to go. In the Marine Corps you never state your first choice as your first choice because they never send you where you want to go. So you make it your third choice. I had learned this. So for my first choice I put down the hated Twenty-nine Palms, figuring if I listed it as my first pick they would never send me there. Then I put down Moffett Field, which was close to San Francisco but not as close as my third choice, Treasure Island. That's where I really wanted to go, so I put it down as my third pick.

Pleased with my strategy, I waited for the results. But once again fate took a hand, and, in a move virtually unheard of in the annals of Marine Corps history, an anonymous clerk somewhere in Washington, D.C., saw that I had just come off two and a half years of embassy duty in Formosa. He felt sorry for me, and with a stroke of his pen, approved my first choice and sent me kicking and screaming back to Twenty-nine Palms, which I regarded at the time as just one short step above hell.

While stationed at Twenty-nine Palms and serving my country as a driver for the base commander, I met and married a lieutenant in the Navy Nurse Corps, Louise Glanville. We had the obligatory Marine wedding and the base commander gave the bride away. But I had to think about our future together, and civilian life began to look more and more appealing.

I left the corps in July 1960, loaded up our '59 Pontiac coupe, and pointed the hood ornament straight toward San Francisco without so much as a backward glance at Twenty-nine Palms. I was twenty-six, full of youthful enthusiasm and vague intentions of becoming a dentist or something. My father had remarried, so upon our arrival in the town of my birth we took up residence with my step-mom and dad for a while in the Sunset District. Louise was pregnant and I set about the business of finding work.

My first stop was the Department of Physicians and Surgeons on Fourteenth Street. If I was going to be a dentist I would have to go to school there. The department head looked at my qualifications, talked with me for a while, and finally let me have it straight and right between the eyes.

"Look," he said. "I want to be honest with you. You have some merit and could probably do some great things in dentistry. But practically speaking, you're not going to make it. People who come out of college, who are used to long study hours and the hard work it's going to take, do not make it through this course. You've been out of school nine years, haven't been studying anything, and your wife is pregnant. You're just going to wash out. You'll be wasting your time and ours."

My hopes fading fast, I sold cars for six months, hating every minute of it. Then I saw an ad in the paper for a police officer, and I went down to take the first test at Mission High School. I think there were thirty-eight hundred applicants. I got as far as the physical, to the point where we were asked to pick up a 150 pound weight. We had to pick it up, put it on our shoulders and then put it down again. It was wrapped in sacking and there was no place to grab it. So I got it on my shoulders and I almost dropped it. I was panicking when a testing officer I had sort of befriended earlier looked at me and whispered: "Four hundred and six dollars a month," the going wage for a police officer at that time. The mere mention of such a vast sum gave me the strength to hang on.

When I got out of the police academy they sent me out to the Taraval District. There was a burglary call out by Ocean Beach one night and I was trying to figure out how best to handle it when up came this dog car, one of our canine units. The sergeant on the scene wanted to send the dog in to search the store and flush the burglar. But the handler was too big to go in through the window with the dog and the sergeant immediately asked for a volunteer. Suddenly all these beefy cops were standing around looking at sea gulls or kicking at pebbles, anything to keep them from making eye contact with their sergeant and being picked to go in with the dog.

After a while I said, "I can do that," and everyone appeared relieved. The sergeant patted me on the back and the handler sidled up alongside me with a tone of new respect in his voice. "You know," he said. "There aren't a helluva lot of guys who would take off their gun belts and go into a building with this dog."

"Why?" I asked, his animal looking at my arm as if it were an hors d'oeuvre. "He's just a dog, isn't he?" He smiled and I began to feel that I may have stepped into something again. "Well, isn't he?"

We searched and didn't find the burglar that day, but when I climbed back out of the building and dusted myself off, I found out the handler had already made plans for my transfer to the canine unit. He helped me write the request and submitted it to the chief of police. I stayed there for many years, mindful of the fact that once again a chance encounter had supplied what would prove to be a pivotal point in my life.

But budgetary cutbacks and the stigma attached to police dogs in the early 1970s finally put an end to the long days spent with Bourbon and Judge, my two canine partners. In 1977 I found myself once again without a mission, assigned to the Tactical Unit at the Hall of Justice but missing the comfort of having a 135 pound German Shepherd with bad breath drooling down my neck all day. I was feeling pretty low when Captain Charles Beene, who had been with me in the Canine Unit and had been named commander of the newly formed Street Crimes Unit, asked me if I wanted to work undercover as a victim officer.

"What's a victim officer?" I asked with my customary alacrity, immediately accepting the assignment.

As it turned out, my job was to go out during the day dressed in plain clothes and hoping to attract the attention of muggers who were robbing people—mostly street alcoholics or the homeless who had taken shelter in doorways—in various parts of the city. Wary of having any potential arrest challenged in court and written off as entrapment, we could not pour alcohol on our clothes or flash large amounts of cash. We worked hard to blend in and appear as vulnerable as possible and we accomplished this in a variety of ways. Capt. Beene, himself an effective decoy officer, once purposely dripped his own blood onto the toe of the hospital slippers he was wearing on the street to create the impression that he had injured himself earlier that morning and was vulnerable to attack. It worked.

We were constantly looking for new props to help us blend in. I was the first one to use a shoe with a sole that flapped when I walked, and sometimes I wore a long, draped coat. Anything to draw the attention of prospective thieves. I started faking falls, something I had mastered during too many liberty calls in the Marine Corps. I learned to look down, to keep my eyes on the ground, because most prospective victims are reluctant to make eye contact with their persecutors. In the urban landscape, the predators are the ones who have their heads up and are looking around.

During the early 1980s, the SCU racked up an impressive string of successes, living up to its name and suppressing crime in problem areas of the city virtually overnight. While fulfilling, duty with the Street Crime Unit was not without its dangers. Tony Rockett had his arm slashed down to the bone while apprehending a suspect, and Officer Doug Gibbs was shot and killed one day after arresting a man who had just robbed a victim officer. Doug was about to put the suspect in handcuffs when an individual unrelated to the initial incident stepped up to him, placed a gun in an area of his chest not protected by his body armor, and shot him once. As Capt. Beene told us later, the gunman shot Doug because he wanted to kill a policeman. And he did.

By 1984 the SCU had arrested more than ten thousand criminals and could boast a conviction rate of ninety-five percent. This compared to a nationwide average of about thirty percent. Walking the streets as a derelict got to be old hat in those early years. I was more than a little surprised when, on the event of my two-hundredth successful hit I found myself surrounded by a squad of disheveled "street people"—virtually my entire backup team—who came out from under cover and proceeded to dump confetti on my head, dancing around me like village idiots, as legitimate street people. The thief we had just arrested stared at the bizarre little scene in disbelief.

Public demand for more uniformed officers on the streets forced the SCU into retirement in 1985. We had cleaned up certain areas of town hard hit by street robberies and everyone seemed grateful, but the brass simply could not justify keeping seventy-five police officers in plain clothes when crime was down. City politics demanded a more visible uniformed presence on the streets.

I returned to my usual duties in the Taraval District. But I missed the action and the sense of accomplishment I had felt while working downtown. So my heart leapt that day in May 1986 when Capt. Beene's lanky frame appeared in the doorway, and he asked, in his customary casual manner, if I wanted to join a scaled-down manifestation of SCU—rechristened the Robbery Abatement Team—tailored to combat a sudden increase in assaults on the elderly. Several people had been killed during home invasions and survivors had told investigators of a man who whispered in their ear to calm them before he beat and robbed them. I would be one of two victim officers to dress as an elderly person and walk the streets in an attempt to find "Whispers" and others responsible for these awful crimes. Most of my original backup team, Eddie St. Andre, Brian D'Arcy, and Ed Dullea, would also be involved.

"What do you say, Bill?" Beene asked.

Once again I felt the hand of fate tapping me on the shoulder. It didn't take very long for me to make up my mind.

"Okay," I said. "When do I start?"

Chapter 2

THE RAZOR

There would be twelve members of the Robbery Abatement Team, nowhere near the seventy-five officers who had worked for SCU during its heyday. Capt. Beene called us to the Hall of Justice on May 15, 1986, for a little pep talk and to outline plans for what the brass were calling "Operation Dismantle."

"It's simple, really," Beene told us. "There's a gang of ex-cons working the Tenderloin and they're attacking older people. They follow them to their apartments, push their way in past the security gates before they close, and confront the victims on the thresholds of their own homes. Then they rush them inside, beat them, and rob them. The victims are either being thrown to the floor or choked into unconsciousness. Sometimes it's going sour. We've had four related homicides so far. We're going to take them down."

I looked around the crowded squad room as Beene talked, peering at the faces of my fellow team members. Any working police officer, no matter how jaded he or she had become after long years on the street, could not help but be affected. There was Sgt. Bruce McEachern, one of the most capable undercover men in the department; Craig Woods, a sensitive, intelligent man with the bulk and focus of a middle linebacker; the ever-reliable Brian D'Arcy, Eddie St. Andre, and Ed Dullea. All were hanging onto Beene's every word, the sense of outrage and feeling of commitment to this latest mission plainly evident on their faces. I sat back and listened as Beene went on.

"Bill Langlois and Leanna Dawydiak will be our victim officers," he said. "They will make themselves up to look like older people and will work from an apartment building we have established in the Tenderloin. Dressed appropriately, they will walk to and from this apartment and hopefully attract the attention of the local bad guys. We've determined that there are fifteen thousand elderly people living in the Tenderloin and at least fifteen hundred ex-cons living out there with them. We're going to square up the odds a little."

Beene stopped and looked straight at Dawydiak and me. "If things go as expected, you two will probably have the stuffing kicked out of you more than once before this is over. Expect it. It will be up to the rest of us to see that it doesn't go on too long and that the people who do it to you are arrested. Just remember that you'll never be alone. There'll be backups walking ahead of you, behind you, and watching from the other side of the street. You'll be triangulated at all times and have one-way radio communication with your team. Listen to them. We don't want the street muggers, we want the people who are going after the victims in their homes. It will be up to the backups to dissuade anyone who might want to snatch your purse or pop you on the street. We want the potential killers."

Beene handed out information on several suspected home invaders, including one the robbery detail had called "Whispers." Little was known about this man, Beene told us, because he was careful to never let his victims get a good look at him. He was also compulsively clean, lingering for hours at the crime scene and carefully erasing any evidence he might have left behind. His victim's first indication that something was amiss came when this predator's arm looped around their neck, pulling them close until his lips were up against their ear.

"That's when he tells them not to struggle, that everything's going to be all right," Beene said. "He says the same thing every time. That's why Robbery has called him Whispers. We think he may be responsible for one murder, maybe more. And we're fairly certain he'll do it again. Any questions?"

There were, and we spent a good deal of time working out who would be doing what. We were excited, going over radio codes and hand signals for the victim officers, eager to get out there and do what everyone regarded as real police work—actually going out and collaring these people before they had a chance to harm someone. But at the same time every one of us knew that things could go wrong out there. There's no way of knowing for sure, of course, but I'd be willing to bet the memory of Doug Gibbs was not far from everyone's thoughts that day.

We agreed right off the bat that the squad would play by an established set of rules. Victim officers would do nothing that could possibly be mistaken for entrapment, which could endanger the outcome of the felony charges once the cases came to trial. Victim officers would simply play the role of senior citizens, posing as potential victims. As in the earlier days of SCU, Leanna or I would carry only small amounts of cash at any given time. There would be a squad critique at the beginning and end of every shift, with every team member expected to participate.

The theory behind Operation Dismantle was very different from previous decoy operations. An entirely different premise, in fact. Leanna and I would truly be "victim officers" in every sense of the word, because we knew we were being sent out with the express purpose of being beaten and robbed and that we were going to have to let the criminals do it to us. Otherwise there would be no crime, no arrest, and no jail time. Once the robbery went down or they began to strike us, then the cavalry was supposed to roll in. In the meantime, we were meant to stand there and take it.

Frankly, the thought ran counter to every instinctive ounce of self-preservation in my body, not to mention the automatic defense mechanisms that tend to set in after more than twenty years of police work. I hadn't yet decided if I would go into this operation armed or not. There were reasons for carrying a weapon and for not carrying one. I knew I would be attacked from the rear in most cases and that there was the good possibility that I would be harmed or knocked unconscious before my backup could get there. In going through my pockets to get the loot or to get the key to my apartment, the bad guys could gain access to a gun—an even better weapon than they would most likely be carrying if they were armed in the first place.

I decided against carrying the gun most of the time. My role was set. It was extremely unlikely that I would have to turn around like Jean Claude Van Damme or whatever, and have to get tough. As a matter of fact, not carrying a weapon helped me with my role because now I really *was* more like a victim. I didn't have anything on me. That helped me look and feel more vulnerable.

Motivation, actually getting up the nerve to go out and do what we were being asked to do, did not prove to be a problem for me. As police officers you see firsthand the impact these types of crimes can have. The thought of old people being slaughtered in their homes, in some cases having their pets killed in front of them to make them divulge the whereabouts of cash or jewels, was repulsive to me. These innocents, caught in the last refuge of their lives and with their sense of self and security invaded by strangers who took so much with so little thought, deserved better.

Some of these unfortunates had been savaged worse than others. Yet all of them had been injured, mentally if not physically. Whether they were killed outright at that moment is irrelevant. They might have died later from the trauma they experienced. There was a woman who was beaten and robbed in 1976, left with black eyes and thrown to the floor. She died within a year. And everybody just accepted the fact that Aunt Nellie was an old woman and it was her time. But Aunt Nellie might have lived to see ninety if she had not been beaten. We'll never know.

Only Aunt Nellie and the few people close to her saw the aftermath of that crime. No one else had a clue. And in a way she was lucky, since many of the victimized people are forced to continue living in the apartments where the assault occurred. The trauma is thus intensified, and they live with it every day, day in and day out, until the day they die. Always in fear.

I left the briefing that afternoon to buy some old clothes from Goodwill, spending a total of thirteen dollars on my wardrobe. A couple of old jackets, pants. Some frayed shirts. Then I bought some makeup, and knee and elbow pads from a sporting goods store. Just to be on the safe side.

We spent the first week blending in with the denizens of the Tenderloin, in an area known as "The Razor" for its toughness. Our backups tried out different clothes and adopted street personas of their own; Leanna and I watched the senior citizens of the neighborhood to see how they reacted to their surroundings. It was a fascinating place, with a crime problem, yes, but also home to an amazing potpourri of people and cultures from all over the world. There were drunks and hookers and their customers, driving into the Tenderloin from all over the Bay Area for a rendezvous with a princess of dubious gender in any one of the thousand or so alleys that laced the neighborhood. I saw all this as only a cop would, picking out the likely strong-arm artists and pickpockets from the crowds walking the teeming sidewalks. And then I would look down and see the children—usually the sons and daughters of Asian refugees who had braved teenage soldiers, minefields, and Thai pirates to get to this country—playing on the sidewalk next to an inebriate or the corner crack dealer.

I prayed for things to go well for us, wanting to do something for this neighborhood and its residents. That night, scribbling in my diary and unable to sleep, I wrote: "Will we get our man? Will this whole operation be a series of 'accidents' or 'incidents?' Is it better to be 'lucky' or 'good?' We shall see..."

The decision was made to introduce Leanna to the neighborhood first, so she went to work on May 22 and scored a hit her very first day. Dressed in an old coat and wearing a scarf over her head to help camouflage her dyed hair, she decided to sit on the front steps of the decoy apartment building, we were using at 555 Eddy Street, riffling through her purse as if in search of her keys. Within minutes a sixteen-year-old male broke away from the crowd on the street and began watching her from a few feet away. When Leanna got up to open the security gate to the apartment building, the suspect followed, holding the gate open and slipping inside. He confronted her the instant she opened the front door of the decoy apartment, strong-armed her, and got all of maybe six feet away before Eddie St. Andre, Brian D'Arcy, Sgt. McEachern, and I jumped out from our hiding places inside the apartment and took him into custody.

"You little jerk," Leanna said, as the would-be thief was led away in handcuffs. We had drawn first blood.

Aside from earlier trial runs, I took to the street for the first time as "the Old Man" on May 27, and while I was followed for several blocks by a likely looking character, I had to wait until the following day to record my first hit.

With my backup team already in place I walked into Boeddeker Park—named after a Franciscan friar, I believe, but known at the time as a hangout for parolees—at two that afternoon, wearing a tan sport coat, plaid slacks and an orthopedic shoe to help me look particularly desirable to any prospective rip-off artists. A pretty little park at the best of times, Boeddeker was loaded that day with tough-looking young men who had taken over most of the benches in the area and sat around drinking out of bottles wrapped in brown paper bags. If I could pass muster as the Old Man here, I reasoned, I could pass anywhere.

Although I was careful to keep my eyes averted, I was instantly aware that I had attracted attention.

"Jeez, Bill," one of my backups murmured over the one-way receiver. "They sure like you. That guy in the blue bandana can't keep his eyes off you."

I waited awhile, tongue lolling feebly, before getting up and dragging myself off to the Roosevelt Market at Eddy and Jones Streets, where I bought three dollars' worth of stuff. I used the reflection in the store's windows to see if anyone was following before leaving the store and heading back to 555 Eddy and my apartment. On Turk Street just south of the park, one of my backups came over the radio. He sounded more than a little uneasy.

"Uh, folks, Bill has several people following him, most of them the same guys we saw in Boeddeker."

I stopped, resisted the urge to turn around and look for myself, and busied myself instead with an inspection of my grocery bag. Several suspects. We hadn't planned on that. How many was "several"? I knew at that point I had Officer Greg Randolph a half-block west of my location and Craig Woods a half-block behind. With only one other man, Bobby Aitchison, in a van cruising parallel to me and the remaining four backup officers out of position back at the apartment building, we could find ourselves recreating an urban version of Custer's Last Stand if drawn into a fight.

I heard Bruce McEachern next, and there was no mistaking the urgent tone in his voice, even over the radio. As "King Rat," Bruce was in charge of the overall street operation and had laboriously tried to plan for every eventuality. But on my first real time out, he was confronted by one he couldn't possibly have foreseen. "How many suspects are we talking about EXACTLY?" McEachern asked, echoing my thoughts precisely. We had always counted on meeting one, two, maybe three crooks—tops. There was no immediate response to Bruce's question and, to my horror, I realized that whoever had the suspects in view was counting them.

"Six. Six suspects."

Oh, man! Six! Three more men than we had on the street to protect me. The decision was made to head back with all possible haste to 555 Eddy, our strongest defensible point. I didn't need to be told twice, and started walking as quickly as I could without giving up my cover. When I rounded the corner onto Eddy and saw that old apartment building looming just ahead, I had to struggle to keep from breaking into a trot, forcing myself to keep dragging my "injured" right foot. The last fifty feet were the worst, as my ears pricked for the sound of approaching footsteps, and my shoulders hunched against the blows I felt sure would be thudding home at any moment. I made for the security gate, knowing how a man swimming for a lifeboat feels with a school of sharks in the water around him.

When I reached the steps I heard one of the backups tell everyone, "He's home. Bill's home," and then, "Suspects have fallen back. Code Four." Only after the iron gate clanged shut behind me did the steel spring that had been steadily tensing between my shoulder blades finally let go. A door opened, Apartment Two, and "Room Rat," Officer Jim Batchelor, peered out into the lobby. The worry in his face was apparent. No one man had ever looked so good to me.

We took a short break, and after a spirited critique of our progress to that point, decided to try again. This time, "the Old Man" would stay a little closer to home, doddering just near the steps of his apartment building. I went back out a little after five. Within forty minutes I had once again attracted attention.

"Okay, folks, we got a live one," Eddie St. Andre said presently, his voice strong and calm as he described the suspect for the benefit of the rest of the team. He gave the color of the man's shirt, and a description of his sneakers. Shoe types had taken on new meaning for me since I had made it a practice to keep my head down as I walked, and I had said so to my teammates. Eddie was giving me information I could use and I was grateful. I turned and climbed the stairs to my building, lingering over each stair as if pausing to catch my breath, watching and waiting for first sight of the man's sneakers.

"He's right behind you, Bill," Eddie said as I unlocked the gate and entered the lobby of 555 Eddy, turning to open the door to Apartment Two and realizing what was to come when I failed to hear the gate close behind me. I had the apartment door open, and heard and then felt the presence of a man behind me. A voice asked me for the time. Then strong arms pushed me hard and fast into the apartment! He was on top of me in an instant and we both slammed hard into the living-room carpet, a blow

```
72   210.02.02.10   01/04/94 16.19 3152
B.DALTON BOOKSELLER OKLAHOMA CITY, OK

  1567960138                        12.95
                    SUBTOTAL        12.95
                    SALES TAX        1.08
                    TOTAL           14.03
                    CASH            20.05


------------------THANK YOU------------------
```

that nearly took the wind out of me and would have done serious damage to a genuinely older person. My earphone had popped out, so the last thing I heard was St. Andre shouting, "It's going down! He's got him! It's going down!" over and over again.

I flailed helplessly, trying to stay in character and resisting the natural instinct to put my thumb into my attacker's eye and pull it out. Then I heard the sound of the closet door opening and Batchelor and D'Arcy boiling out, both shouting "Police! Freeze!" as my assailant's face froze in confusion and terror and I felt his weight come off me. There was the sound of a struggle a few feet away as I rolled over, trying to get to my feet and mindful of the fact that a big and very angry policeman, Eddie St. Andre, was suddenly looming in the doorway of my apartment. Eddie instantly threw himself into the writhing mass of cops and robber rolling around on the floor next to me.

"What is this?" I shouted, leaning on the kitchen counter while I tried to catch my wind and wheezing in my Old Man's voice, grateful I had remembered to remove my dental plate. "What's going on?"

I heard the sound of handcuffs ratcheting closed and Eddie's head finally popped up out of the pile, looking at me to see if I was serious. He peered at me quizzically, wondering what I was up to, and then he went along with it.

"I said, who are you?"

Jim Batchelor and Brian D'Arcy had the suspect prone and handcuffed on the floor, Batchelor rubbing a spot on his left leg where Tyrone Butler, my first customer, had kicked him. They were looking at me too, unsure of how to play it. Eddie came up, flashed his badge and said: "Calm down, Old Timer. We're the police. We happened to be in the area and saw this man assault you."

"Oh," I said, grasping his hand and shaking it wildly. "How fortuitous."

St. Andre's face split into a wide if slightly confused grin, not sure if his victim officer had suffered a concussion as a result of his contact with the living-room carpet. To this day I don't know where the word "fortuitous" came from. It is not a word I use in the normal course of conversation. I guess I thought it was a word the Old Man would have used in a similar circumstance. The old guy was off and running.

Buoyed by our initial success and working out a contingency plan in case we found ourselves outnumbered again, we returned to the apartment building the next afternoon. I made a pass through Boeddeker Park and picked up an admirer who followed me for several blocks and then broke away. Leanna, by then christened "Minnie Rat" by the team, stayed on the front steps of 555 Eddy. She had a man follow her in but lost him when an upstairs door slammed and scared him off. We were about to set up again and try once more before dusk when a narcotics raid a block away scattered everyone on the street and left us without any potential customers.

Changing clothes for luck, I went directly to the Roosevelt Market on Eddy Street the next afternoon. I was wearing a worn-but-snappy-looking blue sport coat, gray slacks, hat, and a regimental tie—the Old Man's upgraded Friday afternoon wardrobe, a proud old veteran still trying to dress the part. I dragged the orthopedic boot along behind me, appreciating the halting effect it had on my step. When I walked like an old man, I acted like an old man.

At the Roosevelt Market I dithered for a while, choosing four dollars' worth of groceries for effect and lurching around inside the store a few seconds before the radio receiver in my ear started buzzing, my backups stepping over themselves in their excitement.

During a practice walk a week earlier I had been followed by what my team felt would be a surefire hit. This young guy had tailed me for about two and a half blocks but broke off just as I got to 555 Eddy. As I usually did when a stalker broke off and failed to complete his attack, I felt I had done something to scare this guy off. If there was something wrong with my guise I wanted to correct it so I asked around to see if any of my backups had noticed anything. Eddie St. Andre, "Swamp Rat" to the rest of the team by now, said the suspect wasn't laughing or anything when he broke away from me at the apartment building. If he had been, it might have indicated he knew what was happening. But this guy seemed content to just follow me home, Eddie said. I was disappointed at the time that he didn't follow through and initiate the hit, but I was soon to understand why.

"Hey, Bill," Craig Woods—"Street Rat East"—said from his position a half-block away. "Our friend is back."

I couldn't see him from my position inside the store, but the backup team had spotted the suspect who had followed me from the market the week before.

"He's going nuts. The guy is so excited he's climbing the walls!" Woods murmured. "Be careful, this guy is really pumping. Stay in there like you're paying for the groceries or something because we're not sure what this guy has in mind."

The Old Man picked over the magazine rack, poked at the frozen dinners and compared the relative merits of ten different packs of candy. But after awhile I just couldn't stall any more. When I turned to leave, the radio receiver in my ear came alive again, buzzing like some sort of pesky insect with the hum of many excited voices all trying to talk at once.

"Be advised the man outside has picked up a friend and they're running ahead to 555 Eddy. Bill, did you hear that? They're ahead of you; they've gone ahead to the apartment building."

I signaled that I had heard him, walking my old man's walk and wondering if they were going to do me on the steps, or wait until I got there, push me down, and then run with the groceries and my wallet. There were people on the street, children. I passed them almost without noticing, fully aware I was walking into an ambush and unable to do a single thing to stop it.

"They're inside the lobby, people. All Rats be advised suspects have entered the building. I don't know how they did it, but they're in."

Exactly what we wanted. These two had obviously done this before. Hall Rat and Closet Rat were scrambling, I could tell from the sound of their voices, to get into position. Apparently the man Craig Woods had spotted tailing me a week earlier hadn't had his crime partner with him at the time and had just been marking my address. It was at that point, that I realized the robberies and murders of recent weeks were something more than opportunistic, random attacks on likely looking victims. These were well-planned, coordinated assaults on people who had been carefully watched and monitored, not at all as spontaneous as everyone assumed they were.

They were much more calculated. The predators knew where I lived and they had gone there to await the Old Man's arrival.

For the first time I really felt like putting the groceries down, getting on a bus, and going home. It's one thing when you're attacked outright, but knowing two guys are waiting in ambush for you is another matter entirely. I had a lot of time to think it over on the way up the stairs to the apartment building. I wasn't getting hazardous duty pay for this, I reasoned, trying to work the whole thing out in my head and coming up with more questions than answers. But to my own discomfort I noticed that I kept climbing those stairs, and the iron gate was suddenly in front of me.

They were waiting in the lobby, the clang of the security gate banging shut behind me eerie as the three of us stood there. I averted my eyes again and one of them, the smaller of the pair, came up to engage me in conversation, asking to use the bathroom in my apartment. I busied myself with the lock, got the door open and turned to face him.

"I'm sorry," I wheezed, wondering if I sounded too much like Gabby Hayes. "The toilet's not working too good. I just moved in and haven't had a chance to fix it."

As we were talking I was aware that his partner had circled around behind me and had pushed his way into the apartment. I pretended not to see him. Someone whispered: "The suspect is inside," and then there was so little radio chatter I knew the Room Rats were in place and staying quiet, inches away from the first suspect lying in wait for me. Hall and Closet Rats were in position, waiting to see how this played out.

"Okay," the small guy said next. "Let me use your phone."

"I don't have a phone," I said, waving my arms around in agitation. "I only been here a week."

It was essentially the truth. Number One backed away and I started to go in, but before I could close the door, Number Two grabbed me from behind and dragged me into the apartment. There was no time to protest. While I was grappling with him, his partner joined the battle, tackling me and pushing me further into the apartment. Then, with a ferocity that would have crippled an older man, both of them picked me up and planted me face-first into the carpet. It was my second close inspection of the rug in three days. From that moment on, my teammates began to refer to me as "Rug Rat."

A pair of hands went around my throat, starting to choke me. I was on the floor, looking at my watch to log the arrest time for the report when the doors to the hall closet flew open and nearly five hundred pounds of cops jumped out, making all kinds of angry noises. D'Arcy and Dullea, who had been watching the proceedings through the louvers of the hall closet were really hot at these guys for treating me so roughly. They piled on until I heard the bracelets going on and these two guys began their litany of innocence. Hall Rat and Closet Rat were putting out the Code Four—No Further Assistance Needed—when a street backup whose name must go unrecorded here charged into the room, shouted curses at the two handcuffed and prone figures on the floor, and then had to be physically prevented from kicking them where they lay.

Both the suspects and the officer in question happened to be Afro-American, and my teammate, incensed that people of his own race could commit such an egregious act against an old man, momentarily lost control of himself. At the unit's inception, this officer had expressed concern that an undercover operation in this part of the Tenderloin would do nothing more than target downtrodden members of the black community, placing before them an enticement so alluring they could not afford to pass it up.

Our superiors assured this officer that going after members of a given race would not be the team's objective, that we were going after a nefarious gang of robbers, be they black, purple, or green. But it was plain to see he had his doubts. Some of us wondered how this officer would react the day black men, like the pair lying handcuffed at my feet, were caught in our net. It came as a great surprise when this man, apparently enraged over what he had just witnessed, charged into the room that afternoon, and instead of taking umbrage at our methods, attempted to mete out a little street justice of his own.

We talked afterward and the officer, a very professional and sensitive man, was profoundly embarrassed about losing his cool.

"I don't know, Bill," he told me. "It just got to me. I was out there hearing what they were doing to you, and I was embarrassed. I couldn't help but think they were doing it to real old people and it just made me crazy."

I understood perfectly and I told him so. I also told him I was grateful for his concern about my well-being. There were no more doubts after that, and the team's resolve about its mission stiffened even more.

Barry Keith Gwen and Perry G. Young, the men who had followed me to the apartment May 23, both pled guilty to assault and robbery charges before their case came up for preliminary hearing, and were sent to state prison.

It turned out that both Gwen and Young had been on parole for knifing an old man during a robbery attempt a year earlier—about a block and a half away from where they tried to drive me through the living-room floor. They apparently hadn't learned a thing from their previous stay in jail, so an unsympathetic judge sent Young to prison for six years and four months. Gwen got three years.

After Gwen and Young entered their guilty pleas, I wore the bruises they had given me like medals. The Old Man appeared to be doing some good.

We took a day off so the team could lick its wounds and the backup officers could visit their doctors and dentists. We returned to the Tenderloin on June 3, still very much interested in the dynamics of street crime, how these people were picking their targets and what the victims were doing to attract them. Leanna and McEachern climbed up onto a roof overlooking Boeddeker Park and studied the reactions of the young men there as I passed through. It was early afternoon, hot, and the alcohol was flowing. Boeddeker looked like a cellblock. A man I recognized as a suspect in several home invasions eyed me as I passed. His street name was "Snake," and he lived up to his namesake's disposition, circling me and looking for a weak spot at which to strike. It looked for a time as if he would try something right there, emboldened by the alcohol and the presence of his friends, so I moved out of the park hoping he would follow and try something back at the apartment building.

But by the time I reached 555 Eddy, "Snake" was nowhere in sight. The team met inside Apartment Two to review things, and once again I agonized over what I had done to put the morning's likeliest candidate off my trail.

"Don't worry, Rug," Eddie St. Andre said with typical wisdom, "Plenty more where he came from."

McEachern decided to try a fixed decoy just outside the building. Leanna took up her position on the steps and stayed there for an hour without attracting anyone's interest. They sent me out next, wearing jacket and tie and my trusty orthopedic boot. I was standing there on the steps when two men walked by, looking at me with thinly disguised malevolence. One of them said something I couldn't hear and they were laughing as they passed me going east. They wanted to do it, I knew. I could sense it. They just needed a bit more incentive. So I fell down.

I had done it before and was actually pretty good at it by then, having used the tactic while working for SCU. I would fall and you could see the heads turn up and down the street. To the street criminal, it showed you were vulnerable. Posing as a street drunk or someone just released from the hospital, it was perfectly reasonable for me to miss a curb or step and hit the deck, going down with a groan and rubbing all the sore spots when I got back up—slowly.

I had used the fall often with SCU. Once, when I fell and stayed down for a longer than usual period of time, one of my backups had strolled past to see if I was all right. "Are you hurt?" he whispered. "You want an ambulance?" I winked and told him I was okay. He shook his head and said, "Jeez, you're getting good at this."

But I would ask myself, if I were a bad guy watching a street full of people and looking for someone to rob, what would catch my eye? Well, if you have a thousand people on a block and one of them falls down, that catches everyone's attention. Now if a bad guy is watching, he's going to think: this is my day—there's an old guy who can barely walk!

I would get followed by someone almost every time I hit the sidewalk. They didn't always try to take me on, but they would follow and give me a good looking-over. Not all of them had the nerve, the opportunity, or their crime partner with them at that moment to help commit the crime.

But that day on the steps, my backups had no way of knowing if I was improvising or not and seeing me go down set the radio humming.

"Bill's down," Swamp Rat said into the radio.

Groaning a little, I rolled over on my side and acted as if I were trying to regain my feet. The next thing I knew a hand was inside my jacket and going straight for my wallet. I was saying "No, no," and trying to hold on to the billfold with its four dollars inside. But another set of hands pushed me down again. "Please," I said.

"It's going down," Eddie St. Andre said into his radio.

"Two suspects. One of them just lifted Bill's wallet."

My two assailants, Kenneth Edwards and Harold Ray, ran off at that point, unaware that three avenging angels were closing in on them. St. Andre, Woods, and Greg Randolph moved in and arrested the pair while they were going through my wallet a few blocks away. The whole episode had taken just twenty minutes and brought the Old Man's arrest total so far to five.

We had been lucky. To that point we had been able to take several very rough customers off the streets with a minimum of fuss or damage to ourselves. I suppose I always knew my luck wouldn't hold forever, but after an operation begins to settle into its own peculiar rhythm and things appear to be running along smoothly, it's easy to get complacent and forget that anything can and probably will happen out there.

That message was driven home the very next day when the Old Man, wearing his trusty orthopedic shoe and an eye patch, strolled through Boeddeker Park and into the market at Eddy and Jones Streets to buy his groceries. Once again, the old guy appeared to have attracted attention.

"Uh, Rug, there are two guys waiting for you outside the store," Woods murmured. It was getting to be a pretty familiar refrain. Everyone was in place, learning to move more quickly after our earlier experience, so I left the store with two men trailing along behind and my backups watching their every move. We wanted to make sure they were after me so I turned south on Jones Street and walked to Turk.

"They're still on you, Bill," Swamp Rat reported, tailing them while they tailed me. "They're talking about the best way to do you."

I didn't like the sound of that. Turning west onto Turk Street I heard next from "Street West," Jim Batchelor, "They got the scent all right, Rug. They're hanging with you."

When I finally turned north from Hyde Street to Eddy I was sweating, a bead of perspiration the size of a marble running down the length of my back and dampening my shirt. It was knowing what was in store for me but not knowing when it was coming that was the worst. I concentrated on my walk, pulling my jacket closed in front of me with one hand and stopping every once in a while to "rest" while every nerve in my body screamed in protest. By the time I got to 555 Eddy I was thrumming with excitement and nervous tension.

"Rug's at the security gate. Suspects are hanging back. They're moving up now. The gate is open. Suspect Number One is moving through with Bill," Woods said.

His name, I found out later, was William Booker. He brushed past me as I opened the security gate, mumbling, "Sorry, old man," as he went by. His partner, Ernest Reed Smith, joined him in the lobby. The two of them went straight to the elevator, waiting for me to make my move to my apartment. Unlike my previous hits, these two men wasted no time on preliminary conversation. As soon as I opened the door to Apartment Two, Booker rushed me, pressed his hand over my mouth and nose to keep me from screaming for help, and, with a twisting motion— something like the move a cowboy would use in a bulldogging competition—wrestled me into the apartment and once again drove me straight into the floor.

For the first time so far in this operation I lost my cool. Booker, who was thirty-seven years old, was also incredibly powerful. His attack had brought me up and back initially, a move that would have resulted in excruciating pain for someone with arthritis or osteoporosis, and when he brought me to the floor he was both choking and suffocating me at the same time. The impact knocked my glasses off. When both men started to beat me with their fists I tried to roll out from under them, filled with a molten hatred and a desire for retribution. I was unarmed that day—I could not help but think it was a lucky thing for them.

Hall Rat and Closet Rat were on us in an instant, shouting orders and delivering punches of their own, when Booker and Smith, intent on their attack, failed to respond to their commands. There was a spirited struggle which lasted for only a few seconds before Dullea and D'Arcy got the best of my attackers and I was on my feet, bleeding from the mouth and hopping mad.

More shapes joined us, more commands were given. Eddie St. Andre got Booker and Smith on their feet and I was looking into their eyes, thinking about how such men could be allowed to live on this earth. Eddie saw what was happening to me and came over to calm me down, patting me on the back and talking to me in a calming, soothing manner. My heart was pounding like a pneumatic drill. "It's okay, Rug," Eddie kept saying over and over. "We got 'em. They're going away."

My face was bruised and swollen, there was a cut to the inside of my mouth and another on my chin. Bruce McEachern arrived, took one look at me and shut down the operation for the day.

"We're going to the hospital," he said. "The rest of you go back to the office and wrap up the paperwork. We'll join you there."

In an unmarked car on the way to the hospital, McEachern could see that I was still hot. My heart hadn't stopped pounding, and for the first time I got a little scared.

"This is nuts, Bill," McEachern said, watching me out of the corner of his eye. "Turning our backs on the bastards like this. Asking for it. I don't know what I'd do if anyone got hurt. It's just not worth it."

"Bruce," I said, when I had found my voice. "I'm not an overly religious guy, but I believe in God and I'm convinced, rightly or wrongly, that I have been put here on this earth to do some good with the time I have. I also believe that he will not allow anything to happen to me. I'm supposed to do something at this place at this time and God will not allow anything to go wrong. I'm convinced of it."

McEachern nodded, considering it. When we arrived at St. Francis Hospital, the place where all the city's cops and firefighters go to get patched up when things go bad, a nurse took my blood pressure and informed me that it was 180 over 110. Due to our rather scruffy appearance, the rest of the hospital staff did not believe we were police officers, even after Bruce flashed his buzzer and ID card. After nearly an hour of inattention, we went away.

I went to my own doctor the next day and he told me my blood pressure was still boiling. He asked me what I had been doing, and when he found out I had been assaulted while working undercover he told me my blood pressure had shot up out of unadulterated rage.

I spent a lot of time in hospitals after that, it seemed. Besides the obvious dangers of the profession, working undercover proved to have other drawbacks as well. While I could find no one to treat me during my initial visit to St. Francis, things took a very different turn a few days later when I accompanied a teammate to the emergency room of the same hospital after he twisted his ankle while making an arrest.

I was wearing a metallic eye protector as part of my disguise at the time, a nice touch because I could see through the gauze wrapping and still look as if I had recently undergone eye surgery. Playing a gentleman of diminished means, I also had a little dirt on my face. The rest of the team had all gone off to grab a bite to eat. My injured colleague and I were sitting in the emergency room when an intern arrived, examined my partner professionally, pronounced that he had received a minor sprain, and sent him on his way. I got up and started to walk off when the intern looked over at me and asked, "Who put on that bandage?" and began to poke at my perfectly functional eye.

My teammate was watching, so I started to play the moment for what it was worth, saying "Oooh, Ahh" as Young Doctor Kildare did his work. He was frowning and quickly ushered me into an examining room, asking for the name of the physician who had applied the dressing on my eye.

Still a little peeved about our reception during my first visit days earlier, I went into my Old Man mode, saying I couldn't remember who had done the operation and that doctors were all alike anyway. Getting my shots in. He started to pull the bandage off and I really began to moan and groan, mumbling about malpractice suits and medical quackery until he finally had my counterfeit dressing off. He stood there, holding the dirty bandage like a used diaper and staring into my peepers.

"What's the matter now?" I asked.

He was really perplexed. "There's nothing there," he said after a minute. "It's fine."

So I walked over to a mirror, looked at myself for a good long time and said: "It's a miracle!" Then I grabbed his hand and started shaking it. "Thank you, doctor. I'm cured! Jeez, I can't thank you enough."

When I finally released his hand he was pretty certain he was being had, but he still wasn't one-hundred percent sure. His mouth was opening and closing. The whole thing had really blown him away. My partner finally put him out of his misery, walking up and flashing his badge and police identification. Even with that, it was plain to see this doctor couldn't believe that anyone who looked as old as I did could be a police officer. He spun on his heel and walked away, muttering angrily to himself while we had a good laugh.

The same doctor came up to me as we were leaving, obviously still a little hot under the collar at being taken like that. "You know," he said. "You gotta stop fooling people like this."

It made my week.

There was just something about doctors and nurses that reminded me of the axiom people use most about cops. When I needed one, there wasn't a medical type around. When I didn't, they wouldn't leave me alone.

Years earlier while attached to SCU, I had been working undercover in the Mission District. We were after a bad bunch of people, one of whom told us later that they went to hospitals to look for their victims because they knew people there would be weakened and less likely to fight back. A particularly animalistic approach, but it made sense to the criminal mind. There had been several sexual attacks on women in recent weeks and so we infiltrated the neighborhood surrounding a likely looking hospital hoping to catch these brutes in the act.

I was wondering what kind of role I should play here when I remembered the absolute agony I had experienced after my hernia operation. So I mentally got into this, the memory so strong that I was able to pull it off, and limped around with a permanent grimace on my face, with some sense of realism. Of the six or seven people on the street outside the hospital at any given time, three were decoy police officers. One day I was laboring up an incline just outside the hospital, my slow pace perfect for observing a carload of likely looking prospects who had been cruising the area, when a shift changed or something and out came a nurse and a doctor. The doctor took one look at me and asked, "What's the matter with you, sir?" I mumbled something and told them to leave me alone but, professional to the end, they started asking all these questions. The next thing I knew they were escorting me into the hospital to admit me. I couldn't do anything to blow my cover on the street so I went along, listening helplessly as this voice came over my earphone: "Jesus, they're taking Bill to the hospital."

Capt. Beene had to send Ed Dullea in to retrieve me.

As the RAT program wore on, the more I got into the role of the Old Man, and the safer I began to feel. We all realized there was a danger factor. And if you didn't play it right, then you were likely to encounter a different type of villain entirely. I found that if I was really into the role, getting all the mannerisms down just right, and doing it the way it should be done, then a bad guy would almost certainly be taken off the streets as a result.

There were a lot of things to consider before setting off as the Old Man. At the Hall each morning I would lay out my clothing, check the fit, check my makeup, look at myself in the mirrors. If something didn't look just right I would experiment, trying to get the posture down and a certain feel for how the old guy would look, how he would act. If I used a certain sweater I would misalign the buttons. Anything to add to my infirm appearance. Other members of the team were invaluable during this time. Often, they would watch me as I dressed, saying a certain item of clothing wouldn't sell on the street, that my posture wasn't right for a certain disguise. I went through this process every morning, knowing that if it were a good day I would probably be robbed twice and, with minor modifications of costume and personality, I could expect to play two different roles. It was exciting to me in that I had no idea what kind of criminal I would be facing and how we would interact and under what circumstances we would meet. There was that edge, that anticipation, that was in a strange way thrilling to me. At that moment, with everything fitting well and armed with the knowledge that I had the best backup team in the world watching my back, my safety factor was way high.

Even so, I was soon to find, things could still go terribly wrong.

By June 6 we had netted a total of ten suspects and gained access to a second decoy apartment at 450 Eddy. Minnie Rat was not having much luck, working hard and getting a lot of "lookers," but proving maddeningly unable to bring any one of them to culminate their intentions. Leanna was furious and tried to find just the right combination of disguise and posture. Her efforts were to pay off in the near future, but that day, it turned out, would not be the day.

McEachern picked me up at the Hall that day at three, dropping me a few blocks away from Boeddeker Park for the start of another shift. I went to my neighborhood market, bought another three dollars' worth of items and drifted off south down Jones Street. It was warm and I was feeling relatively relaxed, working out my expenses for the operation thus far. The department had authorized an expense check of two hundred dollars for me at the start of the program and with that day's purchase I had just gone over the hundred-dollar mark. That included props, makeup, and the occasional pack of chewing gum I picked up during the Old Man's shopping trips to the Roosevelt Market.

It was funny, counting my pennies like that. Once, when I was working south of the Market Area for SCU, a guy came up behind me and snatched my wallet, which contained the usual four dollars—the most we were allowed to carry at any time. It was a clean arrest, the backups moving in quickly and hooking up the thief while I went back to decoy duty. That night, after my shift had ended, Capt. Beene walked up to me and said that the guy who gave up his liberty for four dollars that afternoon turned out to have seventeen thousand in cash stashed in the lining of his coat. And here I was worrying if a pack of gum or a couple of forty-cent soft drinks for my backup team would be considered an extravagant expense.

I tried not to think about it too much, listening as Swamp Rat reported three guys who had suddenly fallen in step behind me. They followed me from Turk and Leavenworth Streets up to the new apartment at 450 Eddy, watching as I went through the security gate and noting which unit I went into before walking away. The team met for a quick critique, sure the latest trio was merely setting me up for a future hit and that we would be seeing them again. We decided that I would try once more before calling it quits.

Traffic was brisk as I set out a little after four o'clock, with kids playing in the street and the hookers coming out for the nightly parade. The sun was just starting to disappear behind the ancient apartment buildings and pretty soon the day people of the Tenderloin would give up the neighborhood to the people who ruled it at night.

An hour later I was returning to the apartment building, tired and frustrated, when I noticed a man who had been standing near the front steps suddenly come alive with the reaction I can only liken to a well-trained gun dog coming to full point. I was just fifteen feet from the lobby gate and the radio chatter at the time consisted of "Bill is finishing his walk" and everyone was about to secure for the day. But this guy was definitely keying on me, looking first at me and then off across the street. My backup team was unaware of any of this.

I could hear King Rat getting ready to shut things down, asking the others where they had parked our cars, telling Hall and Closet Rats to escort me safely out of the area and back to one of our cars after I had made contact inside the apartment. It was my nightmare come true. My backups were shutting down mentally after a very long and uneventful day, with everyone out of position and one very hostile character giving me the evil eye from just feet away. I began to gesticulate wildly, hoping the Street Rats would pick up the cue. Then, to my absolute horror I saw the first suspect, a tough-looking type with scars in all the right places, signaling to a friend across Eddy Street.

This man, a transvestite named Christian Jenson, ran across the street and, as I unlocked the security gate, went in with me. 450 Eddy was very much like the other building we were using, except that there was a long hallway immediately off the foyer. The first man, LaMar Vaughn, brushed past me and took up a position in the hallway to prevent anyone from interfering.

Vaughn took two or three steps up the staircase to see if anyone was on the landing while Jenson positioned himself behind me and to my left. He was closest and had the position of advantage. Just as I reached the stairs, without a word, Vaughn started to hit me in the face. The blows coming fast and hard. I didn't have time to get my glasses off and I was terrified that he was going to drive the glass into my eyes. My arms went up instinctively to fend off the punches. They were both yelling "Give it up, man. Give it up!" trying to get my wallet as Vaughn used my head as a punching bag. He was dishing out the punishment and I concentrated on him, sure he would be the one who would hurt me. Then I heard a tearing and shredding, like some sort of Tasmanian devil, going on behind me, but I discarded the information, figuring the danger was in front of me.

This went on for what seemed like hours before Hall, Closet, and Swamp Rats charged up and tore into these guys, bent on capture. There was a short but spirited fight. It ended like the others, with Jenson and Vaughn face down on the marble floor with my backups hovering menacingly, praying that their prisoners would resist further.

I was shaken, and went up to the stairs to sit down. My head throbbed; my glasses were bent and misshapen. Nothing was said. Everyone was feeling a little sheepish but not wanting to recognize a potentially life-threatening slip-up just then. There would be time for recrimination later, at the critique.

Brian D'Arcy detached himself from the group in the lobby and came over to me. "When did you start carrying a gun?" he asked.

I looked up at him. "I don't have a gun," I said. "You don't think I'm going to give these people access to a gun, do you?"

Hall Rat pointed at my back. "Then what's that?" he said.

He had spotted the handle of a ten-inch-long butcher knife Christian Jenson had apparently used in an attempt to filet my kidneys. The evil-looking thing just sat there, hung up in my belt. I had been wearing a heavy leather belt and the knife had apparently gotten caught in it as Jenson slashed away. The back of my jacket looked as if it had gone through a shredder.

"Gee, Bill," D'Arcy said as I sat there, nursing my aching head. "That was close."

As long as I had been in law enforcement, my fellow officers capacity for understatement never ceased to amaze me.

Chapter 3

FOOTSTEPS

For a brief moment on June 9 we thought we had finally caught up with the one man the RAT unit wanted most—"Whispers."

But, as luck would have it, I had absolutely nothing to do with it.

There was little doubt immediately after my encounter with friends Vaughn and Jenson in the lobby of 450 Eddy that things had gone horribly wrong and that the entire operation could conceivably have ended with a police funeral. Very little was said afterward, but Inspector Tom Vigo, "Office Rat," and Charlie Beene discussed the incident and quietly suspended operations for the weekend. It was good timing, I thought. We had been running hard, perhaps too hard, with everyone keyed up and pushing themselves. Shepherding the Old Man "portal to portal," from the corner market to his apartment and through one of the toughest, most congested districts in the city, was not only time-consuming but nerve-wracking for everyone involved. Perhaps attention spans were getting short.

In any case, the decision was made to give us a rest and I gratefully went home that weekend, soaking away the bumps and bruises of the previous two weeks in a hot tub. On Sunday evening, the night before the Old Man was due to return to the Tenderloin, I received two telephone calls. The first was from Vigo, and he had good news.

"Just thought you'd like to know," Office Rat reported, knowing that the best tonic for a bruised and aching policeman would be news of a guilty plea. "Vaughn and Jenson copped to everything. They can't agree on who used the knife on you—neither of them wants to get pinned with the attempted murder charge—but they've pled out to assault and everything else. It's state prison time for them, Rug. Good work."

With ten suspects in custody and nearly all of them pleading guilty before setting foot in a court of law, I felt a tremendous surge of pride in what we had accomplished. Vigo and I talked a bit more about the operation, exchanged the usual pleasantries, and then hung up. The second call that Sunday evening was from Charlie Beene, and Charlie had something else on his mind entirely.

"How you feeling, Rug?" Charlie asked as soon as I picked up the phone. He had been my commander during the old SCU days and I had known him for years, but something told me I should be listening for anything hidden between the lines of this conversation.

"Fit as a fiddle, Charlie," I said, keeping it light. "I'll see you at the Hall tomorrow bright and early."

"That's what I wanted to talk to you about, Bill," Charlie said, the tone of his voice alone enough to send alarm bells ringing in my head. Of all the men and women involved in SCU at the time Doug Gibbs was shot and killed, Charlie Beene had probably taken his loss the hardest. Hard-working and dedicated, Beene was also openly fond of the people under his command. Such feelings could be both a blessing and a curse, and when Doug had been murdered it had proven a curse. Charlie was inconsolable, blaming himself for scheduling Doug to work backup that day, calling team members for weeks afterward to make sure they were all right. I couldn't hear or see him, but the specter of Doug Gibbs was on the line with us that Sunday night, I was sure.

"What's up, Charlie?"

"I'm worried, Rug. I hear we almost lost you Friday. I wonder if we're not trying to do too much with too little. It's taking a lot of time covering two decoys, pulling you in to put Leanna on the street and all. This going back and forth all the time might be getting to people. I'm really worried about Leanna. She just got married and she's starting a new family and all. She's studying for the bar exam at night. I wonder if the concentration level is where it should be."

"What are you saying, Charlie? Spit it out."

"I just want to know if things should go on. Listen, you won't say it and the other's aren't really talking, but that was really close Friday—too close. Maybe McEachern is right, this operation is just too dangerous. Someone is going to get hurt and I don't know if I could handle that."

He was all right with it, just afraid to lose one of his people. A commander's lot. I don't know that I could have handled it with the same level of professionalism. That's why I had been content to stay a foot slogger all my life.

"Look, Charlie. We're okay with this; it's just time to toughen up a little. People are tired and we could use more backups, but we don't have them. That's just the way it is. Listen, we're knocking them dead with what we have. Vigo just called. Jenson and Vaughn both just pled out. We're kicking their tails."

"I know, but..."

"But nothing. We've been out there, what, a month? We're halfway there. And we've taken some really bad people off the street, Charlie. And they're the RIGHT people, Charlie, the people who are doing these crimes. If it hadn't been for us, how many more citizens do you think would have died?"

"McEachern says we're crazy to be using decoys, that we're going to lose one of you pretty soon. He says we're just asking for it."

That one stopped me. I remembered first the sound of that knife shredding my coattails and then the talk I had had with Bruce on the way to St. Francis Hospital a week earlier.

"Look, Charlie. It's dangerous work, we knew that when we took the assignment. But I'll tell you what I told McEachern. I feel okay about it and I don't think whoever is up there looking out for me is going to let anything happen, you know? I just feel that good about the work we're doing here. See how the rest of the team is feeling about it, but I, for one, want to keep going."

Charlie was quiet, thinking it through and with ghosts of his own sitting at his shoulder, whispering in his ear. At that moment I wouldn't have traded jobs with him for all the gold in Fort Knox.

"Okay, Rug," he said finally. "See you tomorrow."

We had a meeting the next morning at the Hall of Justice, Beene, McEachern, and I, Beene probing for a further assessment of the operation so far. It went well, with Bruce supporting my belief that, while dangerous, Operation Dismantle was proving too effective to shut down just now. "We've just got to be a little more careful, is all," he said.

The team, this time concentrating on Minnie Rat, took to the streets at about two o'clock. Everyone was rested and fresh and with their heads on a swivel, as they used to say during my Marine Corps days. There had been no formal order, no remonstrations, but every one of us, from victim officer to backup Rat—knew that, from that moment on, things were going to have to be different or one of us might be coming out of the Tenderloin in the coroner's wagon. We took up positions in the decoy apartment.

Leanna began her day with a walk down Jones Street, past clusters of likely looking prospects who never even glanced her way, much to her distress. She walked south on Jones to Ellis, then turned onto Hyde. Nothing. No one followed her or expressed even the slightest interest. After an hour and a half she made a trip to the Roosevelt Market, returned to 555 Eddy, and sat down on the stairs, the pronounced stoop in her back and shoulders from depression more than any attempt to affect old age. Leanna, the Street Rats could see, was wondering what she was doing wrong.

At 4:00 p.m. Minnie got up, adjusted her skirt, and began her agonizing climb up the front steps to the security gate. At that moment the two words an undercover cop hates to hear most crackled over the radio.

"Oh, oh."

We came alive inside the apartment, ready for trouble

but unsure of where to look for it. McEachern was on the radio, trying to sort it out, demanding information. "Talk to me, people. We're blind as bats in here."

"Sorry," one of the Street Rats murmured into his microphone. "This guy just appeared. Negro male adult, well-dressed, blue jacket, jeans. He's following Minnie into the lobby and I'm pretty sure he doesn't live in the building. Seems to be loitering in the lobby area. I'd say he's a hitter, King."

We heard Leanna unlocking the door to Apartment Two. If this latest suspect ran true to form, he would strike now, while the door was open, pushing the Old Woman into the apartment where four very uptight and adrenaline-charged cops were waiting to jump on him. But once again, Leanna's luck changed for the worse.

"Folks, we have a civilian coming down the stairs. The suspect looked like he was about to jump her but he stopped when he heard the guy leave. No hit, repeat, no hit."

Leanna was really suffering. Once inside the apartment she looked around, unable to believe her stalker had not carried out his assault. McEachern grabbed her, told her to wait a few minutes and then to go back out into the lobby. Throwing her back out to the lions.

"King Rat to all Rats. What's our man's position at this time?"

"He's still in the lobby. Doesn't appear to be in any hurry to leave now that he's inside. Taking his time."

"Okay. Leanna's coming back out. Be ready to move on this guy if he so much as touches her, got that?"

"We got it."

Our suspect jumped like a startled deer when he heard the door to Apartment Two reopening and saw Leanna, her head down under her scarf, coming back out and walking right past him.

"This guy can't believe his luck, King. He's walking up to her. She's trying to get past the security gate but he's holding it closed. He's on her! It's going down now! He's got the money!"

For the next five seconds the air was filled with the

sound of doors banging open and shouted commands of "Freeze!" In an instant, Craig William Hill, the latest man to fall into the RAT net, turned from predator to genteel thief. He was well-spoken, apologized for being any trouble, and smiled as the handcuffs went on. He was still smiling, in his Jekyll and Hyde personality, while we were booking him an hour later. One minute he had been the strong-arm thief assaulting a defenseless old woman, the next an articulate victim of a police sting.

The abrupt change in his personality was striking. For a brief time the robbery and homicide investigators who had been after him believed we had netted "Whispers." That, however, proved not to be. A check of Hill's whereabouts on the dates of the Whispers assaults showed conclusively that he was not our man.

We were back on the street the next morning.

What we had to do was think of some way to make us—rather than the fifteen thousand bona fide old people who were living in the Tenderloin at that time—the focus of attention for twenty-five hundred bad guys. The only way to do this was to appear more unaware, more sick, more infirm, more incapable of offering resistance. This was an important aspect of what we were doing because the people we were after were, after all, cowards. We had to make it easy for them to believe that they were going to come out on top of any confrontation. Otherwise they would not strike.

Anyone who needs the help of a friend, maybe two friends, to help them rob a seventy-year-old man doesn't exactly qualify for Medal of Honor status. It was up to me to make these criminals reject all the other older people who looked as if they were still aware of their surroundings, who looked as if they could still run and kick, and make them look at me.

I started to experiment with my disguises, mixing them up and attempting to find out if any one thing appeared to work better than others in imparting that sense of vulnerability crucial to my success as a victim officer. The orthopedic shoe had been a nice touch, I thought, because anyone looking me over as I limped down the street knew that this old man would be unable to kick them or chase them after an assault. I got an old cane that looked as if I had had it for a long time, but I only used it with the disguise of the Old Man who was a little better off and could afford a walking stick.

When I first went into the heart of the Tenderloin, I observed that no one down there was carrying a cane. So when I walked down the street with mine it drew attention. That was good in a way because any thief contemplating an assault that day would be more likely to key on me. But it also told the bad guys that I could fight back, that I had a weapon. So I dismissed the cane after a while and used it only with the one persona, to give the Old Man a little diversity.

I next tried wearing a beret because it also drew attention. Besides making me look like a foreigner, it also meant I didn't have to wear a wig that could blow off at a bad time. It meant also that I had no need to color most of my hair—which took a lot of time. Then, I started wearing a hospital outpatient band on my wrist, putting different names on it just to spice things up. For a while I was E.Z. Hitt. There was always the chance—and in fact it happened soon after we thought we had caught Whispers— that someone would actually look at the bracelet and read the name, but no one ever caught on to the pun.

Also, by giving my address on the band as say, Laguna Beach, I felt it would add emphasis to my appearance as a prospective victim, because it told them I was a stranger on their turf and might not feel comfortable in their city. It added to the aura of victimization I was trying to project. It also added to the hate factor. They might say, "What are you doing up here if you're from Laguna Beach? Go back where you belong, old man, or something could happen to you up here that will make you remember that you don't belong."

All these things subliminally told a prospective crook that if they didn't hit me someone else would.

A couple of days after Leanna's encounter, I was in the

Roosevelt Market again. The proprietor there was getting a little confused. He knew me as two different men and was starting to scratch his head whenever I turned up. When I left the market and started to walk along my prescribed route down Turk Street, my nerve endings were on full alert and the hair on the back of my neck was standing up. My backups confirmed my suspicions. I had two very keen guys following me.

I made it down to the corner to head west on Turk and they were still with me. The radio was clicking and hissing, and the emphasis from the Street Rats at the time was "We can't prevent this, Rug, it's going to go down right now. They're going to do it right on the damn street." I'm hearing all this and, of course, a street robbery is the last thing we want. It would draw attention to me and negate our search for the type of criminal who would stalk an older person and attack them in their own home.

The Street Rats were saying "Bill, we're out of position! They're moving in right now and they look like they're going to do you on the street."

They had looked me over in the market, made up their minds and followed me for two and a half blocks. As they got closer my backup was shouting, "They're right behind you! They're getting closer..." And I was tensing, getting ready to take the hits... and then they passed me.

That sort of thing, with its buildup of adrenaline and then its sudden and unexpected release, was perhaps worse than actually being assaulted. It was doubly difficult sometimes, because while my awareness factor had to be very high, at the same time, I was pretending to be oblivious to my surroundings. That was the most difficult aspect of what I was trying to do, and there is no easy way to acquire that skill. I had to really study those situations, learn how to act and react, and get into it.

There were times when I would hear suspects talking about what they were going to do to me. "Let's take him into this doorway, here" or "You take him down and I'll grab the wallet." That was the really unnerving thing. My backup team was not within earshot; they were going to have to let whatever was going to happen to me happen. The only possible comparison I could make to the feeling would be like that of swimming across a lagoon and hearing the sharks talking about how they would make their attack.

I found this doubly difficult to do because, as a police officer, my instinct was to turn around and just take these guys out. Then I realized how much more difficult it would be for elderly people. What do the really old people do, just going out for a walk or to church? It was a mind-boggling thought, knowing that thousands of people were living out their last days with that fear, day in and day out.

To contribute to the lack of awareness I was trying to give off to those around me, I had to take some pretty drastic measures. These included going so far one day as to allow a pickpocket to rummage through my pockets without making any effort to stop her. To do so would have told anyone watching that I was something other than what I was pretending to be, so I kept still, mumbled about the high prices and let this gal rummage around in my pockets until she got what she wanted. I was in the Roosevelt Market again, the place quickly becoming my home away from home, and I cashed a ten-dollar bill, picking up a few things for the trip back to the apartment. This woman, whose name was Barbara, came up and made her move almost immediately. Her hand went in my pocket right off the bat to make the dip, and then off she went.

As it turned out, there were three guys following me at the time, waiting outside the market for me to come out, and they were really angry at Barbara for ripping off a guy on their turf. They chastised her and then they ran to catch up with me as I shuffled off down Turk Street. About a half-block away they moved in, triangulating me in an instant with one guy ahead of me, one behind and the third walking alongside of me. We were walking along like that, my three escorts waiting for the view from the street to be obscured by a parked Volkswagen van, when one of them decided the time was right and stepped in to make his move. The Street Rats told me it was coming so I sort of danced out into the street, right out into traffic, and the car horns are going off as my attacker got nothing but air and smashed his hand into the wing window of the Volkswagen.

I could hear him cursing and yelling and it was all I could do to keep from laughing, I stayed in character, doing a crazy matador's dance out in the middle of traffic while the motorists leaned on their horns and gestured at the crazy old man gyrating and shaking his hips in the middle of the street.

Much has been made about the fact that police officers rely on a peculiar sort of black humor—gallows humor—to hide the fact that deep down inside they've been torn apart by the stuff they see out on their beat every day. Psychologists would say that it is a common thing for someone with a painful job to develop a method of shielding themselves from further pain. Well, it's true, and I did my best to keep things light and lively when time and circumstance permitted.

Sometimes, when we returned to the Hall of Justice to book a suspect, I would duck into Southern Station on the ground floor of the Hall and, still in costume, deliberately walk in and stir things up. If there was a crowd of civilians around, the Old Man would wave his arms and launch into a tirade against the poor, besieged Southern Station guys, muttering things like, "Well, you cops ought to get your story straight," until everyone was looking and every officer's face went red. When the Old Man was through tongue-lashing the grunts for their inefficiencies, he would turn left and head down to the Tactical Division, mumbling to himself and cursing.

One day I went in and spotted Al Bragg, a longtime friend and partner, leaning against the wall shooting the breeze with another officer. I crept along, hunched over and drooling, until I passed them and the second officer was staring openly at me.

"Gee, Al," this officer said, his face pinched and

confused as the Old Man rammed a wall and tottered backwards from the impact. "Isn't that Bill Langlois?"

And Al, bless him, just looked at his comrade and said: "It used to be."

Sometimes, just for fun, I would get into the elevators at the Hall, still in costume and leering at women or doing some of the unseemly things old people sometimes do. Once, I was hanging back and listening as the elevator stopped at each floor, with inspectors from the various details getting in and, once they had determined I was a harmless old coot, talking about the devious nature of some deputy chief or the latest political escapade. I'd sit back, humming to myself without anyone paying the slightest bit of attention to me. When I got home that night I'd call the inspector with the juiciest bit of gossip and cheerfully, in my Old Man's voice, tell him he ought to be more careful about what he said in public elevators. It floored them, and they were supposed to be professional observers. To fool them, in good light and in the crowded confines of an elevator, gave me an added sense of security about my cover identity.

Another time, however, my acting abilities proved too effective for my own good. During my earlier incarnation with SCU, I was portraying a derelict. One afternoon, I had settled down in a doorway on North Fifth Street, the only open doorway on the entire block. Across the street was a parking lot and in the parking lot were two guys who had followed me all the way from Howard Street, about five blocks. They were pacing back and forth, trying to make up their minds whether to hit me or not. I could practically hear them salivating from across the street.

I was lying there, watching an ant trail and knowing a hit was imminent, when I heard footsteps approaching on my side of the street. I heard them stop just inches away and then heard a young woman inquiring about the state of my health. When she got no response she stopped another passerby, gave him a quarter and told him to go call for an ambulance. Inwardly, I was rejoicing that some good soul would actually stop to render aid, but I was also profoundly disturbed that this Good Samaritan was on her way to blowing a truly fine arrest.

I heard the request for an ambulance go out over my radio receiver, then the voice of my supervisor canceling the call, explaining that we were working a decoy operation in the area and that there was no need for an ambulance to respond. After a while it became painfully evident that no help was coming and this woman was really getting upset. She gave a second person a quarter and sent him off with the same mission as the first. Fifteen or twenty minutes had gone by and these two wolves were still hovering across the street, waiting for Florence Nightingale to leave so they could come over and take care of business. My benefactor was kneeling down at that point, trying to rouse me by shaking my arm.

Finally Joe Carlin, one of my backups on this particular operation, told everyone he would make contact with the woman and get her out of there so the two suspects could complete the hit. Joe wandered down, flashed his identification and explained that I was a mendicant known to the police, that I did this all the time and that an ambulance would come along shortly and take me off.

But this woman was having none of it. She said "Fine. I'm a registered nurse. I'll wait until the ambulance gets here," and planted herself until Joe had no choice but to leave us or make a scene. My backup team was on the radio telling me, "Bill, this lady is not going away and there's no ambulance coming. You're going to have to get well and walk out of there. It's the only way she'll leave you."

I stirred, started to rearrange myself, and got ready to stand up, easing out the kinks after all that time on the cold cement. My savior knelt down next to me, making sure this man she'd been watching for almost half an hour and had spent fifty cents on was really all right. She was cursing the ambulance that wouldn't come and asking me questions. I looked up and the two guys were still across the street, pacing up and down and going nuts because they thought this woman was going to get to me first.

When I was almost standing she asked, "Are you feeling better?" I turned to her and, using the only thing I knew that would put her off entirely, propositioned her in a particularly nasty manner. She was gone like a rocket. I couldn't have told her I was a police officer after all that, or she would have been enraged and probably reported my conduct to the chief. But I'd like her to know—if she happens to read this—that I'm apologetic.

Life as a victim officer was fascinating, if a little distressing at times. Aside from the potential for physical danger, there was always the possibility that something or someone would come along and shake my faith in human nature so severely that it would make me even more hard-boiled and jaded than I already was. One of the worst examples of this took place a year or so before Operation Dismantle.

I was hanging out in a parking lot on Eddy Street one day and dressed as a Russian sailor when a woman in her thirties came up and joined a small crowd of people who were watching me shout, "Nyet! Nyet!" and the few other Russian phrases I know. People would try to help and I would push them away, dropping to the ground and rolling around until I could feel the air move the hairs on my leg. Then I knew my pants leg had ridden up far enough to reveal a small eyeglass case I had stashed in my sock.

Another man was already there when the woman with the little girl arrived. I figured he would be the one to make the grab, if anyone, but she strolled up and said, "What's the matter?" And the guy told her this crazy Russian had fallen and his money case was showing.

"Really? Where?" she asked, and he pointed to the case. She reached down and whisk, it was gone. I couldn't believe it. My backup team couldn't believe it. They let her go quite a distance, trying to give her the benefit of the doubt and hoping she would prove to be a good soul and turn the case in to a cop or store-owner or someone. But she walked right past a beat cop a few blocks away, so they finally closed in and arrested her. They found my eyeglass case in her purse, along with a wad of cash, and a couple of items she had apparently just shoplifted from Macy's and I. Magnin. That was the crazy thing. She had money, and her child was obviously well cared for, but she was walking down the street stealing from a distressed old Russian.

I try not to think about it too much. Dwelling on such things is not good for the soul.

After we captured the man we first believed might be Whispers, the RAT unit scaled back its operations slightly. Eddie St. Andre was on vacation, and with a key backup officer gone, no one was eager to take on the bad guys. We kept decoy time down to a minimum, contenting ourselves with identifying potential future prospects. During this time, though, I was followed home on several different occasions by crooks who seemed to be marking my address for future crimes. What they didn't know is that, after they left, backup officers tailed them back to where they lived, identified them, and noted their addresses. After a while we started to see the same faces. Barbara, the pickpocket I had run into at the market earlier, surfaced again. On June 16 she talked her way into my apartment, had a good look around and appeared to be scouting it out. "I'll be seeing you," the Old Man said when she left that day. And he was right.

The next day Swamp Rat was back, rested and telling everyone about his vacation until we begged him to quit. Things started off well with the news that Barry Gwen and Perry Young, the two vicious thieves who choked the Old Man and tried to drive him right through the living room floor on May 30, had pled guilty at their preliminary hearing, thus negating the necessity of a court trial. Gwen got three years in state prison for his sins. His partner went away for six years and four months. The Old Man, needless to say, was elated, and started work with a new sense of purpose.

He celebrated with another hit that afternoon. It was starting to be old hat. The Old Man sauntered through

Boeddeker Park, spent three dollars and sixty-five cents on groceries at the market, and was hit as he returned to 555 Eddy.

The criminal was Leon Dean, and he proved to be a little more refined than the other strong-arm artists I had been meeting lately. Leon tried to ingratiate himself with the Old Man first, saying his name was Bill and that he had just moved into the building. After a few minutes of this he decided the time was right, punched the old guy in the stomach, and reached in for his wallet. He actually had the leather in his hand for about a millisecond before he was buried under a ton of cops. When he had regained his wind, the Old Man hit the streets again and drew two more pairs of prospective clients who followed him home and marked his address. Operation Dismantle, we felt, had hit the Mother Lode of criminals and the vein was far from being played out.

Minnie Rat scored a hit June 18 when two men, Nelson Torres and Pascual Vera, picked her purse and fled, making it to Eddy and Polk Streets before D'Arcy, Dullea, and Swamp Rat scooped them up. Both proved to have previous warrants out for their arrest. The team had nine hits to its credit so far, six for me, three for Leanna. There was a total of fourteen suspects in custody and thus far, not one had been released due to insufficient evidence or faulty police work. Aside from the few blows I had taken, there had been no serious injury inflicted since my run-in with Vaughn and Jenson. That was to change the very next day and, as luck would have it, this time a police officer was not on the receiving end.

Minnie took to the streets first that day without much success. We were keying on what we were calling "Area A," the heart of the Razor, but no one appeared interested in Leanna this day. So we pulled her in, with Sgt. Charlie Brewster of the Robbery Detail watching the operation for the first time. Since few police officers get to watch a felony from the moment the idea pops into the head of the perpetrator to the instant the act is actually committed, Brewster, who specialized in robbery cases, was fascinated.

He would be relieving King Rat—Bruce McEachern—in a few days and was trying to familiarize himself with his new assignment. Little did he know what the day had in store for him.

I hit Boeddeker Park at half past two that afternoon, wearing my trusty beret and the hospital bracelet, and dragging my orthopedic shoe around like a ball and chain. That particular afternoon the park looked like an extension of San Quentin Prison's third tier, home to some of the toughest criminals in California. Nothing was said openly but I could feel the heat of inspection and I sensed that I had attracted attention. Twenty minutes later I got up and moved off, stopping first at the nearby Cadillac Market before making my way back to 555 Eddy.

"Anything?" King Rat wanted to know, his voice clear over my radio receiver.

"Not a thing," said Swamp Rat from his position inside the apartment building.

"He's clean," echoed Street Rat West. "No buyers, yet."

Everything changed as I passed 519 Eddy, just a few doors away from home base. Two men, lean and tough-looking, reversed their direction of travel and keyed on me as I approached the front gate of my building. They were walking swiftly, intently, careful to stay just behind me in order to catch the heavy metal gate before it closed them out. There was little doubt about what they had in mind.

"Bingo," one of the Street Rats said. "I think we have two takers on Bill. Real players. They look like they just got out of the joint yesterday. San Quentin alumni all the way." He gave their descriptions and I tried hard not to overreact to the warning. Instinctively, I hunched my shoulders, burying my face lower to make it harder for them should they decide to take me on the stairs.

"Did you get that, Rug?" McEachern said, trying to keep his voice calm. I signaled that I had.

"He knows," someone else said.

"Right. Get ready to move."

My key grated into the lock on the security gate, resisted

a little, and then slid the tumblers back. When I pulled it open the metal barrier felt like it weighed a hundred tons.

"Where are they?" McEachern wanted to know.

"Right behind him."

I could sense them there, hear them breathing. They were right on top of me, one of them holding the gate open for the other. My feet felt as if they were made of lead. This time, I felt, things were going to get rough.

"Hey," one of them said. I turned and they were on me in an instant, not wasting any time before sinking their fists into me. I curled up, and tried to batten down the hatches and protect my face as they waded in, working me over systematically. I waited for the sound of the cavalry coming, hoping for a bugle call or something to tell me it was going to be all right, that I would make it through this one as the blows kept coming. Usually I could hear the doors springing open and Dullea barking orders or Swamp Rat telling them what would happen to them if they resisted. But this time there was none of that, not a single discernible sound. For an instant I wondered if I had taken a shot to the ear and gone deaf.

What I didn't know was that everyone was screaming in that marbled entryway—Dullea, St. Andre, D'Arcy, as well as Arthur Anderson and Donald Mitchell—my two assailants. What should have been a straightforward arrest had disintegrated into a real dogfight. When Anderson and Mitchell saw the bluesuits boiling into the lobby, a man would have had to scream at a noise level surpassing that created by a jet aircraft taking off to have even made himself heard, much less announce himself as a police officer. It was the sound of sheer human terror and it was bouncing off the walls until it was incomprehensible. They couldn't get out so they started to fight. And that, as it turned out, was not the smart thing to do.

It should be said that, with few exceptions, most of our arrests to that point had been carried out with a minimum of fuss. The opening seconds were always filled with a lot of noise and bluff designed to shock, intimidate, and subdue the culprits quickly, making sure they did not have time to even think about escaping. Afterward, conversations between backup officers and perpetrators were often quite civil, with each side careful to treat the other with respect.

That was how it normally went. But Anderson and Mitchell were not about to go quietly to jail. Anderson, we later learned, had just been released from jail and apparently had developed no fondness for incarceration. Both men fought us. Hard. I lay off to the side and watched as Dullea, St. Andre, and D'Arcy, at first surprised by the stiff resistance, set to the task of subduing the pair. I listened as a baton struck home with a sound not unlike a car tire slapping over a trolley rut, and both sides threw punches and took them with equal measure.

In the end, both Anderson and Mitchell were prone on the cold marble floor, while a squad of red-faced backup cops stood over them surveying their handiwork and blowing like bulls after the charge. Mitchell was bleeding from the head, and it was decided that Sgt. Brewster, who would be taking over the unit in a couple of days, should take him to Mission Emergency Hospital for treatment and then on to County Jail at the Hall of Justice for booking. Brewster hauled his prisoner to his feet and headed for the door, stopping to look back at me, a bemused expression on his face.

"Is it like this every day?" he asked, wondering what he had gotten himself into.

I nodded and smiled at him nebulously. "Every damn day," I lied.

Between assignments as victim officer, I was also expected to appear in court as more and more of the people who had fallen into the RAT triangle made their appearances before the judge.

As I have said, most of them pled guilty outright in the face of such irrefutable evidence, but every once in a while, one of them would try to bluff it out and the case would be slotted for trial. I was scheduled to testify at such a trial one day when the Assistant District Attorney

Michael Williams took me aside during a lunch break and said he felt that the trial could end with a hung jury. Apparently the panel was having a hard time connecting me, a relatively healthy-looking police officer, to the old man they kept hearing about. They just couldn't see how someone would go after me.

He asked me if I would mind if he asked me to do something a bit out of the norm once I was on the stand. He didn't want to tell me about it because my reaction had to be genuine, he said, and I agreed to do what I could. When I took the stand he stepped up to me and said, "Officer Langlois, at the risk of embarrassing you, would you remove your upper dental plate and assume the guise of the gentleman you portrayed in this operation as best you can in your current clothes?"

The jury, every one of them, turned to look at me at the same time and I knew I was on the spot. I could make or break this case with what I did next. It definitely took me off guard, but I said, "All right," sort of hid my face from them as I took out my plate, and turned back to face them.

"Officer Langlois, would you please walk back and forth in front of this jury as you would in your role as victim officer?"

I gave myself ten seconds or so to get mentally prepared, running my hand briskly through my hair, and then I stepped down out of the witness chair. As soon as I hit the floor I was the Old Man again. It came to me that easily by then. Hair slightly disheveled, an old gent with an unfixed direction, just trying to get along. I weighed 190 pounds at the time but I suddenly felt as if I weighed only 160. I walked back and forth in front of them and I could see their expressions change from doubt to outright anger. When I turned and retook the stand I looked down and saw the bad guy slap himself on the forehead. He must have known he was dead. I went out into the hall after a while and the Assistant District Attorney came out a few minutes later. "Well," he said. "You did it again. The guy pled guilty on the advice of his attorney."

The psychology of thieves was a constant wonder to me. I was nearby once when the Street Rats were booking a suspect at the Hall of Justice and it suddenly dawned on this guy, after seeing me walk around in my knickers and out of my old man garb, that he had been suckered. He started to threaten me, full of bluff and bluster, telling me he was going to get even, and if it took him the rest of his life he was going to find me. (He was up from Texas, if I remember, and in town only a short time before he had tried to rob me.) We usually ignore threats of that kind but this man was being particularly offensive. So I walked up to him and said, "Hey, babe, that's fine. But what say I walk down to the crime lab, have them take some pictures of me the way I looked when you knocked me down, and have them sent back to Texas for your mommy and daddy to look at? So they know what a big man you are?"

It was like turning a faucet off. The way he looked at me I knew that if that man's father had any idea what his son had done, he would have killed him. He hadn't been raised to do the kind of things he had been charged with, and he knew it. So he just shut up.

On June 20 Leanna made her fourth hit. A man named Edward James, a career criminal with a history of armed robbery and theft convictions, hit her in the back, choked her, and snatched her purse as she was entering the lobby of 555 Eddy. Closet and Hall Rats found James—the seventeenth unwilling participant in our program—hiding under a parked car in a nearby alley.

Three days later I left Boeddeker Park with a suspect close behind. The Street Rats immediately labeled him "Spider" for his frenetic, agitated manner. He was all around me for several blocks, peering closely at my face, and looking at my hospital bracelet. For long, anxious moments, we felt he was going to try to assault me on the street. Then, without warning, Spider suddenly ran ahead of me, straight to the decoy apartment, perching on the front landing exactly like his namesake and waiting for me to come to him. He jumped me at the security gate, grabbed my wallet, and ran off at speed with Dullea and the Street Rats close behind. He was fast but he forgot to look where he was going. When he turned to see if his pursuers were closing in on him, he ran smack into a parking meter and cracked his melon. No one had laid a finger on him.

His name was Donald Greene. He was my eighth hit. Dullea and Brewster grumbled, but they took him to Mission Emergency for X-rays before booking him. They were getting tired of making hospital runs.

Leanna added two more to the growing hit list on July 2. But she paid for it when the pair, Thomas Clark and Michael Deshay, hit her on the right shoulder and knocked her to the floor as she was entering Apartment Two. Both men had prior convictions for burglary. Leanna, bruised and hopping mad, sarcastically suggested that Clark and Deshay must have been trying to work their way up through the criminal hierarchy by robbing old ladies, but the two men just glowered.

That same afternoon Barbara, the talkative pickpocket, resurfaced and joined me as I was walking along Turk Street. Taking me by the elbow she escorted me home, going on about how she was mad at me because I hadn't been home when she visited the apartment looking for me on Father's Day.

"Yeah, I came by with a turkey and everything. Got my nephew and a friend and we came to see you. We would have cooked the bird and had a good time, but we rang the bell and you weren't home." That was one Father's Day feast I was glad I had missed. She talked her way inside the apartment, making sure the door was locked behind us, and we just let her run, everyone in place but no one knowing what she was going to do. She sat me down on the couch, made a big fuss about getting me comfortable, and went into the kitchen to put away my four dollars' worth of groceries. She took her own sweet time and checked the cupboards out to see if I had anything worth stealing.

"Don't you worry, Honey," she kept saying over and over. "Barbara is here and she's going to take care of everything." After going through every drawer in the kitchen and using my bathroom she came over to where I was sitting and tried to take my hat off—something I definitely did not want her to do since it was covering a very bad dye job. I waved my arms and yelled, "Leave the hat alone!" Then her hands were all over me, looking for my wallet and not being very subtle about it. She finally found it, lifted it out of my inside coat pocket, and then kissed me on the neck, saying she'd be back with her friends soon to cook me a decent meal. "Barbara's going to take care of you, don't worry," she said, unbolting the front door and hurrying out into the lobby with the wallet and all of four dollars. They popped Lavine "Barbara" Logan in the lobby. She pled guilty to two counts of burglary and theft and got a year in the county jail. She still hasn't cooked me that turkey dinner.

After my shopping excursion with Barbara, all of $16.10 were left in the RAT detail's kitty. By all accounts everyone seemed pleased with our success. Leanna had seven suspects to her credit. I could claim fourteen. Expenses had been relatively low and no one could argue with the conviction rate, which still held at one hundred percent. Still, people were tiring again and the team was released to spend the Independence Day weekend with their families and friends.

We returned to work July 7, this time shifting the focus of our operations from the Tenderloin to the south of Market area, specifically the area near the Greyhound Bus depot on Seventh Street. My first attempt to work the area was disrupted when the Street Rats observed a fight nearby and broke away to intervene. When my backups were once again in place I headed north, back to the Tenderloin and wearing a new disguise. I had abandoned my orthopedic shoe for a pair of slippers, and I limped along as if plagued by foot problems. At five o'clock, as we were getting ready to shut down the operation because of darkness, I started to buzz with that old familiar feeling.

Someone, I knew, had taken an interest in me.

Their names were Ivory Walker and Harvey Walton, and both had extensive burglary and narcotics convictions. Both men were career criminals, so tough that for the first time since we had started the operation, one of my backups, Greg Randolph, went to great lengths to "accidentally" run into me on the street in order to give me some very pertinent advice and some much-needed firepower.

Greg, who in his position as Street Rat West had seen these two guys and heard them talking about me, came back down Turk Street and deliberately ran into me.

"Sorry, Old Man," he said apologetically. "I didn't mean to bump you." And at the same time he slipped me a .25 caliber automatic. We were in a very isolated part of Turk Street and the backup Rats thought Walton and Walker were going to drag me into the old cab depot and rob or kill me in there. Walker was an imposing character, six feet seven inches of menace. I was making Old Man noises when Randolph leaned in close and whispered: "If they pull you down into that building, shoot the sonsabitches, they aren't playing around."

That showed how closely my backups had been watching me and to what lengths they would go to protect me. By contacting me openly on the street like that, Greg had exposed himself and jeopardized his own cover. As part of the team, it was the last thing he was meant to do. When he did it, I knew we were in big trouble. I slipped the little automatic into my pocket.

The old depot had a sort of ramp down into the garage and it was dark to begin with, plus we were starting to lose light. Walton and Walker were trying to bracket me, one of them running ahead of me, the other staying behind. I crossed the street, moving away from the cab depot and forcing them to maneuver. Again, one of them ran ahead. He was hanging around, probably so he could pull me down behind some parked cars. I was ten feet away from him when I veered suddenly, and walked past him, and across the street again, this time towards a

construction area where some ironworkers were getting
ready to leave for home. I turned back down Eddy Street,
heading for the apartment and the reassuring presence of
my own troops. Every sense was on full alert and I was
aware of how attuned I had become to the smells and
sounds of danger. While they were walking with me I
could smell the evil—literally smell it. It was like picking
up through smell what you would see when a sudden
concussion shifted the dust in a room. Everything just
sort of shimmered, and I was picking up the vibrations.

As we got closer to 555 Eddy, one of the pair, I couldn't
see which one, stopped to make a drug deal on the street.
For an instant I thought they had been distracted, that
they would leave me alone after all. But as I reached the
familiar steps and unlocked the heavy metal security gate,
the Street Rats reported that Walton and Walker appeared
as intent as ever.

"They're done talking, Bill. They're going to do you,
probably in the lobby," Street Rat West reported. "They're
moving to catch up to you now."

For the last few minutes I'd walked with my hand
around the gun Randolph had slipped me. I surrendered
its reassuring presence and reached for the gate key,
moving in that curious sort of slow motion that always
seemed to come when we reached this stage, the surreal
time when heartbeat and thought processes and sensations
all seem to slow to an impossible rhythm.

"Right behind you, Bill," a Rat reported. "It's going to
happen now."

When the door clanged shut and they were there in
the lobby with me, I remember thinking if people could
be taught to recognize the smell in that lobby, at that
instant, they would know forever what evil smells like.
There was a brief moment of eye contact, something may
or may not have been said, and then I was doubled over
from the force of a blow and a hand was reaching for my
wallet. That curious frozen moment was closely followed
by the familiar sounds of help arriving and the onslaught
of oaths and commands. I lay there, quivering like a raw

nerve ending exposed to air, my hand on the little gun in my pocket. It took a while before I could unwrap my fingers from around the grip.

I was hit again the next night, July 8, by a paroled robber named Henery Scott. It was the team's sixteenth hit. My eleventh. As in the past, I was spotted while spending $3.50 of the $15.00 dollars left in the team's budget on soft drinks at the Cadillac Market. Scott entered the store to check me out further, hovering nearby as I pretended to examine the frozen dinner section. He went back outside, put his coat over his arm and waited for me, following me along my usual route back to the apartment. After a few moments he passed me, waited for me again and tried to push me into a garage at 545 Eddy. I managed to avoid this and Scott, more than a little miffed at missing his first shot at me, followed me to the security gate. There he prevented me from entering and looped one arm around my neck while he searched for my wallet with the other. When he was done, he pushed me to the ground and I rolled down the steps, banging my shin and shoulder as I fell.

Bobby Aitchison, Van Rat, corralled him a short distance away and Henery Scott was booked at the Hall of Justice, spending the next several weeks in jail as a guest of the city and county of San Francisco before he was finally returned to state prison.

After Henery Scott, things began to wind down. It seemed that the press had stumbled to what we were doing and were preparing stories on the operation, something that could be disastrous if the news was broken while our people were still on the street. Apparently a few good souls at the Hall of Justice press room were aware of what was going on and had held back until the television stations and others began to realize something newsworthy was going on and started asking a lot of questions. Charlie Beene, who had lately been spending time with us out on the street, decided it was time to close things down, even though we did not feel we had netted our primary suspect and the reason for Operation Dismantle—Whispers.

"Another time, boys and girls," Beene said. "We'll be back. In the meantime, just know that you've done one helluva fine piece of police work. I've scheduled a press conference for next Monday; we'll shut things down then. I'm very proud of you all."

It came as no shock, but a lot of us, myself included, had mixed feelings about seeing the operation come to an end. Witnessing the end of the RAT unit, to that point the most successful undercover operation ever undertaken by my department, for me was like watching a Super Bowl team retiring. Most of us had been involved in decoy work before and considered ourselves professionals in the game. A lot of my team members, particularly Eddie St. Andre, had been watching my back for years. I have a great deal of respect for Eddie. His brother was a robber who had been killed in a gunfight with San Francisco police, and yet here he was working as an officer himself without ever showing any ties to that affair, or to his brother's life. He was a great police officer, a great backup man. He knew more about me than my wife ever would. The man was really committed.

Everyone had known we'd be able to run the operation only two weeks at a time with the number of officers we had, because the work was just so intense that we couldn't handle a more prolonged exposure on the street. We were expected to be "up" every day, to reach that emotional peak and be ready the minute we set foot on the street. If we didn't it could mean someone's life. After reaching that level every day, day after day, seeing it all come to an end left me with a curiously empty feeling.

On Friday, July 11, some members of the media who had been good to us and refrained from plastering details of the operation across the front pages of their papers or on the six o'clock news were brought in for a firsthand look at Operation Dismantle. Photographers were positioned on rooftops near where we were working and others were loaded into our van, shooting video through the one-way window.

Leanna went out first. We had a lot of bites but no takers, which was a little disheartening. It would have been nice to end the program with a videotaped record of an actual hit, so that the general public could have an objective look at what exactly it was that we were doing out there. The press photographers, pleasant enough guys but used to having things wrapped up nice and tight for them, grumbled a little about the lack of photos, but hung in there.

A little after four, dressed in a black coat, white shirt and tie, and with one foot shod in a slipper, I entered Boeddeker Park for what would prove to be the last time. At least two possible suspects were warned away by residents of a nearby crack house who had come to realize that the Old Man was not what he seemed to be. At 4:44, I picked up two new-found friends and the radio began to buzz and hum with warnings and admonitions. They played the usual game of cat and mouse, passing and then falling behind me, a half dozen still and video cameras watching their every move, until I crossed to the north side of Eddy Street and they paralleled my route from the opposite side of the street.

It had been decided that we would use a different apartment this last time out rather than jeopardize any possible future use of 555 Eddy, and I stepped up to the security gate of 450 Eddy as the press cameras ground on. Brewster asked me if I felt these two were the ones and I nodded, sure I would be hit. The photographers, who were at first slow to rise to the game we had been playing every day for the last eight weeks, reacted with excitement as the two men who had been following me suddenly crossed Eddy Street, rushed me into the lobby and attacked me on the stairs.

Both suspects, Stephen Simmons and Douglas Jeffers, resisted as the backup Rats materialized and swarmed all over them. It turned out to be perfect theater, with local television using footage of the arrest on the evening news and still photos planned for use in the *San Francisco Examiner* and *Chronicle* the next morning.

We returned to the Hall of Justice that last afternoon with Simmons and Jeffers in tow, and reporters and photographers hovering and asking questions as we booked the last two members of the Rat Trap Club—numbers twenty-five and twenty-six. After explaining for the hundredth time how it felt to walk down a darkening street in an old man's shoes and with two or more predators snapping at my heels, I could see the reporter's eyes glaze over with boredom and move off in search of another news snippet. Only a few seemed to have a real sense of what it was we had been doing for the last two months and fewer still seemed to realize what we had accomplished. Not one asked me if I had been hurt during my last encounter.

After it was over and the press had drifted away to file their stories, Charlie Beene walked up to me with that smile of his and asked how I had known that Simmons and Jeffers were going to try and take me down.

"Charlie," I said. "They were hungry and I was the plate of the day. They would have followed me if I had gone out to Land's End and walked out into the surf."

That night the entire team, with the exception of Bruce McEachern and Bobby Aitchison, attended what we thought would be a farewell dinner held at a Daly City restaurant. It was a grand evening. I gave identification bracelets bearing each individual's RAT unit name and badge number to my partners as a small expression of my appreciation and good feelings toward them. We had been blessed. For a time I had had a chance to do something really worthwhile. We had taken some truly dangerous people off the streets and put them in jail where they belonged. That's what really thrilled our team. So often in police work, officers do their duty and it's months or years down the line before they see any results. But this operation was very satisfying. The people who slept behind bars that night were the right people—caught in the act, predators in the worst sense—and we had nailed them every time.

But none of the dozen police officers who gathered

and tipped their glasses over the starched white tablecloth of that restaurant that night, nursing our bruises and filled with pride, could possibly have known that within a year we would be called on to do it all over again.

Chapter 4

COMEBACK

News of the RAT unit's accomplishments in the Tenderloin spread quickly that summer of 1986. Team members basked in the warm glow of public appreciation few police officers ever experience. Requests for interviews, appearances on radio talk shows, and newspaper articles commending our work followed in the weeks after Operation Dismantle. It was the sort of attention police officers secretly long for but know deep-down inside they're not likely to get.

I was proud of what we had accomplished and of my part in it. Soon after the RAT unit was disbanded and its team members shuttled off to their regular duties at district stations, I was nominated for a Gold Medal of Valor—the department's highest award for bravery—in connection with three separate cases undertaken during the 1986 operation. Leanna Dawydiak was nominated for a Silver Medal.

Any exultation I may have felt from news of my nomination was tempered in late July when we received word that a ninety-three-year-old woman returning to her home in the Duboce Triangle area of the city had been beaten, robbed, and left for dead by a suspect who matched the profile we had been given of Whispers. The woman, caught on her doorstep and pushed inside her apartment by her assailant, remained in critical condition at a local hospital for several months after the attack. We could not help but wonder if our efforts in the Tenderloin had merely driven this predator out of the neighborhood and into other areas of the city in search of new, less aware victims. The thought haunted me for months.

While the Robbery Abatement Team had, for all intents

and purposes, ceased to exist, it was difficult to entirely erase the memory of my two months in the Old Man's shoes. I returned to my former beat in the Sunset District with mixed emotions, getting used to the feel of a uniform again and missing the excitement of my work in the Razor. Every so often, when things were slow, I would take out a dog-eared copy of a *San Francisco Chronicle* editorial published the day RAT was disbanded and read it for what seemed like the thousandth time. I carried the clipping in my wallet and dragged it out to remind myself of what RAT had been able to accomplish and the support we had engendered in a town as politically, ethnically, and culturally diverse as ours.

"A nationally innovative program of the San Francisco Police Department, launched to protect the elderly infirm from hit-and-run robbery attacks, has resulted in twenty-six arrests in just six weeks.

"The novel, decoy experiment was begun after one hundred robbery-assaults were reported on aged victims last year, with four of the crimes resulting in fatalities. Old people in the Tenderloin District have been particularly vulnerable to criminals who stalk their victims from the street into a building, where they are viciously attacked and robbed.

"Members of the special police anti-robbery unit are doing their job with courage, skill, and daring. They have earned the community's commendation and gratitude."

High praise from a newspaper which, in the very recent past, had found more to fault than to praise where the activities of the police were concerned.

Behind the clipping I had tucked away another little souvenir token, a lucky charm I've kept to this day. On the night before Operation Dismantle got underway I took my wife Kitty out for Chinese food, carefully steering the conversation away from any discussion of my team's mission. Kitty didn't know everything about the RAT unit's purpose and I saw no reason to worry her. Even so, I could tell from her expression that she was uncomfortable with my involvement and nothing I could do or say would be enough to put her mind at ease.

Things brightened considerably when our waiter arrived with dessert. I grabbed my fortune cookie and, on a whim, told Kitty my fate would be guided by its message. Then I snapped it open and extracted the fortune inside.

"See," I said, sliding the slip of pink paper across the table. "I told you there was nothing to worry about."

Kitty's expression changed from one of consternation to outright amusement as she picked up the little piece of paper and read my fortune aloud: "Among the lucky, you are the chosen one."

No fortune, I felt, would ever prove so true.

After the daily rigors of Operation Dismantle I settled back into the routine of a district station officer, walking my beat on Irving Street, capturing the occasional felon, and enjoying my conversations with the area merchants and local characters I had come to know and love over the years. Life was good, if a little too comfortable for my taste, and although Kitty was happier knowing I was out of the mix and working a low-crime area, I secretly longed for something more challenging.

The opportunity presented itself in early summer when investigators in the Fencing Detail asked if I would like to participate in an undercover sting operation, posing as a larcenous pawnbroker and part-time fence named Bill "Tiger" Taggart in the city's Mission District. It sounded like a fulfilling assignment. I would work from a storefront with a Daly City police officer, gradually letting it be known among the shop's customers that we sometimes bought stolen goods. After we had established our clientele, dealing with the neighborhood burglars who brought us their "merchandise," we were to take them into a back room and, offering just pennies on the dollar, carefully record each transaction with hidden cameras and sound equipment. It would be another new role for me to play, another challenge. And I leapt at the opportunity.

Once I agreed to take part, everything was set in motion.

Backup officers were chosen, the equipment was in place and my cover identity was being nurtured and established. In the meantime, though, an old scourge had returned to the city and—once again—fate and the toss of chance combined to put me in the right place at the right time.

On June 12, as the final touches were being made at our Mission District storefront, Lt. John Brunner of the Robbery Section sent an inter-departmental letter to Deputy Chief of Investigations Larry Gurnett. Brunner's memo cited the sudden "dramatic increase" in the number of strong-arm assaults against the elderly in the Tenderloin in recent weeks.

"Within a five-block area of the district we have noted a marked increase in the number and frequency of attacks against the elderly wherein the suspect follows the victim into the residence then proceeds to beat the victim into submission before searching the residence for valuables..."

Brunner concluded that: "Normal police operations have not been able to bring the suspect(s) to justice. The Victim/Officer program utilized during 1986 should once again be placed on-line for a period of two weeks utilizing personnel from TAC, Field Operations Bureau and Investigations in order to locate and arrest the suspect(s) preying on the elderly."

Attached to the memo were the case numbers and details of sixteen separate assaults—on people ranging from sixty to ninety-nine years of age—which had taken place in the Tenderloin over the last two months. In most of the cases the victims had been followed for several blocks by one or more suspects, assaulted on their doorstep, and pushed into their homes. Once inside, they were beaten or choked into unconsciousness. Several revived to find themselves lashed to chairs, forced to sit by while the intruder methodically ransacked their home, looting family heirlooms, and making off with any cash they might find.

Descriptions of the assailants were understandably shaky. But under close examination a common thread began to emerge. Six of the victims reported seeing a lightly complected black male ransacking their homes, carefully wiping down counter tops and anything else he might have touched. In at least four of the cases, this man put his finger to his lips and "shushed" his victims when they began to protest his intrusion, telling them in a hushed, whispery voice not to make a sound.

It was warm in San Francisco that summer, with spectacular sunsets painted in red and gold. But as the temperature climbed, so did the number of reported assaults and thefts against the elderly. All the good weather was bringing more people out into the streets. And while nearly every one of the bad guys we had bagged the year before was still serving out his sentence in prison, our detectives felt a new breed had stepped in to pick up where they had left off—either forgetting the lessons learned by their less lucky brethren or choosing not to care. It didn't matter. What did matter was that old people were once again being victimized, and the decision was made to do something about it before someone was killed.

I was first contacted by Commander William "Bud" Scheffler who, with Charlie Beene, had been tapped to come up with a plan to knock down the type of crime we had seen the year before. Both men were comrades from my old days with the Canine Unit. My heart began to race when Scheffler called with a familiar proposal. He told me that running a second RAT program with two victim officers would be too complicated, that the training phase for the number of backup officers needed to cover two decoys would take too long.

Instead, if I agreed to it, we would use just one decoy this time around—me—in a concentrated effort to combat these crimes and catch the crooks in the act. Scheffler said the Fencing Detail and its Mission District sting operation had been asked to take a back seat for one week while I did this, and they had agreed, using the time to complete the wiring job on the bogus coin-and-stamp shop we would be using as a front.

One week didn't sound too bad, even though I would be the only one out there taking the hits, but Scheffler must have thought I needed another hook because he threw me one I simply could not pass up.

"By the way, Bill," he said casually. "We think one of the guys we want is Whispers. Robbery thinks he's back in the Tenderloin."

Those few words seemed to ring in my ears for minutes after Scheffler hung up. I put the phone down and walked around my apartment aimlessly, my brain on overdrive. Whispers was back.

I went down to the TAC Squad office at the Hall the next day to meet with Beene, Scheffler, and Lt. John Brunner. Someone must have been in a real hurry to see these crimes knocked down because none of my superiors was wasting any time. They laid out all the latest crime statistics for me, filled me in on all the suspect information they had, and said, "Bill, we're going to go right into the teeth of the lion."

There was a pin map in the office showing where the most recent victims had been found, and Beene pointed to an area of the Tenderloin where the concentration of pins was thickest—good old "Area A." The Razor.

"My home away from home," I said, trying to conceal the shiver which corkscrewed down my spine. "Once more into the breach..."

"Right. It's the same drill as last year," Beene said. "All the victims are elderly, followed home, pushed inside, and brutalized. It's all going down off the street. These guys must be related to that bunch we got last year. They're tough and they're ruthless. You can expect to take some licks."

Charlie's evaluation of the working relationship between these crooks proved to be spot on. "Area A" was, in my estimation, a sort of watering hole for humans set up in the middle of the urban jungle. We had roughly fifteen thousand wildebeests who left their shelters during daylight hours to go to the hole to drink and twenty-five hundred lions waiting for one of the weakest ones to make a wrong move. And there was no doubt that the lions controlled the area. It was their turf. And now some of them were together and on the hunt again.

Senior-citizen bashing was fast becoming the new crime of status among the Tenderloin's parolee population. A low-risk endeavor which carried the added attraction of potentially high rewards for the perpetrators, they had it down to a science, leaving little evidence but terrorized seniors in their wake. Although public attention had peaked during the weeks and months following Operation Dismantle, the citizenry's notoriously short attention span had once again reasserted itself. Older people who had felt safe in the relatively crime-free months which followed the RAT unit's first effort were now being picked off at a record rate. But, not happy with only worldly goods, their assailants were also taking the very fabric of their victim's lives and unraveling it thread by thread.

Our budget for the one week the RAT unit was supposed to return to the Razor was once again a whopping two hundred dollars, this time generously donated by Chief Investigator John Majka of the District Attorney's Investigators Division. Almost all of the money was devoted to my transformation back into the Old Man.

Not only had Majka come up with the money for the operation but he had volunteered some of his troops as well. Four of his investigators were provided, working alongside veteran RAT unit members for the first time. As it turned out, the resulting partnership between working cops and representatives of the DA's office surpassed everyone's expectations.

Joining us for RAT's latest manifestation were District Attorney's Investigator Karen Hibbitt, who posed as a lady of the evening while working backup and who ended up with the unfortunate sobriquet "Hooker Rat" ever after; Lee Tyler, also known as "Cab Rat," who wore the most outrageous aloha shirts he could find while driving a borrowed taxicab with Karen in the back seat; Vanetta Pollett, who shot surveillance photos of suspects from the team's van and who was quickly named "Photo Rat;" and Ron Leon, "Pocket Rat," whose ability to blend in with the tawdry background of the Tenderloin earned him the admiration of team members who were still trying to perfect the art.

Joining them as "Street Rats" in a concentrated effort to protect the Old Man were some old and trusted friends: Eddie St. Andre, Craig Randolph, Bobby Aitchison, Craig Woods, and Tony Rockett, men to whom I would gladly entrust my life. Joining Ed Dullea and Jim Batchelor on duty as "Closet Rats" this time around was Officer John Chestnut of the Tactical Division, and I wondered how we would manage to hide these three giants in one tiny closet. Another new officer, Jeremiah Morgan, would serve as "Lobby Rat" during this effort, this new position created to enhance response time in the event the Old Man was assaulted in the lobby of his building, as had happened several times in 1986. Still another RAT unit veteran was Reno Rapagnani, an experienced Tactical Division officer who, it so happened, was married to Leanna Dawydiak, my decoying partner from the previous year. Reno would serve this time around as "Room Rat."

Inspectors Jim Bergstrom and Tony Camilleri, on loan from the Robbery Detail, were dubbed "King Rat III" and "Office Rat II," respectively, and were responsible for coordinating the program and making any necessary changes to its mechanism.

We decided to work out of three apartment buildings. One was on Sutter Street, the second on O'Farrell, and the third—and best of the lot—was the Ben Hur apartment building on Ellis. I decided that it would be best if I slipped in and out of three different roles, interchanging props from each for diversity, and matching personalities to whatever apartment we chose to use that day. I would become the Hospital Releasee, fresh out of surgery with a bandaged foot, and still wearing my hospital admitting band; the Pensioner, a gentleman who lived on a restricted income, but still wore a snappy hat and jacket when he went out for his afternoon stroll; and The Veteran, still proudly wearing his VFW pins, but fighting the greatest battle of all—age.

While the stated purpose of our mission was to arrest the people responsible for the latest round of elderly assaults, every one of us knew we were also after one man—Whispers. It became plain to me, judging by the set and determined looks on the faces of my colleagues, that this man's criminal career would be coming to an abrupt halt if we were good and lucky enough to find him.

LEE TYLER, "CAB RAT."

I was first approached and told I would be taking part in the RAT program that summer by my boss, John Majka. John called me into his office one day, looked me up and down, and immediately told me to stop shaving. He said that I would be going to a briefing the next morning and would eventually be assigned to a new task force targeting crime in the Tenderloin. That's how I got my introduction to RAT.

John knew I had previous police experience. I was, I suppose, "volunteered" along with three others from my office who had also been out on the street and who, John felt, would be most comfortable doing the things we would be called on to do.

That was another innovation of the RAT program. Usually, the police department and the district attorney's investigators office operated as two separate and distinct bodies. While we occasionally ran across city police officers, we had never worked with them. Looking back on it, I don't think the department could have fielded the number of people they needed for a RAT operation at the time. There was an acute manpower shortage within the San Francisco Police Department at the time—and still is— and the department just couldn't give up that many people to staff the task force. So we were called in to help.

My initial reaction to news that I would be joining RAT was one of great anticipation. I thought it would be a terrific opportunity to do some police work. A task-force assignment usually means something out of the ordinary, that things would be getting exciting. I looked forward to that. I was also looking forward to working with the San Francisco officers, many of whom I'd come to know while assigned to the district attorney's office. All of us were very eager to see what the brass had in mind.

We met in the TAC Squad office the next morning and Lt. Brunner told us about Whispers. Beating and robbing an older person was, as far as I was concerned, the worst type of crime. And Whispers was the worst type of criminal.

No one said much during that first meeting. Everyone just listened. Then Jim Bergstrom put our respective assignments on the board and told us how we would go about them. Jim assigned us according to what he perceived to be our individual talents. I don't recall ever volunteering to drive the cab, but when I found out what was going on—that there would be an outside team and an inside team responsible for keeping an eye on Bill—I knew I didn't want to be one of the guys on the inside. As demanding a job as it was, I just knew I didn't want to spend all day sitting in that apartment and waiting for something to happen. For some reason Jim tapped me to be Cab Rat and, boy, was I happy with his decision.

My job was to follow Bill in a taxi we had borrowed from one of the local cab companies, staying just behind and keeping an eye on Bill as he moved along. If he got into any trouble on the street I was supposed to move in. I had a microphone I kept out of sight and just under steering-wheel level. It was a great setup because I could talk without bringing the microphone to my mouth, something that would attract attention in that part of town.

For some reason, the cab made me invisible. It was like I was not even there. Several times I witnessed drug transactions being made within feet of me while I was parked in a loading zone, keeping one eye on Bill and feeding him information as he went. The only people who saw me were the people who happened to want a cab, and I would have to shoo them away if they got persistent. It was easier with Karen riding in the back seat.

With "Hooker Rat" riding as my fare, I was pretty much left alone.

I learned a lot in the Tenderloin. The longer I drove the cab, the faster I learned that elderly people were generally being regarded as easy prey. We could see the psychology behind each hit. Karen and I would watch them, the old folks carrying bags full of groceries, trying to make it past these groups of young guys who stood on the street or in doorways and sized them up as they went by. Sometimes it was just a glance, a change of pace, but you knew what they were up to. I had never before realized it was so bad. It changed my perception of growing old.

Living in the Tenderloin had taken a lot out of these old folks and they had pretty much given up hope. They were walking along with tunnel vision most of the time, thinking that if they kept their heads down and their eyes away from people, the bad guys would not see them and they would be able to make it back home that day, wrapped in their own protective bubble, with their money or their groceries. It was disturbing for me to see this because, of course, simply ignoring the threat was not enough to make it go away.

When we first started the program I had the feeling that some of the San Francisco officers were looking at those of us from the DA's office and wondering, what we were doing there. They were the veterans and we were the new guys. I caught that at the briefing. I knew a couple of the cops, but not all of them, so the next day I made it as clear as I could to a couple of the San Francisco people that, "Yeah, I'm a DA investigator but I'm also a cop. I've been a cop for twelve years and I like putting crooks in jail. If you think I'm here to watch you, you're wrong. I'm here for the same reason that you guys are here, and that's to catch these people and put their butts in jail."

They took it pretty well. Actually, it didn't take us long to start to work together as a team, and things really began to come together after we made our first arrest.

Watching Bill turned out to be like putting a piece of

cheese on a string and dragging it through a rat's nest. He was a born actor and definitely one of the best cops I ever met in my life. He's got more heart than anybody I know. When Bill got out onto the street and into character, the thought that he might be a policeman would never cross your mind. He was just that good.

We could see the transformation in the morning, when Bill would start to change his clothes, mixing this jacket with that shirt, always trying out new things to look even more convincing. Karen and Vanetta would help him with his makeup, putting gray in his hair and beard, darkening his eyes, and we would all stand around and watch him transform into this Old Man.

After a while, he even started talking like him. On the street Bill would shout and jabber and rant. At the end of a shift, while the rest of us were getting ready to go home, Bill would be over in a corner, staring into a makeup mirror and playing with a false beard or some new prop.

We all knew why Bill worked so hard at becoming the Old Man. We also understood why it was so difficult for him to leave the character behind sometimes. When you're asked to play a certain role for hours every day and your very life depends on how well you play that role, it's not so easy to just step out of it when someone says the game is over and everyone can go home. It is an awful lot to ask of someone.

When I stepped onto the streets as the Old Man in 1987 it dawned on me just how dangerous the next few weeks would be. The whole thing suddenly seemed to take on a dimension of its own, becoming something larger and potentially more lethal than I had anticipated. For the first time in my many years as a decoy, the threat of impending violence loomed in my future. Big time.

I became aware of an exceptional feeling between my teammates and myself, an almost indescribable sense of attachment fueled by that most powerful of emotions—fear. It was the same fear civilian victims must have felt, I reasoned, yet it was somehow different. A real bond was forming between team members that not even other cops, let alone the general public, could never fully comprehend and would always be excluded from sharing.

Those outside my Robbery Abatement Team would have no earthly idea of the magnitude of what we were attempting. I resolved then and there that we could not, would not, lose the battle to come.

With the Street Rats already in the area and Cab Rat always close behind, I returned to the Tenderloin with the entire team in place for the first time on June 19, concentrating on routes and responsibilities and cursed by radio problems as well as other glitches almost from the beginning.

Although I was followed to my new home after only a few hours on the street, my stalker broke off his attack at the last moment, possibly because he spotted a backup officer with a camera across the street.

That night, scribbling in my diary again, I wrote: "Interest in the Old Man seems high his first day back. It would have been nice to have gotten a hit our first day out but this sort of work is not exactly easy. Only when everyone does their job perfectly will the bad guys feel comfortable enough to make their moves. It will come!"

We spent the next day meeting and "dressing up," traveling to the local Goodwill to buy clothing for the backup team. It cost us a total of $18.98, which says something about the quality of the clothing we were seeking. Army fatigue jackets were *de rigueur* for the Street Rats because they were commonly worn in the Tenderloin and because their baggy shape made it easy to conceal the bulk of a bulletproof vest and whatever weapons the street team decided to carry.

Earlier in the morning we had traveled to an apartment building in the eight hundred block of Sutter Street to take a look at a basement storage room the building owner said we could use as a dummy apartment. It had possibilities, we decided—a double door setup at the end of a dead-end breezeway and isolated enough to make

interference by an unwitting passerby unlikely. We decided
to give the storage room a try, returning later to paint the
door and nailing a big, brass number two on the front. A
few days later we would find out what a truly lamentable
decision we had made.

The paint on the storeroom door was still drying when
we took to the street June 23 and the Old Man, creaky
and cranky, arrived by cab at Boeddeker Park. After
complaining mightily about the cost of the cab ride to
the cabbie—a big, sturdy-looking fellow with a brush
mustache and a day-glo aloha shirt—I crept into the park
dressed in a light gray coat, green tie, and my trusty black
beret. But where Boeddeker Park had looked like a state
prison annex just a year earlier, this day found it filled
with families and young children taking the afternoon
sun. There were still empty bottles of whiskey littering
the grassy areas and the odd hypodermic syringe could
still be seen rolling with the breeze under the park benches.
But the daunting presence of parolees which had marked
our first excursion into the area a year earlier was nowhere
to be found. Their departure, I thought, was testimony to
Operation Dismantle and the follow-up work of the
Central Station officers who had retained control of the
area after the RAT unit had pulled out.

I left Boeddeker, fulfilling a private vow I had made
not to conduct decoy operations in an area where women
and children were present, and headed toward our dummy
apartment on O'Farrell, using Jones and Ellis Streets and
keeping my eyes open. It was hot. I found it very difficult
to work for any length of time without having my makeup
run. Even if I had wanted to, there was no way I could
wear body armor—I would have died from heat
exhaustion. It would have been like a sauna.

I made it "home" without incident and set out again,
this time catching my personal cab to Taylor Street, where
I attracted attention as soon as my feet hit the pavement.
My radio receiver came alive with the sound of excited
voices.

"We have a fish on, folks," a Street Rat reported

instantly. "Black male, brown sweater. He's behind Bill but hanging back, heading north on Taylor toward Sutter. Fish on. Did you copy that, Bill?"

I signaled that I had, charged with excitement and feeling the first rush of adrenaline tingling at my fingertips and the back of my neck. It was an intriguing sensation, with each of the senses snapping on one after the other, as my body prepared itself for the ensuing game of cat and mouse. The Old Man was back. From Sutter I walked a block west to Jones and turned south back toward the apartment on O'Farrell, wanting to see if my shadow would stay with me. I got my answer within minutes.

"He's sticking, Bill. He's still on you." It sounded like Craig Woods but I couldn't tell for sure. "Fish on. Fish on."

The other Rats began to check in and I became more aware of the security network around me than at any other time. Nine police officers were on the street, in vans and a dummy taxicab, moving like a destroyer screen around a damaged and listing aircraft carrier as I walked haltingly along O'Farrell to the private entrance of my decoy apartment at 801 Sutter. All things considered, it was a massive police presence. It wouldn't take much to tip off the lions that the hunters were in the area. I prayed that things would hold together as we neared the building.

Our suspect really had to slow his walk down to keep pace with me. Half the time he was across the street, crossing over and watching me from there while Tony Rockett, Curb Rat, sidled up alongside to look him over. Our man was clean-cut, sort of portly but not out of shape, Rockett reported. He had a folded newspaper in his hand and he kept playing with it. Rockett and the other Street Rats were going crazy trying to see if he had a gun or a knife tucked away in there.

When I stopped to catch my breath the suspect would also stop. I could see him, hands concealed by his newspaper, reflected in the shop windows. We played a little game. I would walk along, stop and peer into a store window and he would do the same, maintaining his distance but never getting too far behind. When I was sure that everyone was in place, I turned into the alley and headed for our newly painted "apartment."

It was situated at the far end of what was actually a closed alleyway, ringed by the four-story-high walls of adjacent buildings. While we had all agreed at first that it would make a perfect decoy apartment for the Old Man, its shortcomings quickly became apparent. Not only was the alley too long, with no place to hide our troops and with my having to travel unescorted along its entire length, but to add to our problems a huge dumpster had materialized there overnight. This blocked out any view the Street Rats had of the Old Man as he neared and entered what was actually the rear basement door of the apartment building. Our dummy "Apartment Two" was immediately inside the door and on the left.

"He's right there, Bill. Right behind you. I still can't see his hands. If you hear that paper rustle, turn around and take him out, partner, because we don't know what this creep is going to do," Curb Rat advised.

That sort of radio traffic was really hyping up the Room Rats, who couldn't see a thing but were, of course, listening to every word. Reno Rapagnani was positioned just on the other side of the apartment door when I reached it. He was trying to stay calm, wondering if the next moment would see me being slaughtered on the very doorstep, when someone said, "He's inside with Bill. I can't see what's happening. The Room Rats are going to have to take over."

That was enough for Reno, bless him. I was fiddling with the apartment key when the suspect, who went by the street name of "Chevalier," slid his arm around my neck and attempted to pull me down. I needed another second or two for him to follow through and make it a strong-arm robbery, but Reno couldn't stand it any longer and he materialized, standing there with a baton in his fist and a wild glare on his face. He frightened the stuffing out of our suspect. At that point we really only had Chevalier for burglary, but Reno's unexpected appearance was enough to convince him he had erred, and the next thing I knew he had dropped his newspaper and taken off out the basement door and back down the alley like a scalded cat.

About the only good thing to be said about our choice for the Old Man's apartment was that there was only one avenue of escape for Chevalier and it was easily blocked. The Street Rats, with Lee Tyler and Karen in their trusty cab, rounded him up in seconds.

It turned out our suspect didn't have a knife or gun or anything in that newspaper after all. He had been so keyed up, so excited by the chase and what he was going to do to me that he had been masturbating into the paper as we walked along, playing our game of cat and mouse. He was booked and we left it to the district attorney to decide what charges to file against him. Reno, with a playful reminder not to be so hasty next time, was left behind to book the rumpled newspaper into evidence.

TONY ROCKETT, "CURB RAT."

I was working out of Southern Station that summer of 1987 when one of the other guys told me there was talk that the old Street Crime Unit was being reformed, only this time with a twist. I didn't need to hear much else. I told this person that whatever operation was being planned, I wanted to be included, and a couple of days later I got the call. It turned out to be very satisfying work. It's not too often that you actually see a crime happen and you're able to make an arrest at that time. We were able to see the whole thing develop, the look the suspect gave his victim, the approach, the actual hit.

I had been a member of the SCU prior to the existence of RAT. As it turned out, it was pretty much the same guys who were with SCU in those early days who were later asked to work with RAT. They took me on because they knew I had the experience and also because of the part of town we were going into, the Tenderloin. It would be easier for me, as a black officer, to blend into that area because of its racial fabric. Everyone knew it would have been virtually impossible for a white guy to stand on the corner of Eddy and Leavenworth unless he really looked like a dirt ball.

Some of those guys, like Eddie St. Andre, might have been able to pull it off, no offense to Eddie. It's just that he was that good. But to be there on a consistent basis for a very long time with apparently nothing else to do was a little difficult.

RAT was an invaluable experience. Maybe because of a particularly nasty experience I had had in my SCU days, I knew it could also be damned dangerous. No matter how hard we tried to blend into the area, I just never knew when I would run across someone who recognized me as a police officer. Several times we would be watching a certain guy as he followed after Bill and he would turn and look at me, dead in the eyes, trying to figure out if I was a cop or not, and then his eyes would pass me by.

We had no idea who we would be dealing with at any given moment out there. There were just so many different variables to consider. Communication breakdowns, having a bad guy spot you, losing Cab Rat because he was pinned in traffic—there was so much that could go wrong. A family friend spotted me one day, scratching on the street corner like the heroin addict I was attempting to portray, and that night my wife got a very polite phone call.

"I saw Tony today," our friend said, trying not to sound the alarm prematurely, but still curious and concerned enough to call. "He was down on Eddy Street. Didn't look very well, either. Is he okay?" That sort of thing. My own sister walked by me one afternoon and ignored me when I called her over. She didn't recognize me.

My wife was not happy with the work I was doing but I couldn't let it go. It was fun in a way, a real test of my talents as a police officer. But more than that I felt we were doing some good, going after the worst breed of criminal and putting them away. I would say that ninety percent of the guys we arrested had a long history of the same type of crimes—robbery, assault. And when they started hitting the elderly, everyone knew something had to be done.

Hearing that Whispers was working again really got us going. We knew he was young and black. I remember they said he always wore a green leather jacket, that he had a strong body odor, and that he always spoke softly to his victims just before he struck. He was working the Upper Tenderloin–Lower Nob Hill area because there were a lot of elderly people living there and it was very quiet. The guy was like air. One day he'd move into an area, make his hit, and then be gone. Every one of us wanted him in the worst possible way.

My job as Curb Rat was to serve as Bill's close cover. Out on the street, I would be the one closest to him. If anything went wrong I was supposed to get there first and bail him out. That's why it was difficult for me, because I had arrested some of the guys we were dealing with.

Many times a guy would catch my eye and I just knew he was trying to remember where he had last seen me. Naturally that would have been when I was slapping the handcuffs on him and taking him to jail. It was the last thing we wanted them to remember. That's when I would do something really strange to throw them off—urinate in the street or pick my nose—things a police officer would never do but which we had to do to protect our covers. Sometimes I'd scream at a woman as she walked by, "Hey bitch, where's my money?" And she'd scream back and we'd have a little scene right there on the street because that sort of thing was the norm in the Tenderloin and it was the last thing the Kronks, the bad guys, expected a cop to do.

The whole exercise was a form of acting, pure and simple, and the people who were the best at it, like Bill, made the best undercover officers. We had to play a role depending on the area we happened to be in and we had to be able to walk the walk and talk the talk of that neighborhood to be convincing.

Bill called me Curb Rat because I was always just on the opposite side of the street from him, walking along with him as he shuffled along in his Old Man character. I was watching him, but at the same time I had to look like

I wasn't watching him. That's when I'd play the part of a junkie, hanging on a parking meter or pretending I was breaking into cars—anything to keep my cover and stay in a place where I could watch him. Pretty soon he had given the entire team new names, to the point where we not only used them over the radio but also in private. Bill would say, "Curb, do me a favor and run this guy through the computer for me," or "Hey, Street West, there's someone on the phone for you." To an outsider I guess it might seem a little silly, but it added to the sense of camaraderie and helped keep things light.

Costuming was important for the Street Rats as well as for Bill. We were always looking for something different to wear that would make it easier for us to blend in. Bill used canes and makeup. Craig Randolph and I did a lot of shopping around at Sallies and Goodies (that's what we called the Salvation Army and Goodwill), and we would pick up something that looked as if it would work on the street, or use something a family member would give us.

There were times when this was next to impossible. I mean, on a ninety-degree day, how do you cover a radio, a gun? We never wore body armor, because some guys would walk up to us out there and run their hands all over us while saying hello to see if we were wired or carrying a gun. Besides, the body armor always showed, no matter what we did to hide it. We'd get that telltale hump along the back or a bulge in the front which made it easy for people to spot us. So the Street Rats didn't wear it. Part of the decoy element was to attempt to look like everyone else on the street that day.

I had a radio I wore under my coat or shirt. Then I covered the earphone with headphones so I could bounce and beep and bop along without arousing suspicion, just another guy on the street listening to his favorite tunes. Usually I would pretend to be an addict, scratching from drug withdrawal, rubbing my hands together, and jerking around. I was constantly wiping my face. It made it easy for me to talk into the microphone and give Bill information. The only difficult part of it was when someone tried to engage me in conversation on the street at the same moment that one of the other Rats was trying to tell me by radio someone was following Bill.

And that happened quite a lot. Just when you started thinking nothing else could possibly go wrong, something would. It was that kind of game.

"Jeez, Bill. I'm sorry."

Poor Reno spent the day apologizing. Room Rat thought he had screwed up our first hit by opening the door prematurely. I told him to forget it, that I was glad he had come to my rescue. But while my encounter with Chevalier had been relatively painless and his arrest relatively free of incident, it was clear that our plan of operations still had some kinks to be ironed out.

At the critique that night we decided to dump the apartment at 801 Sutter as just too dangerous. We couldn't watch it correctly, it was agreed, and everyone resolved to find another, more suitable place, for the Old Man.

The next morning we started again, working on tactics and trying hard to smooth things out. I was out for a morning stroll, head down as usual and careful to mind my own business, when I saw a young man waiting in a nearby doorway. The Street Rats advised me that this man was definitely interested in me. I continued, happy to have a client so early in the day. But minutes later I was dismayed to see that another potential victim, an elderly woman between sixty-five and seventy years old, was approaching from the opposite direction and had also attracted this man's attention. The look he gave her was unmistakable. As she approached him he stepped out, requesting a cigarette. His eyes flickered slightly at the sight of the few dollar bills she had stuffed in the cellophane of the cigarette pack. They flickered again a moment later when he spotted even more cash in a semi-clear shopping bag she was carrying—one of those see-through things with her money showing through as plain as day. I couldn't believe the soon-to-be victim could be so careless. A lion had selected his prey right in front of me.

Moving as fast as I dared, I edged closer to the suspect, watching as he attempted to put his victim at ease by thanking her politely for the cigarette. Then he walked quickly around the corner to lie in wait for her.

Before we took to the streets each morning we took the time to carefully diagram each of my walks so that every team member would know my intended route and direction of travel. All had agreed that I should not just meander according to whim. When I doubled back on my route and headed for the suspect to keep him in sight, the Street Rats knew immediately that something was amiss.

It was painfully obvious to me what this man had in mind. I had seen the predatory look he had given his prey before and I trailed after her as she rounded the corner. Sure enough, she ran right into the guy. This time he was not so polite. As I watched, he snapped a headlock on her, wrestled her purse away, and knocked her to the ground. I was pointing, signaling, doing everything but tapping out a Morse Code SOS with my cane to get my team's attention, but I needn't have worried. They were already on the radio, summoning a marked patrol car to make the arrest rather than expose our backups.

Still, I had witnessed a crime and I decided to see it through for as long as I could without blowing my cover, shuffling after the thief as fast as the Old Man could go. Our suspect disappeared into a nearby market and I followed him inside, standing there watching as he went back to the freezer section to rifle the woman's purse. She had also seen this guy go into the market and she walked up to confront him, demanding her purse back and getting knocked down a second time for her efforts. She fell headlong into a display, took some cans down with her, and started to scream.

This did not please the thief, a twenty-nine-year-old, 195-pound package of muscle named Michael Gordon. As I stood there watching this scene play itself out, Gordon threw the ransacked purse back at her, less the money of course, and said, "Here's your damn purse, now shut up!"

By then she was screaming, "Yes, but you took my money! You took my forty-six dollars!" and with that Gordon ran out the door, his shirt drenched with sweat.

What Mister Gordon didn't know was that Curb Rat and Street Rat West had watched him from the moment he ran from the store, with Randolph following along behind and giving minute by minute updates on his location as they went. When the local beat car arrived seconds later, Randolph pointed the suspect out and a very surprised would-be thief found himself on his way to the Hall of Justice. Cab Rat located the forty-six dollars in Gordon's right front pocket. Although the victim drifted away after the incident and could not be located, the rest of the team was not so hesitant. In the end, Gordon was sentenced to six years in state prison, with three years suspended, on the basis of the team's testimony alone and despite the fact that the victim had not come forward.

Gordon, it turned out, had been arrested for eleven felonies and ten misdemeanors that ranged from robbery, rape, and assault with a deadly weapon up to that point in his career. I had to wonder what a guy with that kind of history behind him was doing out on the street to begin with, but after a while those sorts of thoughts can weigh a cop down. So I moved on to other things.

While Old Bill was being a good citizen at the neighborhood market, the Room Rats back at our second apartment on Sutter Street were playing with the intercom system, inadvertently listening in as a male-and-female robbery team discussed the merits of taking down "the old guy with the cane" while standing around on the front porch. The duo was weighing the likelihood of success when neighbors from the nearby Hacienda Hotel, a hostelry known at the time as a notorious crack cocaine den, sauntered over and advised them to look elsewhere, that the area was "swarming" with cops.

Although no one seemed to have tumbled to the fact that the Old Man was something other than he appeared to be, it was plain that it was time for another move. We ended up using a large apartment building at the corner of Hyde and Ellis, the Ben Hur Apartments. It was perfect, an ideal location with a large, marble foyer and a spacious, ground-floor apartment to the immediate right of the front door. The manager was cooperative. We decided to try it right away and I set out from Eddy and Larkin Streets, attracting attention from a pair of thugs who followed me north on Hyde to Ellis, looking as if they were going to take me on at any moment but suddenly breaking off the hunt.

I couldn't figure it out. I reexamined my clothing and assessed my vulnerability factor. Craig Woods, who had gotten close to the pair during their stalk, said one of them turned to the other and said, "That's one lucky old man today!" before the pair decided to break things off.

"Discouraged," I wrote in my diary that night. "Possibles all seem to have something else to do today. They seem to be buying the performance, I don't think I've been burned, but they are not following or attacking and I can't fathom exactly why. Maybe I'm trying too hard. Maybe I don't appear vulnerable enough. Something's wrong but I can't quite place it."

The very next day, June 26, my luck changed. A little after two, I started out from the unit block of Taylor Street, across from the famous Original Joe's Restaurant, when a slender, grungy-looking kid in his mid-twenties fell in behind me. My backups reported his every move but for some reason he was not acting like a candidate. Instead, he was observed walking ahead and talking to two local transvestites. All three waited for the Old Man and then hit me right on the street and in the open, standing me up and surrounding me.

"Don't I know you, honey?" one of them said before they pushed me up against a wall, a hand darting in and going for my wallet.

The Street Rats, more precisely the district attorney's investigators, couldn't believe what they were seeing. While Vanetta Pollett filmed the entire sequence from our van, I was pushed into a doorway and beaten, the blows coming in salvoes, hard and fast and aimed at my face. My glasses were knocked askew. I covered up, trying to protect my eyes, when I saw a hand reach in and snatch my wallet. Feeling a little feisty and stalling for time, I fought back as the Old Man would and actually managed to regain control of my billfold for a moment before more blows slammed home and it was taken for a second time.

"I don't believe it," Pocket Rat said over the radio. "They're beating the hell out of him and he's looking at his watch to log the arrest time!"

It was over in seconds. The Street Rats converged and braced my three assailants against a wall. I was shaken but determined to remain in character, praising the brave officers for their fine work and muffling a tirade against criminals so insidious they needed three people just to rob one tired old man. "It's a damn shame!" I railed. "What's this country coming to?"

I was bruised for a week after that. Worse than the physical injury was the realization that literally dozens of people on the street that day had witnessed the attack and had done nothing to stop it. Looking at Vanetta's pictures afterward, we saw several people who had walked past, stopped to watch as the Old Man was attacked and then continued along on their merry way. One of them was laughing, telling a friend he never knew "queers could hit so hard."

It was a sad commentary, and although I was roundly congratulated for the arrest by my teammates, I was left feeling really down. Later, as we were booking the trio of strong-arm robbers back at the Hall, one of the three men looked at Swamp Rat and said he was glad he would be going to prison. "I've got to get off the street, officer," he said. "And I've got to get off this junk. Maybe a little time inside will do me good." It turned out he was an intravenous drug user on parole for previous strong-arm robberies. He was obviously desperate. I felt for him but couldn't quite bring myself to feel that sorry.

"Good luck," Eddie said, leading him away. Sometimes it was all you could do for them.

We went back out that afternoon and almost scored again right away. One team of prospective muggers gave way to a second squad of thieves who had me staked out. The confusion put them both off, I guess, because neither group carried out the attack.

I was creeping north on Hyde, getting passed by toddlers and everyone else on the street while cautiously maintaining my snail's pace, when two men—both looking lean and mean—broke out of the crowd on the sidewalk, crossed the street and ran ahead to the Ben Hur Apartments, their arrival sending shock waves through my backup team.

"Where the hell did these guys come from?" muttered Craig Woods. "How'd they know Bill lives in the building?"

Both men made it inside the Ben Hur and spent a considerable amount of time surveying the lobby. My backups thought the attack, if it came, would go down there and they told me so. It came as some surprise, then, when my two shadows abruptly left the lobby and returned to the corner of Hyde and Ellis, where I was chugging steadily home, and took me by the arms.

"How you doing, Old Man? Need some help?" one of them said, not waiting for an answer. I began to protest, feebly, but they pretended not to listen and escorted me straight into the lobby like a couple of overly attentive nephews, patting my pockets as we walked along. My radio buzzed in my ear and plans were made to pounce on the pair as soon as they made their move. But as my helpers were ushering me into the lobby, they were suddenly and loudly confronted by two absolutely stunning old ladies on their way outside who sized up the situation for what it was and did what they could to rescue me.

"Well, my Lord, look who it is," one of them said to the other, declining to call me by name because, of course, she had never seen me before in her life. "How have you been, dear? It's been such a long time since we've seen you."

They were glorious, and my two escorts were momentarily paralyzed, unsure of themselves for the first time and afraid to move a muscle. I waved my arms a little to free myself and tried to make conversation, unintelligible to the last, but the two old dears hung in there, explaining that they had known me for a year and that I was a longtime friend of their mother and sister. They were moving in, trying to get me away from these two obviously nefarious characters, when Batchelor sent the apartment manager into the lobby from his hiding place in the laundry room to shoo his two well-meaning tenants away.

Initially put off by all the attention, my escorts quickly regained their composure and sense of purpose when we were once again alone, asking which apartment was mine and running their hands over my pockets as they walked me over to Apartment 102. "See, we told you we'd get you home all right, Mister," they said as I fumbled with the key, finally getting it into the lock and pushing the door open.

They treated me very carefully up to the moment we were alone. Then, as I heard the door close behind me, their manner changed as swiftly and distinctly as if someone had thrown a light switch. "Look out, Old Man," the first suspect, a prolific burglar and ex-convict named Willie Bell, said menacingly as he pushed his way past me into the apartment. His partner, Terry Xavier, unmistakable in his bright red shirt and striped purple pants, was busy holding me against the apartment wall, going through my pockets in search of my wallet. While Bell was checking the rest of the apartment for more loot he stumbled across Ed Dullea, who glared at him from his cramped hiding place in the hall closet and, knowing he had been discovered, barked for Bell to "grab a wall." Both Bell and Xavier were taken into custody without further incident, absolutely dumbstruck that they could be caught so completely by surprise.

"This is the same kind of thing that happened to Chevalier," Bell said to his partner during the ride back down to the Hall of Justice for booking. "The same damn thing. It ain't fair. It just ain't fair."

Although booked for three felonies each, both Bell and Xavier made bail. When they failed to appear for their court appearances they were rearrested, found guilty during a September trial and sent off to state prison—two more lions removed from the water hole.

"Word is getting out," I scribbled in my diary the night after we took Bell and Xavier into custody. "Hopefully, news of our return to the Tenderloin will not reach Whispers before we do. So far, since we started this project on June 19, we have spent eighteen and a half hours of actual decoy time on the street. Our net so far: three hits and one "on view" strong-arm robbery. We have seven suspects in custody and so far I have been meaningfully followed four times without a hit. Will try again soon. Onward."

By June 29 we were nearing the end of our allotted time on the streets and there still had been no sign of Whispers. Investigators from the Robbery Detail were looking into a couple of recent assault cases which might or might not have been linked to our elusive quarry but, once again, there was nothing solid for them to go on. No fingerprints, fiber samples—nothing. He was like the wind, everywhere and nowhere. Still, the detectives had some foggy descriptions of a silken-voiced man in a green leather jacket, but no one description ever seemed to exactly match another and very little physical evidence was ever found.

It was getting a little frustrating. We were out there, taking our lumps and getting the bad guys off the streets, but at the same time our principal target continued to evade us. Seventy dollars and seventeen cents were left in the team kitty by June 29. I was cutting back on the soft drinks and fruit I usually purchased for the backups during my sojourns at the local markets in an attempt to make the cash last a little longer. No one wanted to quit until we had the one man everyone was looking for, but the deadline for ending the operation loomed.

I took to the street one morning dressed in regalia I

thought would prove irresistible to someone like Whispers—a black sport coat, black hat, and tie. The Gentleman of Diminished Means, forced to live in the Tenderloin but with money enough to keep up appearances. I brought along a cane as an added touch and leaned on it heavily as I made my way along, stopping for a rest and to pay my respects in McCauley Park—named after a long-dead hero police sergeant killed in the line of duty.

When I left the park I turned north and walked up Larkin to Geary because there were more people there. At most, I felt I would pick up a shadow or two from the small knots of young men loitering in the doorways and alleys, but as I neared the intersection two men passed me on the left, gesturing at me as they went by. Something was said but I couldn't make it out. It was the only chance for preparation that I had. Both men were young and as slender as racehorses. Each was wearing the expensive, high-tech tennis shoes cops call "Felony Flyers." These two, I remember thinking, looked like they would try to run.

They walked ahead to a phone booth and pretended to make a call, waiting for me to catch up. When I passed the booth they jumped me and I immediately began taking punches. We were doing our level best to avoid street crime but these guys just couldn't resist me. I fought with them as the Old Man might but I ended up on the ground, covering up and waiting for help to arrive.

They were not only vicious but they were slick. The first suspect, a guy named Baron Penny, lifted my wallet and was off with it before I knew it was gone. His partner, Reginald Bennett, was not as lucky and found himself surrounded by a squad of scruffy-looking street people who brandished handcuffs and ordered him to lie face down on the ground. I heard the sound of squealing tires as Cab Rat blew a red light and pulled his De Soto cab up alongside the phone booth. Lee and Karen were there in an instant and Bennett quickly surrendered to Karen, preferring to give himself up to beauty rather than the beast.

Penny, meanwhile, turned out to be something of a

sprinter. But his luck and youthful speed deserted him that day. He was off down Post Street, moving like a Tarzan movie extra being chased by an angry elephant, and well on the way to having the worst day of his life. I watched the back of his black jeans and green-striped shirt fade as he bolted away. Only the bottoms of his shoes showed as the Street Rats took off after him in hot pursuit. Then, miracle of miracles, a citizen actually did the improbable... he got involved.

The chase down Post was in full cry. The Street Rats were cursing the weight of their guns, radios, and other hardware, and steadily dropping back as Penny pulled away. Then a South San Francisco man who had been driving in the area with his girlfriend stopped his car in the street, got out and launched a flying kick at Penny— and missed. Still, it was a noble effort. If Baron Penny was stunned, we were flabbergasted. We were used to seeing people close their doors or windows and look the other way when someone was in trouble, and we were beginning to believe everyone was like that. This individual, even though he had nearly hurt himself in the process, helped restore our faith in humanity.

We watched as Penny, going for a world record in the hundred-meter dash, continued up the hill and headed straight for Craig Randolph, who is built along the lines of a hungry drug addict and who was picked to serve with RAT largely because his diminutive physique was not likely to be mistaken for that of a cop's. Randolph was poised there in textbook police fashion, a recently purchased burrito in one hand. Penny hit him like a freight train, ran up his shirt front and just kept right on going. Randolph, knocked ass over teakettle, scrabbled along after him on his hands and knees, and angrily tried to sweep Penny's legs out from under him. He failed, but did manage to salvage the burrito.

While all this was going on, Lee Tyler jumped back in his cab and, with tires screeching, caught up with and cornered Penny in a garage. There the huffing and puffing robber surrendered to Cab Rat without further incident.

Even though we were grateful for his help, our good Samaritan could not be told that he had come to the rescue of an undercover policeman. The Street Rats carefully scooted him away from me, continuing with the role and asking, "Are you okay, Old Man? Do you need an ambulance? Would you like a ride somewhere?" the whole time looking into my eyes to make sure I had survived the assault.

To top things off, we were about to embark on a search for the Old Man's wallet, which Penny in his wisdom had decided to ditch somewhere along the route of escape, when a Post Street resident walked up with the billfold in her hand. The money, all five dollars of it, was still inside. Our citizen piped up, told my backups how she had seen these two thugs beat up the Old Man over there and take his wallet. She agreed to give a statement. As much as I wanted to thank her for coming forward, I said nothing. I couldn't.

One bad thing about being a victim officer was the realization that loose lips, parted even in innocence, could still sink ships. This person was obviously a very fine, wonderful woman, but she could walk into the hairdressers one day and tell a friend that she had just stumbled into an undercover operation where an old, slightly decrepit looking, police officer was made to look even older and more decrepit and sent out as bait to catch the neighborhood crooks. Next thing we know the beautician would tell a friend. And so it would go, until the whole operation went down the tubes. People love to talk and gossip. Most cops do, too. I'm one of them. But attracting attention and getting talked about is a bad set of elements for the success of a victim officer. Instead, we kept these fine people and even other officers in the dark about the Old Man and continued to play our roles.

Still, it had turned out to be an exceptionally, successful morning. While not entirely happy about having to abandon our principle mission—the search for Whispers—the entire team had been left with a warm feeling. It got even better when we returned to the Hall to book Penny and Bennett and found out that both men were scheduled to appear in court for robbing and beating a sixty-two-year-old man on the very same street corner just one week earlier. We asked ourselves, if society had demanded that these two be kept in jail at the time of this last offense and the courts had followed through, how many other crimes would have been prevented? Certainly the one against me.

I changed clothes and we went back out that afternoon, using the Ben Hur apartment as home base and hoping someone would try to hit me there. There were some lookers, men and women who passed me by muttering darkly about how I "should be more careful," and two guys who followed me for a couple of blocks before breaking off and returning to their rooms in a notorious drug hotel near Larkin Street.

We pulled out of "Area A" and returned to the Hall of Justice for the evening critique. While there, we were informed that Chief Jordan had ordered the program extended for another week. There was the usual banter—some good-natured moaning about having to go unshaven and looking like true dirt balls, with marriages in jeopardy for another week—mixed with some scattered applause. The DA's people seemed happy that we had been continued, having fallen in love with the work in the short time we had been up and running.

"I have another announcement, people," Charlie Beene said, waiting until the squad room had quieted down. "Two nights ago, a ninety-three-year-old woman was assaulted and robbed outside her convalescent home in the one hundred block of Dolores. Out in the Mission District. At this point we don't know if she's going to make it. I guess she broke some bones when he knocked her down, and then he thumped her around some more once he was inside. It looks like a Whispers' assault. Robbery will be following that up in the next couple of days and we'll let you know what they find. In the meantime, we're still on the job so let's stay on the ball."

It was suddenly very quiet, the brash rowdiness usually

present at our end-of-watch briefings swept away like sand from a beach. The accomplishments of the day were forgotten in an instant.

Whispers had struck again.

Chapter 5
PURE MENACE

We reassembled on June 30 and, almost from the outset, things began to fall apart.

During our morning briefing in the TAC Squad office we were surprised to see that a television crew from Channel Five had joined us. Bulky coats and cameras all over the place. It turned out they had been invited in by the brass after the station's reporter tumbled to the fact that we were once again at work in the Tenderloin. They started asking questions and a deal was struck. In exchange for an invitation to film the operation in progress, they promised not to air their story until we had closed things down and had our people off the street. Even so, the effect that camera had on a room full of undercover officers was palpable. Several team members grumbled about having to baby-sit a camera crew as well as the Old Man on his daily stroll through the heart of the Tenderloin.

And, of course, as soon as the glare of media attention was on us, the gremlins went to work. We were hurrying, trying too hard to get out on the street and to what to us was by now more familiar territory, when I realized my decoy receiver was malfunctioning, a glitch which would leave me entirely cut off from my backup team. While the electronic problems were being dealt with I began applying my makeup, a ritual which had become almost second nature to me. On that day, though, with the camera grinding on, it seemed to take forever. To make matters worse, my makeup job looked woefully inadequate under the unforgiving lights of television, a revelation which did nothing to boost my confidence level that day, but rather left me with a lasting sense of dread.

We had hoped to get into the Tenderloin before noon,

but the gremlins were not through with us. As we trooped
out to the small convoy of vehicles waiting to take our
rapidly growing entourage into The Razor, I heard Lee
Tyler groan and then utter a string of curses. Our cab, it
seemed, had selected that moment to have one of its tires
go flat. Someone wondered aloud if it was meant as some
sort of omen. Cab Rat fumed and hissed even more when
the television cameraman moved in for a tight shot of
the taxi as it rested on its tire rim—the "Ace Undercover
Team" swinging into action. Things were not going at all
the way we had planned.

Radio problems continued to plague us when we finally
made it to Larkin Street shortly before one. I was getting
bits and pieces of transmissions with the radio cutting in
and out, and although we got lots of lookers and I executed
a rather nice fall for one gentleman who looked very
keen, something always seemed to come along to scare
off any potential customers.

We returned to the hall that night for a desultory
critique, the team's disappointment evident. It grew even
more pronounced when the Channel Five crew promised
to return for another try the next day.

"Hey," I told a dejected Tony Rockett before leaving
for the evening. "It can't get any worse. We'll nail them
tomorrow."

But our luck continued to sour. In addition to the
television crew, we found ourselves serving as chaperons
for five additional newspaper photographers and their
reporters the next morning. Our morning trip through
the Tenderloin must have looked a lot like one of P.T.
Barnum's parades through town. The undercover van was
stuffed with so many photographers it had begun to
resemble a safari wagon. There was no possible way we
could operate with that many people aboard. Try as we
might, Lady Luck had stacked the deck against us and
there seemed to be nothing we could do to get her back
on our side.

On Eddy Street I attracted the attention of a likely
looking candidate who was only moments away from

making his hit when Van Rat, angling for a better camera position for his covey of demanding shutterbugs, got in too close and scared the suspect away. Later, I had three suspects on the line when a black-and-white from Central Station cruised past at just the wrong moment and ruined the caper. What's the old axiom, never a cop around when you need one? It happened again the very next day and I was about to toss in the towel. My confidence level was at an all-time low when I took a walk that I will never forget the afternoon of July 2.

It started on Hyde Street, with the summer breezes that come in fresh and cool from the bay whipping my coat around as I trudged south toward Eddy Street. A good number of people were outside, their children playing on the sidewalk.

At 2:31 p.m. I passed a man at 425 Eddy Street, going in the opposite direction. He was well-dressed for the area, wearing a black baseball cap, gray jacket, blue jeans, and immaculate white tennis shoes. He held a bag in one hand. When he glanced my way, I heard his intake of breath and his tennis shoes scrape on the sidewalk as he changed his course. He stopped and, without hesitation, began following me. White shoes. It didn't mean much to me at the time, since almost everyone in the Tenderloin wore white tennis shoes of some kind or another, but I made a mental note of it just the same. Deep down inside, that old feeling, the one that came when something bad was about to happen, began to percolate.

I knew he was interested but I wanted to make sure. Crossing the street to the Cadillac Market on the southeast corner of Eddy and Leavenworth, I tried to get the message across to my backup Rats that this guy was targeting me. I went to the fruit rack at the front of the store so my backups could see me through the glass and, using hand signals, conveyed the message that I had picked up a customer. It was a difficult thing to do as there were about 150 people in the immediate area.

"Wait one, everybody. Bill's in the market." It was a departure from the day's normal game plan and the Street

Rats picked up on it right away.

"How come you went in the store?" Curb Rat asked. I made a sort of nonsense gesture, the Old Man reacting to the high price of fruit or something, and Curb Rat was back on. "Is somebody on you?"

I nodded. At that point I realized that White Shoes had slipped through my safety net of backup officers. He was just another face in the crowd of people on the street this day. Was he just that good or had someone's inattention given him the initial advantage? Using hand signals, I attempted to press home the message that I was being followed.

"Okay, people, Bill says he's got somebody on him. Is it the guy in brown?" They were describing the man nearest to me, again overlooking what, to me, seemed to be the obvious choice. I waved my arms again, shaking my head. "Is it the guy in the windbreaker and blue jeans?" I reacted the same way. "Okay, how about the guy in white tennis shoes?" I nearly dislocated my arm signaling in the affirmative, and I heard the Street Rats begin to move in on our man, sizing him up.

"CURB RAT"

Sometimes there would be dead moments and I would have to check my radio to see if it was still working, pretending to wipe my face and whispering into the microphone: "Can anyone out there hear me?" It was like that sometimes. We'd be out there for hours, trying not to look too obvious but with absolutely nothing happening, no suspects around, and everything just real quiet.

Actually, that was the hardest time, when things got like that and the hours started to drag, and we had to fight to keep our minds from wandering, thinking about whether or not we had gotten the kids to school on time that morning. And then your head would snap up and you would say, "Where's Bill?" and he would be gone.

The Street Rats keyed on the man Bill thought was stalking him. Craig and I moved up and, looking him

Bill Langlois at ten years of age, fifth grade at St. Joseph's Military Academy, outside Grandmother Alice's flat, at 4th and Lake Streets, San Francisco. February 1944.
Credit: Langlois Collection

USMC Training Center, 29 Palms, California. In early 1955, Lt. William L. Ehrle, Sgt. William Langlois, and Lieutenant Colonel R. D. Wright of the 1st 155 mm Gun Bn. received a trophy from Colonel Ivy as winners of drill team competition. The team eventually won USMC West Coast championship. *Inset:* Embassy duty, November 1955. *Credit: Langlois Collection*

Officer Langlois with Bourbon, Police Dog No. 7 and Bomb Dog No. 1. Bourbon served until 1972 and once caught five suspects at the scene of a burglary and held thirteen suspects with Officer Langlois until help arrived. *Credit: Langlois Collection*

With Judge, Bomb Dog No. 3. Judge served with Langlois until 1977. He was a direct descendant of Rin Tin Tin and weighed 135 pounds. *Credit: Langlois Collection*

91st Division Association solid gold medal, awarded annually to San Francisco's bravest police officer. This one presented – on the occasion of the association's 50th anniversary – to Officer Langlois in September 1968 for actions in 1967.
Credit: Langlois Collection

Bill's portrayal of a wounded down-and-outer
waiting to be victimized, 1978. *Inset:* Officer
Langlois preparing for his role as a victim.
Credit: Langlois Collection

Officer Leanna Dawydiak, "Minnie Rat," preparing for the street, 1986.
Credit: Langlois Collection

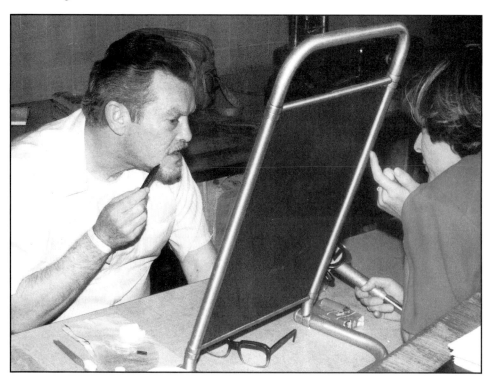

Officer Langlois turning into "the Old Man" while talking to Rita Williams of KTVU, Channel 2. *Credit: Langlois Collection*

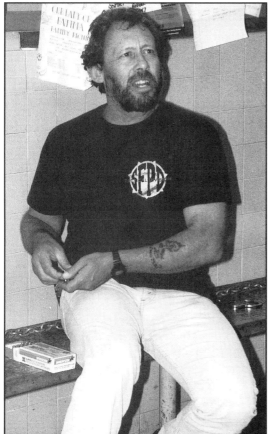

Officer Craig A. Woods, "Street Rat East," checks out one of several undercover vehicles prior to operations.
Credit: Langlois Collection

Officer Eddy St. Andre, "Swamp Rat," preparing for the street.
Credit: Langlois Collection

The "Rug Rat" ready for the street.
Credit: Chris Hardy, *San Francisco Examiner.*

Suspect begins to follow "Rug Rat."
Credit: Chris Hardy, *San Francisco Examiner.*

Suspect checks the street while two women confederates bracket victim/officer.
Credit: Chris Hardy, *San Francisco Examiner.*

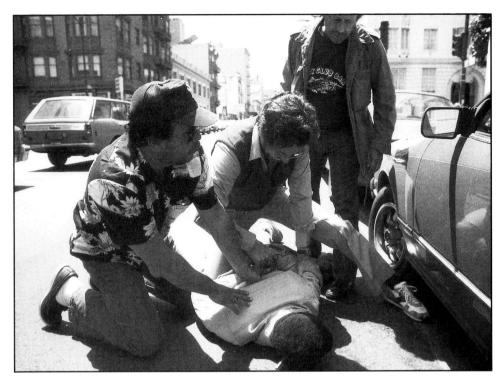

Officer Dullea, "Closet Rat," Officer Morgan, "Lobby Rat," and "Swamp Rat" take suspect into custody after robbery. Female suspects captured by Rat members, July 1987. *Credit:* Chris Hardy, *San Francisco Examiner.*

The "Rug Rat" addressing media, July 1987. *Credit: Langlois Collection*

Chief Frank M. Jordan's news conference. Officers R. Aitchison, "Van Rat," R. Rapagnani, "Room Rat," and J. Chestnut, "Closet Rat III," back up chief. *Credit: Langlois Collection*

Officers C. Woods, "Street Rat East," "Closet Rat III," "Room Rat," "Van Rat," V. Pollett, "Photo Rat," R. Leon, "Pocket Rat," and L. Tyler, "Cab Rat," with chief. *Credit: Langlois Collection*

Officer Langlois in police squad room wearing Robbery Abatement Team T-shirt, reading some of the 450 letters he had received by the end of 1987 operations. *Credit: Paul Bannister, Fleet Street West*

Jeffry S. Langlois – Senior Prom, 1989. Died in a car accident, May 1990.
Inset: June 1989. Three generations – Grandfather Lee, Jeffry, and William.
Credit: Langlois Collection

Officer Langlois as escort for ladies from a retired home. Mother's Day, 1989.
Credit: Langlois Collection

Officer Langlois says goodbye to members of mounted unit, Dennis, Bruno, and Bill with horses "Ray," "Lucky," and "Joker."
Credit: Langlois Collection

One last tour of the beat, January 2, 1991. *Credit: Langlois Collection*

Secretary Linda Pate, Lawyer J. Riordan, and Langlois. *Credit: Langlois Collection*

A. Nucup, E. Go, and J. and N. Salangsang, Langlois, W. Ocasio, and M. Salarno. *Credit: Langlois Collection*

Owner, A. Azadkhanian, and employee, R. Avery, of Alvin's Coffee and Teas bid farewell to Langlois. *Credit: Langlois Collection*

Last day on beat, January 2, 1991. Kiss goodbye for Lisa Marie "the Elf" Rico, nine years old.
Credit: Langlois Collection

Goodbyes at local finance office, January 2, 1991. Bill Wolfe, Cindy Nesler, Langlois, Manager Bill Barnickel, Mary McQuiller, and John Okabe. *Credit: Langlois Collection*

Helen Swee, Frank Wierdt, Langlois, and Vince and Doris Gallo.
Credit: Langlois Collection

The author, Bill Langlois, as a civilian in 1985. *Credit: Frank Castro.*

over once, we narrowed the list of possible suspects down to him. Bill was really agitated and we were talking the whole time, "Is it this guy? This one?" And he would shake his head until we finally pointed out a guy who was totally unassuming and plain as a blade of grass in a meadow, and Bill gave him the nod.

We weren't exactly sure what to look for. The profiles we had of Whispers and the other Kronks who were out there doing these jobs were just so slim. It was extremely difficult to get a good description because they hit from behind, and all the victims were elderly. I remembered they thought Whispers wore a green leather jacket or an all-white get-up, like a hospital attendant or something. In fact, I think the Robbery Detail started checking out workers at all the local convalescent homes after Whispers started hitting the Tenderloin. He was also supposed to have a strong body odor. That was all we had to go on and, frankly, it didn't narrow the field much.

Craig and I looked Bill's suspect over. He was wearing white tennis shoes and carrying something in a bag. When we got close we could see it was a shirt. Really, there was nothing remarkable about him. But Bill had a sixth sense when it came to these things, so Craig and I began to tail him.

"He's moved across the street," Curb Rat said. "He's on the northwest corner, pretending to make a phone call. I checked that phone this morning. It's inoperable."

I bought something and left the store, heading north up the steep, cluttered stretch of Leavenworth and mindful of the fact that Tennis Shoes was careful to keep a respectful distance between us. Street Rat East said: "You must be mistaken, Bill, the guy's back on the corner. He's not even looking at you."

Then, five minutes later, as I was about ten feet from the top of the hill and about to turn west onto Ellis Street, up he came. The Rats, who had had their doubts that our man would turn out to be a player, changed their minds quickly when White Shoes turned, altered his course, and then ran up the other side of the street to parallel me. That's when things got intense. This guy was really good.

"Bill's right, Bill's right. This guy's in the game," Curb Rat said. "Fish on, fish on." The Street Rats were naturally tuned in now. I could imagine the Room Rats waiting just blocks away, dropping their cards as the radio chatter went up a notch, checking their weapons and hiding places, hearts pumping hard with anticipation. Rug was bringing a suspect home to them.

It was now plain to everyone that this man meant business. The most amazing thing about the entire episode was that, had you been a cop going by on patrol that day, you would not have looked twice at this man. He carefully followed me for several blocks, coming up fast behind me and moving to my side of the street to join me in the entranceway of the Ben Hur apartment building at 400 Hyde. He was in his early twenties, well-dressed, clean-shaven, almost collegiate in appearance. Nothing remarkable about him. There were mailboxes and doorbell buttons on the left of the entranceway and he appeared to be studying them, leaning on the wall, and to all outward appearances looking for the name of a friend. Totally innocuous.

But as it turned out he was not standing there innocently studying the names on the mailboxes, he was waiting for me to go through the front door. When I did, this well-dressed guy with his cleaning in one hand and an upright look on his face, moved his hand just slightly and held the door open just an eighth of an inch as it swung shut behind me—just enough to keep the lock from slipping into place. God, he was slick.

For all intents and purposes the door appeared locked. I think it was Ron Leon who said, "He's not going to get in, Bill. The door is locked behind you." And there was no way of telling him that I *knew* our man was holding it open. I moved into the lobby, heading for the door of Apartment 102, the only apartment on the ground floor, waiting for him to follow me in. When he did, it caught nearly everyone off guard.

"No, no, no! He's inside. Repeating, suspect is inside the building," one of the Room Rats with a view said. At that moment everyone knew we had a specialist on our hands. The Street Rats closed in behind us, perfectly in sync.

"Stall him a little, Bill. Fumble with your keys or something, like you're having trouble. Let's see what he does."

I was having trouble. My forehead was bathed in sweat and my black beret was slipping. It felt as if my makeup was sloughing off in rolls onto the marble floor and I was so keyed up I knew I was sweating through my dark suit jacket. To make matters worse, the slipper I was wearing on my right foot was not slipping gracefully. If this guy was who I hoped he was and believed him to be, he was definitely taking the slide out of my glide. "Hang on," I said to myself. "Just a little longer. Hang on."

The Old Man had his keys out, picking through them one by one and grumbling. I heard the sound of tennis shoes chirping on marble and saw our man go over to a marble bench in the lobby and sit down about twenty feet away. At that point I thought he might be the type who waited in the lobby of a hotel or apartment building, selected his targets, and then rang their doorbell later, overwhelming them as soon as they opened the door. So I slid my key into the lock and prepared to shuffle inside.

On the right-hand side of our apartment was a desktop table about four feet long and waist high. It served as a sort of divider from the living room. There was an oval dimmer switch on the wall to my immediate right, parallel to the door and turned on but dimmed to minimum light. Immediately in front of me was the door to the bathroom and to the right was the door to the kitchen. Further right was the door leading into the living room, which was open. Ed Dullea was hiding in the living room. St. Andre was in the bathroom and everyone else had packed themselves into the kitchen area. I went on in.

The light in the apartment was murky, about one

candlepower. I did not think my shadow would try anything at that moment, believing that he was still waiting on the bench outside. The thought crossed my mind that maybe this whole thing had just been a practice run for him, that he was saving the Old Man for later and just wanted to see where he lived. My plan was to get inside and wait for him quietly to see if he would knock. I could hear my heart thumping in my chest and wondered if White Shoes could, too. At that moment the most we could charge him with would be trespassing. I put my package down on the top of the desk, and reached behind me to get the door closed. Suddenly there was a hand above mine, and I realized that White Shoes was behind me, helping me close the door.

I had been robbed over 250 times to that point. And while I count myself as among the more vigilant of people, I simply did not know this guy was there. He was that slick. I saw his hand above mine and inwardly I said, "Oh, oh," because I wasn't ready for him. Oddly, with patience and care, he took my right hand and moved it down behind me into the small of my back. Then he took my other arm and did the exact same thing, gently, just like an attendant helping an elderly person in a hospital. Only now he had both my hands behind my back and I could feel his lips up against my right earlobe. He began to whisper, "Everything's okay, everything's going to be all right."

That whispered admonition hit home more than anything else. My fear factor went up exponentially, and I could feel the sweat rolling off my neck and soaking my collar. There was only one man we knew who whispered reassurances to his victims, and I knew at that moment that he was standing behind me. When he told me everything was going to be all right, I said to myself, "It is now, you bastard!" The adrenaline began to flow through me like water through a spillway.

My whispering friend changed his grip and his tactics then. He had my arms, I was under his control, and we were inside the apartment, away from prying eyes. That's when he went from his Dr. Jekyll into his Mr. Hyde mode. As he threw his right arm around my throat, he hit me on the right jaw, corrected himself, and then slapped a choke hold on me. The last thing I needed was to black out with this monster on top of me. I began to fight him. Through the fog of combat, with the two of us dancing back and forth in that darkened foyer, I was vaguely aware of a hand reaching in and plucking my wallet from my inside coat pocket. I struggled to reach the dimmer switch, hoping to get the light level up. The Old Man was in distress, wheezing and puffing. When he finally managed to turn the light up he could see Ed Dullea charging in, head down and ready for a fight. Behind Dullea and looking equally pugnacious was Swamp Rat, and behind him was a veritable wall of anxious Room Rats, composed of Officers Morgan, Chestnut, and Batchelor.

Dullea hit my attacker solidly, knocking him off me and loosening his grip on my wallet. The billfold hit the floor and our man, whose name was Glennell Witcher, was placed under arrest after a brief struggle. Then there was another immediate transformation on the part of the suspect. He started yelling, "I know it was wrong. I'm sorry. I've never done anything like this before. Check my record!"

As Swamp Rat put the cuffs on him, Witcher began to look around wildly, panic in his eyes. "Where is the old man?" he yelled. "I want to apologize to him."

I got out of the way and let the backups take over. I think I was in shock, still feeling the grip of Witcher's fingers around my throat. And then I went into my Old Man thing saying, "Who are you people? What's going on here?" and our man added to the general din by yelling even more loudly. Dullea and the others got him down and dumped him into a little niche by the doorway. Ed came over to check me out.

"You okay, Old Man?"

I nodded that I was, rubbing my jaw and staring at the man lying handcuffed at my feet. Almost from the moment Witcher had clapped his hand over mine and begun to whisper in my ear, I had felt we had finally come up against the one man the Rat unit had wanted most. Now, if I could just get my knees to stop shaking.

"I'm fine, son," I said, smiling at Dullea and the others as Witcher was hustled out of the building and off to the Hall of Justice for booking. "Couldn't be better, in fact."

When Witcher was in custody, he constantly apologized to the booking officers about his personal hygiene, saying: "I'm sorry if my body odor is offensive to you, officers," or "I hope my socks aren't too bad." That sort of thing. It turned out he had outstanding warrants for robbery and assault, which contradicted the statements he had made at the time of his arrest. For me, everything he did and said fit the profile of the man we knew as Whispers. Could there really be two men out there with the same hunting pattern? I doubted it.

Witcher appeared very genteel on the surface, well-mannered and respectful. But I remembered how he had reacted once he thought he had the Old Man under his control, how he had transformed himself into this sort of evil twin. I felt if a person had really resisted him he wouldn't have stopped until they were unconscious or dead. He had to be a practiced thief because a beginner simply does not do things with the ease that this man had exhibited. Take the way he had caught that door before it closed: I lived in that place and I don't know if I could have done that as neatly as he did. He was really good at his art, and that sort of proficiency can come only through repeated trial and error.

There were other signs, as well. He worked alone and he was very good at tailing someone without arousing suspicion. Besides that, no two guys were going to grab someone the way he had grabbed me and then whisper the same thing in his victim's ear. "It's okay. Everything's going to be all right." It just doesn't work that way. I knew when I saw his hand above mine on the apartment door that this guy was the ace of aces, super slick. Out of all of those we had arrested in weeks and years past, he was the coolest. A man of ice.

Surviving witnesses had told us this thief would assault and rob his victims and then meticulously clean the victim's apartment, spending hours wiping and dusting everything until no trace of him was left behind. Our suspect also exhibited those tendencies. While it was evident Witcher had been living on the streets, we would never have known, just by looking at his clothes, that he was living rough.

That night I wrote: "This suspect's moves and his stalking method were just too perfect. I was unaware the suspect had entered the apartment until I saw his hand pushing the door closed. This, along with the almost gentle way the suspect attacked and that damned whispering, makes me think we may have finally gotten our man. The entire team believes we have snared Whispers. Perfect m.o., right size, age, complexion. Right down to the body odor. How many guys in the world attack like this?"

More unsettling were the memories of the terror I had felt, the feeling of helplessness. I was a police officer but I was the Old Man, too. I now fully understood what victims of these terrible, cowardly crimes had experienced, what it was like to reach the pinnacle of fright. It was not a game. I had entered the age of fear.

My life would never be the same.

A few weeks later robbery investigators following up on another set of leads arrested a man they felt was Whispers. They found him sleeping in a parked car. I didn't want to make a big thing out of it, but I've been a cop a long time and there just aren't two guys who work in exactly the same way. Neither Witcher nor the man arrested weeks later was ever charged with any of the assaults which had prompted the formation of the RAT unit in the first place. There was no physical evidence to link either man to the crimes. But to this day, even though we could never prove that either man was directly responsible for one of the most heinous and shocking string of crimes ever perpetrated in our city, I feel the man we netted in the Ben Hur Apartments July 2 was Whispers.

There was other, more significant evidence. After we netted Witcher the crimes stopped. That fact alone told me more than anything else that we had finally gotten the man we were after. We'll never really know for sure, I guess. That secret lies with Whispers himself. Our man Witcher, who had training as a computer programmer and thus had more of a chance than most to make it in life, decided against a jury trial, pled guilty to second-degree robbery in a plea bargain, and was sentenced to state prison in October 1987. As this book is written, he is once again back on the streets and living in a town in northern California.

INSPECTOR TOM VIGO, "OFFICE RAT."

I don't think we'll ever really know what happened to Whispers.

The sad fact is that, at the time when crack cocaine was just starting to flood our streets and people were doing anything to get more money to buy their drugs, there were a number of thieves out in the Tenderloin who spent their days searching for an old man or woman to rob. We've never been sure how many there were, exactly, but most were parolees just out of prison who talked it over and realized that robbing the elderly was not only relatively safe but profitable.

We had informants tell us that ex-cons were conducting informal "classes" on how to go about robbing the elderly. These intended victims were less likely to resist and their eyesight was bad, so you could just follow them home, choke them once you got inside, and ransack their home at your leisure. One guy, we heard, actually led a few disbelievers on "field trips" to show them how easy it was, making the hit while his "students" watched. It was that bad.

It would be hard for me to tell Bill, who was on the receiving end of all those assaults, that the man who tried to rob him in the Ben Hur was not Whispers. Bill knew better than anyone else at that time what he was up against. To have a man attack you like that, say the things he said to Bill, to have all that happen, would tend to reinforce your beliefs, and I have to respect those beliefs.

But we were able to locate and arrest another man a few weeks after the RAT ceased its operations and, although we could never prove that he was responsible for all the assaults, I believe he was our strongest candidate.

As I said, we'll never really know for sure.

What we do know is that these types of crimes stopped soon after the RAT pulled out of the Tenderloin in 1987. No one had ever tried this kind of thing before. It was a completely new and innovative approach to the problem. And it worked.

Everyone associated with RAT worked hard to make it a success, but I would have to say old Bill was the key to the entire operation. He used to just dazzle the guys out on the street with that act of his, falling down, walking out into traffic. There wasn't another officer around who could do it with the same dash. He would take his dental plate out, daub on some makeup, and he would look eighty. Sometimes I think Bill actually thought he *was* eighty.

It took a lot of courage to go out there every day not knowing what you were going to come up against, and Bill had what it took. He was out there getting thumped regularly and he would tell you he was happy as long as it was him and not someone's father or mother. Lately, we've been seeing a recurrence of the type of crimes against the elderly we first experienced in 1986 and 1987 and, while it would be nice to re-form the old RAT unit, I don't think we could do it today without Bill. The department tried to run a few similar operations after he retired, but the bad guys would get up close to the decoy, say, What's wrong with this picture? and back off.

When Bill was on the street as the Old Man, his most pressing concern appeared to be where he could buy the best brand of orange juice for the money, or how to avoid falling down, all the things a genuinely old person would be worried about. That was his world. A young guy would cruise him, maybe mumble something about robbing him, and Bill would hear it all but say nothing, careful not to put the guy off by glancing his way. I really think that's what made the RAT thing go. The thieves and robbers working in that area at that time truly believed that the Old Man had moved into the neighborhood and that he was there for their pleasure.

I wish I could tell Bill for certain that his man was Whispers. I know he wanted him more than he's wanted anyone in his career. What I can tell Bill is that he gained my lasting admiration as well as the admiration of many others during those two years.

And while I can't be sure he got the one man the RAT unit wanted most, I can be sure of one thing—having the Old Man out there saved some lives.

After the fireworks created by my encounter with Witcher, we took the weekend off and spent July 4 with our friends and families. The night before we were to return to work I sat down in my den and tabulated our efforts thus far. Since the first day the RAT was mobilized on June 19, I had spent over twenty-nine hours as the Old Man, pounding the pavement a couple of hours each day over ten working days. In that time I had been "robbed" five times and had stood by as the rest of the Rats took ten suspects into custody. On an average, I figured, the RAT unit could expect to witness a hit every other day or make an arrest once in every three working decoy hours.

Although a passing police car or the presence of a camera ultimately put them off, I was also followed by thirteen suspects on six other occasions. If they had followed through with their intentions, I reasoned, we would have had a total of eleven hits and twenty-three suspects in custody, not to mention the arrest made after we witnessed the assault on the elderly woman outside the market June 24.

"This is a great deal of criminal activity against one

'elderly' citizen," I wrote that night. "But it will all be worth it if Hit Number Five is proven to be Mr. Whispers! We shall see."

That Monday dawned clear and warm, brightened even more by the news that Chief Jordan had ordered the operation extended until the end of the week. The team was pleased, we were on a roll, but several of them had planned vacations or court appearances for the week in the belief that RAT would be discontinued as planned. Vanetta, Tony Rockett, and Craig Randolph had gone on vacation and Tony Camilleri was in Texas on a case. We juggled assignments at the morning briefing and worked out a plan to try our luck again.

Our first day back went quickly and without incident. But the following day, July 7, I was hit for the sixth time, and we added Ronald Morgan to our growing bag of suspects.

Morgan attracted attention right away. He was a compact, tight little guy dressed in snug blue shorts, a light blue horizontally striped tank top, and blue-gray tennis shoes with white socks pulled up to his knees. He looked like someone trekking through the tropical regions of the British Empire in the 1930s, or maybe some eccentric soccer player.

I was dressed on the loud side myself, with a blue and white baseball cap, light blue sport coat, tan pants, and my good-luck slipper on my right foot.

Morgan first approached me in the two hundred block of Taylor as I was walking north, coming in head-on and going straight for the twenty-four dollars I was putting in my wallet at the time. He snatched the bills. It would have been an easy arrest, with at least six cops witnessing the entire episode. But we didn't want the street crooks. We wanted the ones who followed victims into their homes. So I took the money back, snatching it out of Morgan's hands and putting it back into my wallet. The Old Man made a few pointed references about Morgan's character, or lack of same, and then resumed his usual shuffling gait, heading for home.

After a few seconds Morgan recovered from the shock of having the money he had just snatched from his victim snatched back again. Head swiveling, he looked around and then set out after me, eventually following me the four and a half blocks it took to reach my apartment at 400 Hyde Street. The stalk took over twenty minutes. He would walk ahead, pretend to talk on a phone, let me pass him, and then fall in behind me once again.

Once inside I was quickly joined by my latest friend, who hovered nearby as I fiddled with the keys to my apartment and eventually let myself in. Morgan came to the closed door, seemed to change his mind, and abruptly sat down on the marble bench. Then he got up and started to leave the building. Although he had not consummated his attack, at that point Cab Rat and Inspector Bergstrom detained Morgan as he tried to leave the building.

Under questioning by Jim Bergstrom Morgan admitted to "bumping" into me on Taylor Street and thinking how easy it would have been to rob the "Old Man," and then how he had followed me home after failing in his initial attempt out on the street.

Morgan, it turned out, had a record of armed robbery convictions. Even though he did not get a chance to attack me, his presence in the lobby and the statements he made to Bergstrom and the other Rats after he was detained were enough to prove criminal intent. He, too, was taken away.

Subpoenas whittled the team down even further the next day as several of us were called to Department Twelve to testify against Timothy Wilson, known to us as Chevalier. We ended up sitting around for three hours before we learned that Wilson's case had gone the way of most other suspects'. Faced with nearly incontrovertible evidence, Wilson, like most of his predecessors, had elected to enter a guilty plea.

We broke for a quick lunch and were out at the corner of Leavenworth and McAllister a little after two. I headed north in my Old Man shuffle, happy to be outdoors but trying not to show it. It was warm, over seventy degrees, and the wind was whipping the trash around. There were many people in the street, lots of hustle and bustle. At 2:10, I was in a grocery store at the corner of Leavenworth and Turk when the Street Rats reported seeing a suspect hovering outside. He was young and tough-looking, on the small side but heavy with muscle and built like a boxer. Street West listened as our man, later identified as Jerome Butler, attempted to enlist the aid of another man loitering in a nearby doorway.

"It'll be easy," Butler reportedly told the second man who, lucky for me, declined to take part in the robbery.

Alone now but unwilling to let such an easy target pass him by, Butler waited for me to leave the grocery store and then fell in behind me as the Old Man made his way north up Leavenworth, huffing and coughing from the exertion and toying with his room key. Butler, the Street Rats agreed, looked very anxious.

"He's coming up behind you, Bill. Just behind you now. I think he's going to make the hit..."

I hunched my head down even farther into my suit, tensing out of reflex at the sense of urgency in my backup's voice. There he was, just behind me and coming up fast, just as the Rats had said. And then, at the precise moment when I was sure he was going to clobber me, our man walked swiftly past one very keyed-up victim officer, whose nerves were drawn as taut as bowstrings.

"What the hell was that all about? This Kronk must just be looking you over, Rug. That must have been a dry run," Curb Rat said.

It was possible. I could also have done something to put him off. I wondered if he had seen my earphone or something else to make him think twice about taking me on. The answer came seconds later when Butler stopped dead about ten feet in front of me, turned and then ran back down the hill straight into me, trying to knock me off my feet. It was like being on a football field, and finding out I was the ball.

"Hey," I wheezed. "What are you doing?"

Butler threw me up against the wall. I had just removed my room key and had my coin purse in one hand. I realized he had been trying to assess my awareness factor the first time he came alongside me, taking one last look to make sure it would be a confrontation he could win. I flailed like the old man, spitting mad and fighting to keep my feet under me. People stopped to watch what was turning out to be a real cat fight. But Butler just kept banging away on me, scratching at my hands and drawing blood in a clumsy attempt to get inside my jacket and to my wallet.

"No, no, no," I said. "Leave me alone."

Lee Tyler was right there in his trusty cab and he put out the word that it was going down in the street before he came running. Butler was so intent on getting my wallet that he didn't see the cavalry closing in on him. We fought. I grabbed his hands. I could hear him saying, "C'mon, c'mon, give it up you old bastard," as his hands darted inside my jacket and finally found the leather. Then he was off, running south on Leavenworth and making it all of about twenty yards before the Street Rats closed in and bagged him.

They had him handcuffed and back on his feet in seconds. The Old Man, not nearly as winded as his would-be assailant, got off his butt and strolled over for a look. There was something about Butler's face and I looked at him long and hard. After a minute or so I was vaguely aware that I had met this man somewhere before, I just couldn't remember under what circumstances. I gesticulated and waved my arms, loudly denouncing the type of person who could perpetrate such a crime and singing the praises of the police department. Later, during booking, I learned that Jerome was the twin brother of Tyrone Butler, a strong-arm artist who had robbed me during RAT's earlier tour of duty the previous year.

"I'll be damned," Jim Bergstrom said when he had divined the connection between the two Butlers. "Who would have thought we'd run into this guy's brother?"

"Crazy," I said. "The family that preys together..."

"Yeah," Bergstrom said, scratching his head.

It had taken Butler only a few minutes to make his move on the Old Man and we still had a lot of daylight left, so the decision was made to try again before sundown. We started at Turk and Taylor, with Cab Rat dropping me off in the heart of the Razor with a cheery, "Good hunting."

"CAB RAT"

I was constantly worrying about my access to Bill. Could I get to him in time if someone tried to take him down in the street? Would I get stuck in traffic at the moment he called for help? What would happen when I got there? Would the guy hurt me? All those things were enough to keep the backup Rats worrying. On top of that, the adrenaline rushes, the times when we would see someone keying on Bill and everyone starting to pump up, kept us on a constant emotional roller-coaster ride.

When I got home at night after a day on the job I was completely worn out. I couldn't have been more tired if I'd spent the last eight hours digging a ditch.

But we all knew why we were there. It was sad when you stopped to consider the reason. I mean, we were watching this one old man. How many older people out there were going through this, living in fear for their lives every single, solitary minute? Every time Bill got hit it scared me. Some of the shots he took would have killed a real old man or woman. But every time he got hit we knew that we had saved someone else from experiencing that fear, that pain.

After each hit we'd stand Bill up and brush him off, asking him if the guys we had were the guys that robbed him, knowing full well they were, but playing the game just the same. Anything was possible with Bill. Sometimes he'd start ranting and raving, calling the bad guys all sorts of names only an old gent would use and calling us his "boys." We had to bite our tongues because we didn't want to crack up in front of the suspects and witnesses.

For us, the bottom line was that someday we were

going to walk into a courtroom with these jerks and the Old Man was going to walk in and start testifying as a San Francisco police officer. We knew going in that we would have the last laugh.

And that is a rare thing for a cop to be able to say in the best of times.

Ten minutes after Cab Rat dropped me off at Turk and Taylor—for over forty years one of the most notorious intersections in town—I attracted the attention of two more suspects who began to follow me north on Taylor to Ellis, despite the presence of a uniformed patrol officer walking his beat nearby. That afternoon I was playing the role of the Old Veteran, dressed in a black beret, gray sport coat, gray pants, and wearing a slipper on one foot. For an extra dose of luck I had pinned the 1881 regimental badge of the Twenty-Fourth Regiment of Foot, a famed Welsh infantry regiment, to my lapel.

"Two fish on, people," Street East chirped when he spotted my shadows. "They have the look. Lean and mean and probably fresh out of the joint. They're staying about fifty, sixty feet behind Bill but they're definitely on him."

The first one was about six feet tall, 165 pounds. He was wearing a blue baseball hat, dark gray jacket, black pants, and tennis shoes. His pal was a little taller, dressed in a blue sweat shirt, blue pants, and blue shoes. I listened as their descriptions were given out to all the Street Rats. Both men were in their mid-thirties.

Turning west on Ellis Street I crossed immediately from the south to the north side of the street to make sure Street East's fish were still following the bait. Both men paralleled my route block after block, skulking along, sometimes a hundred feet behind and not always together, while Photo Rat filmed their every move. When I reached my apartment building they crossed the street at speed, separated a minute, looked around, and then closed in behind me, pushing their way into the lobby.

The now familiar feeling of fear enhanced by the proximity of evil overwhelmed me. I controlled the sudden urge to run, to just get out of there. These guys, I knew instantly, meant business. One of them barked, "Give it up," and pounced hard on me from behind before I had a chance to get the door to my apartment open. It was a true attack out of the blue and I took several shots to the face, my head snapping back with each impact. My slipper came off straight away. For some reason I decided to fight them a bit more vigorously than usual, sick of being everyone's punching bag and more out of stupid pride than anything else. It took them off guard. They went slack-jawed and got in each others' way. Both men were trying to throw me down, probably surprised that a seventy-five-year-old man would resist them at all, and the three of us battled back and forth for control of my wallet. One of them hit me in the back of the head, knocking my beret off, while the other guy started cursing and tried to stand me up so he could get his arm around my neck. I heard my jacket rip as the first one tried again to reach the billfold. I'm sure the whole thing lasted only a few seconds but it seemed like hours. Sometime during the struggle they managed to get the billfold.

Finally I heard the shouts and hunting cries of the Room Rats and then the terrified noises of two men who realized they had been caught in the act. Ed Dullea shouted, "Police, hold it!" But if it had been a battle up to that point it was unconditional warfare from that moment on. I was grateful a hapless tenant did not wander into the fray.

The lobby of the Ben Hur was nicer than most in that part of town, with marble floors from the thirties and two nearby planter boxes filled with ferns and other flora. I have to say that the normally clean marble floor looked like a ravaged garden after my assailants, Ronald Flenoy and Nathaniel Burton, attempted to fight it out with the Room Rats. Potting soil was everywhere, planters were overturned and uprooted ferns tilted at odd angles toward the ceiling. Odd articles of clothing were strewn about. Five very large men fought it out in that little lobby, two of them fighting for their freedom and the other three fighting to make sure they didn't get it. Everybody was slipping and sliding, their blood mixing in with the dirt and uprooted palms. I remember huddling in a corner and listening to the shouts and curses, watching the ferns sail by along with the occasional human body. I was yelling, the Rats were yelling, Flenoy and Burton were yelling. The damage done in the lobby that afternoon was appalling. It was a real donnybrook.

In the midst of the battle one of the pair, Burton, managed to extricate himself from the melee and ran out the door and onto Ellis Street. The promise of freedom must have blinded him because Burton ran straight into the arms of "Pocket Rat"—Ron Leon—who KO'd the running man in honor of his own fortieth birthday while a crowd of appreciative street people stood by and cheered.

After the battle our guys were standing there, huffing and puffing. The lobby looked like ground zero. His timing couldn't have been worse but the manager of the Ben Hur chose that moment to come down and see what all the fuss was about. It was plain to see by the look on his face that he was staggered by the extent of damage done to the property under his care. We were, I thought, just moments away from a severe tongue-lashing.

Once they had regained their wind our guys fell all over themselves apologizing, straightening up their clothes and weapons and trying to make this man feel a little bit better about agreeing to let a bunch of cops use one of his rooms in the first place. I mean, that lobby was a mess.

Dullea started to say something, trying to get the manager's mind off his troubles, but the guy just waved him away. Judging from the look on the manager's face, I thought we'd all be out looking for a new decoy site the next morning, but I misjudged him.

"Wreck the whole place if you have to. Tear up as many plants as you need," he said after a while. "Just catch the bastards."

The manager turned on his heel and was gone, leaving us standing amidst the wreckage of his lobby with stupid grins on our faces. My face was cut and bruised and

Dullea had suffered a cut to the hand which had gone right down to the bone, but we were a happy crew, setting a new RAT record by arresting three suspects from two separate hits in just one hour and fifteen minutes.

Flenoy was searched and Swamp Rat relieved him of a butterfly knife. Outside, Ron Leon and the other Street Rats were still enjoying the admiration of neighborhood residents who offered words of encouragement as they led Burton to the van for the short trip back to the Hall of Justice.

Public reaction to our work varied. Since my guys often looked more despicable than the people they found themselves chasing, the average Tenderloin resident could not be sure if he was watching a gang fight or a police undercover operation. The picture was usually one of great confusion until the unshaven men in the dirty clothes pulled out their handcuffs or brandished their badges. Then people tumbled to what was going on. Until that moment, though, most people on the street took great pains to avoid whatever calamity they saw going down before them.

A lot of times, if the public saw me assaulted while in my role as the Old Man and then saw the cops coming out of the woodwork to catch these people, there were some hoorays. It was sort of surprising because you wouldn't expect that from a populace many people felt was on the edge of the law itself. Had it been any sort of drug deal, the arresting officers could have expected to have catcalls, insults, and maybe the odd bottle thrown their way. But there was a code of honor when it came to older people. If they saw the Old Man down on the ground and ranting, many of them would point me out to an officer and say, "Hey, take care of the old guy."

Perhaps it was because they had mothers and fathers of their own and they could picture them in my place, on the ground and bleeding after a particularly vicious assault. Or perhaps it was because they could see themselves succumbing to the universal and inevitable changes of old age and did not want a world where the young were allowed to prey on the elderly. Whatever it was, I found the concerns exhibited by the people of the Tenderloin gratifying.

Court time ate into our plans once again on Thursday, when several team members were summoned to appear in connection with the arrest of Michael Gordon, the man who had had the great misfortune to commit a strong-arm robbery on an elderly woman in full view of five undercover officers—all of whom had shown up to testify to what they had seen. The rest of us caught up on paperwork or made repairs to our equipment until after noon, when we decided to try Leavenworth Street again.

Short-handed and with *San Francisco Examiner* Photographer Chris Hardy along for the ride, we moved into the Tenderloin on another fine, clear day and I began to walk north on Leavenworth from McAllister. After the Great Fight I didn't have to fake any disabilities. I was sore as hell. Five minutes after I set out, the radios began to buzz as the Street Rats chimed in, one after another, with information on three people who had taken an unnatural interest in my progress up the street.

"Hey, there's a guy crossing the street with Rug, looking at him over his shoulder. I think we have a player." Hardy captured the moment on film, the exact moment one man made up his mind to rob another.

Our suspect was five-foot-eight, about 145 pounds. He was wearing blue jeans, a beige shirt, and a black baseball cap. The Street Rats were all over him, watching his every move as he watched mine. Two women we'll call Betty and Marilyn soon joined him, the three of them walking back toward me as I continued to chug along. I wanted to cross the street and get into a store to prevent them from hitting me on the street, but at that moment a gust of wind blew my jacket open, exposing the billfold in my inside left coat pocket. I heard one of the women say, "Just take it," so I left the sidewalk and crossed the street, with the male suspect following along so close behind I thought he was going to jump me right there in the middle of the street.

The radio came on.

"Uh, folks, I think our suspect is with those two gals, the ones standing on the corner there. They were walking behind Rug and then they went ahead of him and both took a good hard look at him as they went past. Then they had words with Number One. I think the three of them are setting him up for a hit."

I clutched both my hands to my chest as the Old Man would, knowing that my backups were sizing up the situation. Walking at an easy pace, I headed north for the Ben Hur. At one point the three of them passed me and I could hear them discussing what they were going to do. "You stay with him," the male member of the trio stated. "We'll take him if it looks good for us." They took up a position ahead of me, the three of them leaning against a parked car and eyeing me as I shuffled past. I thought I heard the guy tell the girls, "Stay with him now, no matter what," and they left the car and fell in behind me once again. Following me wasn't good enough for these three. They wanted to be in front of me, too, in case I changed direction or scooted into a building or doorway. That way they could stay with me and keep up without making it painfully obvious that they were on my tail. This went on for several minutes. The three of them got in behind me and then passed me, fell in behind me again, and then passed once more, all the way up to the Ben Hur.

At Hyde and Ellis I had to turn right to enter the apartment house. I stopped at the corner mailbox to rest a second, and the male member of the trio passed me by, stopping at the entrance to the Ben Hur and pretending to tie his shoe. They were now playing "bookends," with me in the middle. The whole thing was sort of comical in a crude way, a crazy takeoff of a Charlie Chaplin movie. I had to resist an urge to yell, "Boo!" just to see if they would scatter.

When I reached the entrance to the apartment building they hung back for a moment, crossing the street when I got near the door and then coming in right behind me.

They sidled in, the last girl squeezing through the front door as it clicked shut. One of them said, "Yo, how you doing?" It was painfully obvious they did not have any business in the building, that they really didn't care a whit about my well-being, and that the girls were waiting for the male member of the cabal to make the play. They hung just behind him, looking at me and trying to make conversation as I headed to my apartment with my key out and ready.

"Are you the manager?" the man asked me once I was inside my apartment, with the door still open. I pretended I didn't hear him too well. He asked me the same question two more times before I shook my head no.

"Got a light?" He moved in closer. I moved my hand down as if to go for a cigarette lighter. Then he pushed me backward. Hard.

I was off balance but did not go down. My assailant grabbed for the wallet inside my coat pocket and began to yell, "Give me the money!" I reached up and grabbed the leather with both hands just as he took it, and a bizarre game of tug of war ensued on the threshold of my apartment. Suspect Number One, Earl Douglas, removed the rubber band from around the wallet and took the money, then snatched the glasses off my head. I guess he was trying to blind me to stop any possibility of my giving chase. The two women, Marilyn and Betty, pushed me around and made sure I couldn't fight back until it was plain that Douglas had scored what they had come for. Then all three bolted out the front door, slipping and sliding like dogs on a waxed kitchen floor, all of them running into the waiting arms of the Street Rats.

"Code Four, suspects in custody," someone said when all was over but the shouting. The entire process was getting to be old hat. Even so, we were gratified to hear that the *Examiner* man had gotten some terrific shots of the arrest. With one day left to go in our extension, it would be a nice way to end things. The pictures would play well and, after the trials and tribulations of the prior few days, it was reassuring to know that things could still go our way.

We were told at evening briefing that the program had been discontinued. A press conference had been called for the next morning. We sat there, absorbed in our own feelings, some of us glad it would be ending, others not so glad. My own feelings were mixed. The Old Man had become a part of me during the last two weeks and I wondered how easy it would be to leave him behind. One by one the team got up and went home. No histrionics. No teary displays of emotion. Professionals sad to see a great operation come to an end but happy to be returning to their private lives once again.

It was finally over.

I went home that night thinking about what I would say to Kitty. While I would no longer be walking the Tenderloin as the Old Man, the Fencing Detail still had plans for me and pretty soon I would have to become Bill Taggart, pawnbroker. The juxtaposition of personalities would be jarring. It was a whole new identity to slip into and hone. Still, I had learned a lot about people during the last two weeks—the law-abiding sort and otherwise—and I wondered if any of what I had learned could be used on my next assignment. At least on my next job I would be able to face my antagonists.

That night I sat down in my den and outlined some of the things I would do differently if and when the time came for the Old Man to return to the streets.

"Final tally: nine cases, seventeen suspects in custody, one on-view felony arrest. Not bad for two weeks' work.

"Next time more 'pre-time' should be given prior to the start of any RAT program. Any actual attempt to draw hits on victim officer should wait seven to ten days while team members, especially new ones, become used to assignment and practice blending into target areas.

"More time and effort should be put into obtaining good, working undercover vehicles such as utility trucks, parcel delivery vehicles, and cabs, anything which would cover further the identities selected by members of the backup team.

"In addition to vehicles, all other equipment—especially communications equipment—should be checked and rechecked until it is in good working order.

"Quiet areas of the city should be used for dry runs, with team members playing various roles, thus working out any bugs. It is crucial to develop a high degree of confidence, especially among new decoys.

"Anyone in the team who does not fit into the concept or does not want to be there should be required to leave the team.

"A study should be made of all previous operations and used as a guide. After all, you can't know where you're going if you don't know where you've been..."

I sat back, listening for a moment as Kitty fussed with something in the other room. I let my eyes wander to a nearby shelf and rest on a statue of Robert E. Lee, one of my heroes. My badge number, 1870, happens to match the year he died.

Then I bent over my diary once again and began to scribble an afterthought.

"Account balance for RAT operation: $29.82, less $21.00 to replace the watch Ed Dullea lost in the struggle during our last arrest. That leaves us with $8.82, to be returned forthwith to the District Attorney's Investigators Office.

"That's it for now, past the Old Man's bedtime."

I got up, switched off the light, and padded around, tidying things the way I normally do before going to bed. When my head finally hit the pillow, I was overcome by the sudden, blissful contentment of exhaustion and was asleep in minutes.

Chapter 6

LIMELIGHT

A week after the end of the 1987 program and the debacle of my on-camera breakdown, I was approached by a reporter from the *San Francisco Chronicle* who said she wanted to do a feature story on the Old Man and his alter ego.

There had been many requests for interviews since the press conference. While I was still mortified by my display of emotion, the media, it seemed, was intrigued. I couldn't figure it out. They must have thought that anyone who cried on camera had to be telling the truth, or at the very least might be good for their ratings.

In the days following the end of the 1987 program, local television aired several stories on the RAT unit and its work. My blubbery few seconds figured prominently in each one. At home one night, watching in mortal embarrassment as television brought in the videotaped image of my contorted face and heaving shoulders for what seemed like the thousandth time, I couldn't help but think about how bad the Old Man really looked.

Then, by the end of that first week, when we were well into our sting operation in the Mission District, working out of a small coin and stamp store, I was approached by *Chronicle* Reporter Elaine Herscher. Although I was working hard to nail down the characteristics of my latest persona, that of a larcenous pawnbroker named Bill "Tiger" Taggart, Elaine explained that a considerable amount of public interest had been generated as a result of the RAT unit's efforts, as well as by my lamentable performance at the press conference. She wanted to do a follow-up story on the Old Man and his work.

Try as I might, it was hard for me to understand why

the public would latch onto the image of a bawling cop, but for some odd reason they had. It seemed that my display of emotion had somehow touched the public consciousness, as many people had called the paper to express their concerns. When Elaine asked if I would consent to an interview, I agreed, on the condition that my face not appear in the newspaper undisguised. Seeing my battered old mug on page one of the morning paper could seriously jeopardize our growing relationship with the Mission District's resident felons—many of whom were starting to come see us on a daily basis.

The interview went well. I behaved myself and did not say anything too nasty about those people in the Tenderloin who had used me as their own personal sparring partner for the last few weeks. And I managed to hide my anger about a breed of cat who, because of an ignorant or uncaring society, had been allowed to turn an area of the city into their own private hunting ground.

"Nobody likes to cry publicly," I told Elaine when I met her days later and she asked the inevitable question about my dismal performance before the cameras. "But it was an honest reaction and the tears were honest tears. There's just nothing more I can say about it. I wish it had never happened, but it did."

Things grew more comfortable as the interview continued and I began to talk at length about the city I had grown up in, my life with my grandmother, and the subtle changes which seemed to have overtaken us in recent years, few of them for the good. Elaine listened quietly the entire time, nodding when appropriate and taking copious notes. I prattled on to her about the San Francisco I had had the privilege of knowing as a youngster and about how much things seemed to have changed— how the old morality seemed to be evaporating, only to be replaced by violence carried out against the innocent with little thought and less remorse.

"I remember the time in this city when women wore veils and gloves, and there was gentility and sophistication and respect. Somewhere in the years since World War II, we have lost that.

"This city has always been a place for Bohemians, and that's good. That's not immorality. But what we are allowing to happen to old people here— anywhere for that matter—is immoral. Why should they spend their twilight years living in fear of being attacked by predators? Why should an old person have to risk his life going out for a pint of ice cream at five o'clock in the afternoon?"

The next day I was back behind the counter of Mission Stamp and Coin, picking through pillowcases filled with jewelry stolen from homes in the area, and offering cents on the dollar to grinning thieves who joked about how easy the pickings were out there. While one particularly cocky burglar bragged about how he had gotten into a home across town, I picked a wedding ring out of a cigar box he had brought in. The gold band was still marked with the owner's name and wedding date. I held it up to the light appraisingly.

"Yeah, got that from an old lady," the thief said, eager to please. "Been living in this house up on the heights since pioneer days. She's so senile she probably doesn't even know it's gone."

He smiled wolfishly at me and I leered back at him, but for an altogether different reason. My new friend was proud of his prowess and accomplishments as a thief—a despicable life form who could rob an elderly woman. I, on the other hand, was thinking about how effective it was going to be to play the videotape of his over-the-counter confession to the jury at his trial. I held the ring even closer to the hidden camera on the wall above our heads, the one recording his braggadocio for posterity.

Business at Mission Stamp and Coin was good that day. So good, in fact, that publication of the *Chronicle* story slipped my mind entirely. As it turned out, my few innocuous words and the resulting article stirred a groundswell of reaction and support unheard of in the history of the San Francisco Police Department. This tidal wave of reaction, an outpouring of emotion the likes of which I had never seen in my twenty-six years in law enforcement, was overwhelming. It seemed that people from every element of society, from pipe fitters to corporate presidents, had been touched by a simple message I thought no one had wanted to hear.

Their reaction provided me with the impetus to try to implement a plan I had been toying with since I first joined the RAT unit in 1986, a plan designed to help protect senior citizens in our city and cities like it across the nation.

I was behind the counter at Mission Stamp and Coin, scratching at the beard I had grown for my part as "Tiger" Taggart, pawnbroker with an eye for eighteen-karat gold and a heart of pure obsidian, when the *Chronicle* article finally hit the streets. My new partner, Daly City detective Bob Blazer—or "Dom," as he was known to our customers, and I were between deals. Except for a few early risers (crack addicts who slept very little anyway), we were finding that most of the neighborhood burglars preferred to visit the shop in the late afternoon. Then, after they had gotten a little beauty sleep and had rested from their night's work, they would haul in loot pilfered the night before.

Bob held down the fort while I strolled out onto Mission Street in search of a morning paper. When I found a rack I saw the story featured prominently on the front page. There was a photo of the Old Man, stooped and bent and looking like a target, making his way down a garbage-strewn street in the Razor. Above the picture was the heading: "The Decoy Cop Who Couldn't Help Crying." I moaned at that one, fearing that I had been typecast as an emotional basket case for the rest of my life.

Flipping through the paper to the features section, I found the bulk of the article and read through it quickly. It seemed fine. I had not been quoted saying anything inflammatory and my fellow team members had been prominently mentioned, which has always been my foremost intention when talking to the press. Elaine ended the piece with a simple quote I had offered at the end of the interview, almost without thinking: "You get tired of putting on the makeup and going out there. Last year I did it for six weeks and got robbed twenty-six times. It was in all the papers. I didn't get a single letter from a single person saying thanks."

Well, that was true enough. I regarded it as a harmless statement, even if my jaded fellow officers could construe it as a little whiny. I read through the article again, searching for anything I might have said that could jeopardize my current assignment or somehow get me into trouble with my superiors. After the second read-through, I could not find a single thing to fault. I tucked the paper under my arm and hiked back to the store without a second thought.

The next afternoon I left Mission Stamp and Coin once again, this time to make my daily rendezvous with investigators from the Fencing Detail. Deeply undercover and not wanting to risk being seen with uniformed police officers or anyone else who could be regarded as the law by the band of cutthroats we were dealing with, we found ourselves going to great lengths to meet far away from Mission Stamp and Coin. We had discovered early on that using the store phone to contact our overseers at the Hall of Justice could be dangerous. Once, with a bad guy just across the counter from me, I had taken a call from a supervisor down at the Hall and whispered "Ten Four," the police code for "message received."

"Damn, Bill, do you know what you just said?" my supervisor hissed over the phone, sure he was seeing the entire operation going up in smoke. I froze, aghast at my own stupidity and knowing that the entire operation was now teetering in the balance. Everything hinged on what I said next, since the Kronk across the counter was listening to my every word.

"That's right," I said quickly, thinking fast. "Ten to four if you can get it. Fourth race. Yeah. Put me down for a hundred on the nose." It was all I could come up with. I put the phone down and turned back to my burglar. "You ever bet the horses?" I asked.

He shook his head, suspicion etched into every line of

his face.

"Don't," I admonished. "Sucker's game. Now what did you bring me?"

That had been close enough for me. Now we relied on afternoon meetings in randomly selected locations across town to catch up on departmental news and to give updates on our progress at the sting site. My contacts always arrived in plain clothes so as not to draw attention to them and to lessen the slim chance that someone who knew "Tiger" would see him talking and laughing with uniformed police officers. These meetings provided a welcome break from the routine skullduggery of business at Mission Stamp and Coin. They were also my only real opportunity to catch up on the latest departmental gossip.

Three days after the *Chronicle* article came out, I was greeted by a particularly stern-faced inspector from the Fencing Detail, who met me in the middle of a large parking lot just outside the Mission District.

"What the hell did you tell that *Chronicle* reporter, Bill?" he asked, without so much as a "Hi, how are you?" My heart dropped like a shotgunned mallard, then leapt in a spasm that nearly took my breath away. I remained fixed in the front seat of my car, trying to remember all the things I had said in the article, running it all back in a vain attempt to pin down what it was that had turned this man against me. So I had missed something in the article after all.

"Oh no, don't tell me," I moaned. "What'd I do?"

The Fencing Detail inspector got out of his car and went to the trunk, still spearing me with his patented Clint Eastwood "Make my day" glare. He rummaged around for awhile and came up with a bulging plastic garbage bag. Then gliding with the sinister intent of the Grim Reaper to the passenger side of my car, he held the bag away from him, as if it were filled with dirty diapers. I squinted to see what was inside, thinking how appropriate it would be to have the three things a cop fears most—a chief's reprimand, a subpoena, or his termination papers—hand-delivered in a plastic Hefty bag.

Damn, damn, and double-damn.

My fun-loving colleague stuffed the bag through the window and dropped it onto the front seat. The top opened then and I could see that the bag was stuffed with envelopes. Dozens of them. Whatever I had done had really stirred people up. The letters spread out into a small pile. It was as if someone had reached through the window and dropped a live cobra on the seat beside me. I stared at them, then looked expectantly into the blank face of Inspector Eastwood.

"They're all for you," he said, his face finally easing into a semblance of a smile. "Something about a lot of people wanting to say thank you. Apparently they're getting a lot of calls down at the Hall, too. Nice job, Rug." He gave me a little pat on the arm, got into his car, and drove away. Another example of cop humor at its finest.

I was floored, suddenly remembering the last quote in the *Chronicle* story. Gingerly, still filled with a cop's inherent belief that nothing good can ever happen to him, I opened the bag and rummaged around. They *were* thank-you letters. At least a hundred of them. Maybe more. Mostly from people in San Francisco but some from other parts of the Bay Area, as well. Oakland, Concord, San Rafael. Each one written in a separate hand. Postcards, funny greeting cards of the "Far Side" variety. Some were just quick notes, offers of dinners, drinks at a local watering hole. Others were pages long, obviously with some thought behind them, the pen strokes bold with the writers' passion.

I exhaled for the first time in minutes, picked out a letter from the pile and began to read.

Dear Officer Langlois,

I think it is a very fine and brave thing you have been doing and I thank you for it. I'm in my fifties and one of my greatest fears of growing older is the danger on the streets today.

I'm not a very religious person, but I do firmly believe that one day we will all have to answer for the lives we have led on earth. I worry about that because I'm not contributing much of anything. You, though, should have the comfort of knowing you have made your space on this earth a cleaner, safer place to live for thousands of people. And I think God will be well pleased with that, and with you...

I put the letter down thrumming with emotion, and picked up another. This neatly typed letter was from a woman in Oakland. Finally, I felt as if I were making contact with people other than my team members—people who cared about what was happening to their town and their relatives and who felt the same way as I did about the problem.

"... It's so hard to understand why anyone would attack old people. The thought is so repulsive that I suppose most people put things like this out of their minds unconsciously and don't give any real thought to them.

"Obviously, you're very different..."

Bob Blazer looked up at me when I sailed into Mission Stamp and Coin a half-hour later, the plastic bag full of letters in one hand. I had taken the time to read about six of them. By the time I arrived back at our bogus storefront I had resolved to reply to each and every one.

"How you doing, Bill?" Blazer said, looking at me quizzically. "Everything all right?"

It felt like I was walking on air. "Absolutely first rate," I said, stashing the bagful of letters under our counter and casting an appraising eye over a load of stolen jewelry Bob had bought from a local thief just prior to my return. "Things just couldn't be any better."

As it turned out, that first batch of mail was only the precursor to a torrent of response which flooded my old station in the Taraval District and Chief Jordan's office on the fifth floor of the Hall of Justice in the weeks to come.

The sheer volume of mail received became something

of a problem. According to departmental policy, I had to officially acknowledge each letter addressed to the chief on my behalf before the letter could be placed in my personnel file. Going to the Hall was out of the question. As a result, my overseers in the Fencing Detail would bring the latest batch of letters out to me during our daily meetings away from Mission Stamp and Coin.

Although there were a few cracks from fellow officers about having to serve as "mailmen," I believe they were offered in jest. Most of my colleagues seemed pleased that our work with the RAT program had resulted in a welcome shower of good publicity, a phenomenon police officers seldom see.

The *Chronicle* story also touched off a flurry of calls from interested parties who phoned from all over the world to tender their best wishes or to request an interview. I talked freely about RAT in the few moments I had when I was away from my post at the coin shop, doing a live interview with a Salt Lake City radio station while standing in a foul-smelling phone booth a few blocks away from the store. The announcer was an enthusiastic guy who praised the team and its work. I could not bring myself to tell him that I was watching a very different kind of rat— the kind with teeth and a tail—as I explained how our Street Rats went about their business. I was, nonetheless, amused by the coincidence.

Other calls came in during the days to come. Over two hundred of them. I found myself dashing from phone booth to phone booth to keep up with demand, talking to a reporter from a student newspaper in Des Moines one moment and the BBC station in Cardiff, Wales, the next. People were kind, wishing me well after we were off the air or they had finished taking notes, many of them expressing fears about the privations exacted upon senior citizens in this country and abroad.

Meanwhile, the sting was off and running well, with more and more customers arriving every day as word slowly got out that the boys at Mission Stamp and Coin paid cash and asked few questions. Even so, there were periods when things were slow and I would seize the opportunity to read the letters that were still coming in every day. (Ultimately, over four hundred letters found their way to the Old Man. Several were even addressed that way, care of Officer Bill Langlois.) I used the downtime to read each one and pen a response, sitting at the counter and enjoying the contact with the very people I had sworn to protect. It was a rare connection with the citizens of this land and I relished their words. With every reply I enclosed a small picture of the Old Man, taken while he was out on the street. Most of the time I added a sentiment on the front of the photo.

In the year we stayed in that little shop, crooks of all descriptions coming through its doors at all hours, no one ever tumbled to what I was doing. If anyone came into the store I would just shove the letters into a drawer and give them my "Tiger" Taggart greeting: "Whatcha bring me today?"

During the fledgling first few weeks of the sting I was able to respond to a lot of letters that way, writing a few at a time. Many of them were unsigned, though, their authors saying they merely wanted to express their good wishes and did not feel it necessary for me to take the time to reply. Many did not give a return address. As my dad pointed out, they just wanted to reach out and communicate with someone they felt was on their side.

In addition to the number of letters I received, I was amazed by the diversity of the people who wrote. Everyone from politicians to pipe fitters, airline captains to housewives. Young and old alike. I even received a laudatory letter from a convicted murderer doing time in state prison; he called the people I had helped send to the cells next to his "the worst of the worst."

The degree of apprehension being felt by young people—with many years of life left to live—was particularly striking to me. Many of them were already living in dread of their own old age.

"I am not a senior citizen yet," one woman wrote. "In fact, I have forty-three years left to go before retirement.

But when I reach that time, I hope and pray there are people like you still around."

Another woman, from Marin County, was thirty years old and already frightened by the way this society treats its elderly people. She said she had worked in nursing homes when she was younger, had watched how people age and how a society that is becoming more and more infatuated with youth treated them. Just thirty years old! It was so hard for me to grasp.

There was another letter, from a student at Stanford University, which left me virtually inconsolable for several days. In the letter she told me of her grandmother's last days.

"You are the unknown soldier, my grandmother's knight in shining armor," she wrote. "She died this last year. Before her death she suffered one of the indignities of growing old. She was mugged and robbed and unable to protect herself.

"She had always been such an independent lady. The experience took that away from her, made her know her vulnerability. It pushed her over an edge that she never returned from and made her frightened for the rest of her life.

"It makes me sad to know that the elderly of my grandma's generation are made to suffer from the blatant ignorance of mine. I thank you, Mr. Langlois. You are most certainly my hero."

I moped around the apartment for a couple of days after that one, thinking of Grandma Alice on the bed in her walk-up flat in the Richmond District, her dress arranged neatly around her while Gengembre slept forever at her side, neither of them hearing the bells from the Little Sisters of the Poor across the street. My wife Kitty sensed something was wrong and left me alone, content to let me work it out in my own good time, knowing that I would talk about it when I was ready. As usual, her quiet but unwavering support got me through that bleak spell as it had through others.

And then one day in August my daily mail carrier

from the Hall of Justice handed me a letter bearing the embossed seal of the President of the United States. Being an old ex-Marine and one who is generally impressed by rank, I swallowed hard and almost came to attention.

"They can't draft me at my age, can they?" I asked, opening the letter with trepidation. It read:

Dear Officer Langlois,
Word has reached me of your years of devoted service to protecting the elderly, and I wanted to let you know how much I think of your actions.

Crimes against the vulnerable elderly are especially detestable. Your courageous efforts to deter these crimes demonstrate the finest qualities a human being can possess—selflessness and a willingness to assume risks for the sake of others. Although you may never fully know the good you have accomplished, without doubt, many lives have been protected through your courageous actions. You are a credit to your department, your city, and our nation.

Nancy and I are proud to send you our commendations and best wishes for the future. God bless you.
Sincerely,
Ronald Reagan

Many more people went beyond a simple expression of thanks. They wanted to know what they could do to help, where they could go and be directed to help combat the problem. I had been giving that a lot of thought myself, roughing out and setting to paper a loose set of ideas that I often toyed with as I walked the Tenderloin as a victim officer. It all seemed so simple and clear to me: increased penalties for those convicted of crimes against the elderly; a portion of the gate taken during sporting and cultural events to go toward existing but financially strapped senior service organizations. One day, while staring at the growing list of ideas, I went to the top of the page and penned "SOS—Save Our Seniors." It was a simple concept and SOS, I believed, would help impart the sense of urgency I feel is needed to help solve this problem.

The thrust of the plan is simple. Under SOS, a one-dollar surcharge would be added to the ticket price of sporting, entertainment, and cultural events in a given city. Just one dollar. I have seen people give more than that to panhandlers on the street. But under SOS the giving becomes automatic and the money can be accounted for.

The money means very little when counted individually. Even the Sunday paper costs more these days. But when you consider that the average attendance of a San Francisco Forty-Niners football game on any given weekend is sixty thousand people, it does not take much to work out the sort of revenue SOS could expect to have in its coffers. That would be sixty thousand dollars *every Sunday* during football season alone, with approximately ninety percent of that going directly to the SOS program and the rest toward administrative costs.

About this time I became aware of the Senior Escort Service, a well-run civic organization in San Francisco made up largely of volunteers. These kind and good-hearted people donated their spare time to taking the elderly wherever they needed to go during the course of a day. Some folks had remained virtual prisoners in their own homes due to the increase of street crime in their neighborhoods. Now they had only to call a given number and an able-bodied escort would be dispatched to walk or drive them to the doctor's office, the pharmacy, or to a friend's house for afternoon tea.

It was a great service, with many fine and devoted people serving selflessly to make it work. One area of the Western Addition known for the frequency of purse snatchings and other crimes against seniors was particularly well served when Senior Escort Service concentrated its efforts there. The number of crimes perpetrated against its grateful clients was reduced to nearly nothing.

This success bore out what had been hammered into me during my time in the Old Man's shoes: It is wise to have a friend along whenever venturing out. The extra person is paramount in preventing this insidious crime. With the added person there are two sets of eyes to watch and record a thief's face when he makes his move, another voice to yell and draw attention. The addition of a second person on the street poses new and insurmountable problems to all but the most determined thief.

But the financial pitfalls of the late eighties were having their effect on volunteer organizations of all kinds, and Senior Escort Services proved to be no exception. Volunteers who could afford to donate a couple of hours each week found that their time was now required elsewhere, and agency officials found themselves cutting back more and more. As a result, the number of crimes against the elderly began to creep up again in various parts of town.

By the time Senior Escort Services was kind enough to honor me with its Humanitarian Award for my work with RAT, I was already trying to tell anyone who would listen about my plan to bolster and expand the fine work of this organization. Given the response to the effectiveness of the 1987 operation in the Tenderloin, I thought local politicians would be interested in hearing of a cheap, effective way to provide for the security of the elderly in our city. It did not take long, however, for me to realize that some politicos had been to shake my hand when the spotlight of publicity was shining my way, after all the hoorays were over, I was once again nothing more than a simple patrolman with questionable ideas and doubtful political clout.

Little by little, during the few conversations or written communications I had with the powers that be, I discovered that people could not stand to think that a lowly patrolman had come up with a rational idea to solve a growing crime problem. Those who requested copies of my outline of SOS began to change certain elements, picking at and eventually eroding the entire concept until it was whittled down to bare bones. The whole procedure left me feeling more depressed than during my worst moments on the street. For the first time, I felt, there was a chance for a city to take direct action and now, because of petty politics, the opportunity was slipping from our grasp.

Disheartened but still believing I could do some good, I met with a former police commissioner I had come to admire during his long years of service. We talked about my ideas over lunch and I lingered over his every word, hoping for some sign of encouragement. At one point he stopped my passionate discourse on the problem when he reached across the table and touched my arm. "That's all well and good, Bill," he said gently. "It's a sound idea. But you don't grasp the issue here. No politician is going to latch onto an idea that has nothing in it for them."

My friend said that unless an elected official felt they could secure a voting block good for fifty thousand votes or be seen receiving a plaque from the American Association of Retired Persons, they wouldn't want to take such a project on. This message was driven home especially hard because it was a politician who told me this. It left me feeling completely, totally helpless.

There was no real reason why a plan like Save Our Seniors could not be implemented. But there was no one in a position of power willing to stick their neck out to see it done. It didn't make any sense to me. We had eleven supervisors of what was supposed to be one of the most progressive cities in the nation, who seemed to be more concerned with the politics of El Salvador than they were with the problems of the elderly in their own hometown. It boggled my mind.

After the *Chronicle* article came out I was besieged by requests from local television to further discuss the issues of crimes against the elderly. It was a Catch-22 situation for me. As much as I wanted to trumpet the cause and get people fired up, I was still actively involved in an undercover operation. Appearing on television could be suicidal. As it happened, the Old Man saved the day once again. When a producer from the local NBC affiliate called to ask if I would come and talk about the problems, I suggested that I appear as I did when the RAT unit prowled the streets. They loved the idea.

I was nervous about appearing on television, but I was elated that I would be given the time to air my ideas. Hopefully, we would be able to come up with some answers. The initial story went well enough, current shots of me in disguise cut in with file footage they had taken of the Old Man during the operation. My voice was electronically altered and, when I finally saw the story on the evening news that night, I had no fear of being recognized. Filmed against the backdrop of the Tenderloin, I talked at length about a generation of apparently disposable Americans who had devoted entire lifetimes to their jobs and families only to find themselves alone and unneeded in their waning years.

Where the *Chronicle* story seemed to have touched a nerve in the public consciousness, my second attempt at television attached a live wire and sent a wave of electricity through it. A second flurry of letters rivaling the first quickly followed, along with a new spate of requests for television interviews. Someone out there was listening, I reasoned, or we would not be getting this kind of response. The problem was to present the ideas of SOS to the right person, the man or woman who had the power to carry out at least some of the things I was suggesting, at just the right time.

Eleven days after the chief's press conference, I was approached by a producer for a local talk show called "People Are Talking." The producer told me they were lining up a show which would key on the problem of crime against the elderly. Audience participation would be encouraged, she said, with questions directed to me, other members of the RAT unit, and a panel of experts who worked with older people. When I told her I was still undercover, the producer said there would be no problem since coming as the Old Man would actually be a benefit. I agreed to come, as did Craig Woods, Lee Tyler, and

Vanetta Pollett.

Craig and I drove down to the station together, telling war stories on the way down and glad to be together again. I had my favorite props—a polyester blazer, a beret, and a hospital slipper—in a brown paper bag tucked under my arm. An aide greeted us and brought us into the studio, showing us the platform at the front of the sound stage where we would sit with four other panelists. She then ushered us into a small anteroom, showed me a small desk and mirror arrangement so that I could fine-tune my makeup, and left us alone with the pastries and doughnuts. Craig settled back on a couch and I began to resurrect the Old Man, daubing gray tint on my sideburns and beard. I was nearly done when show hosts Ann Fraser and Ross McGowan came by to introduce themselves and get a feel for our stories. We shook hands all around and spent a few minutes locked in small talk until another aide came along to give us the ten-minute to air time warning. I put on my slipper, adjusted my beret, and followed Craig out into the studio, amused to see myself limping along out of habit.

The harsh white glare of the studio lights brought back memories of the chief's conference that I tried hard to push away. We settled into our chairs as technicians scurried. Lee and Vanetta smiled and waved from their seats in the audience.

Everything moved very quickly after that, with the audience settling down and watching the monitors as a pre-produced tape of the RAT unit in action flickered across the screens. When it ended, the floor manager signaled the hosts, a red light blinked on over one of the heavy studio cameras, and Ross McGowan introduced the day's show to enthusiastic applause. After a brief round of introductions he directed the first question to me, asking me to describe the typical scenario for these crimes.

"I don't know that there is a typical scenario," I said, "but let me tell you about the eighty-three-year-old woman who decides to go out for cake one afternoon because she is going to have a friend over. On the way home from the bakery, this woman is followed because she is old and frail and because she is unwittingly projecting a victim aura. She is followed back to her apartment house where the criminal, usually young and very tough, uses some sort of subterfuge to make his way into the building with her."

The glare of the studio lights made it virtually impossible to see more than a few feet past the stage, but out of the corner of my eye I noticed a woman, probably around thirty-five, lean slightly forward in interest.

I continued: "In this case the thief volunteers to help the woman enter her apartment. She allows him to do so. Once inside, his arm goes around her neck and across her eyes. Her glasses shatter. If the initial blow is forceful enough—and the victim is brittle enough—the thief may break her cheekbone or her jaw. When he throws her down, her hip may go. Now regardless of what injuries she may receive physically, an eighty-three-year-old will not recover from this type of abuse in the same way as a twenty-six-year-old who breaks her hip on the ski slopes. This probably takes years off the old person's life. It strips her of her dignity, of her personal sense of well-being. Not only is there physical pain, but now this person is afraid to go out."

A murmur, barely perceptible, spread through the audience. The woman in the front row was nodding.

"The victim's apartment is ransacked, her personal memories destroyed, her sense of self violated. And for a few bucks or whatever these people get in the course of their attacks, they have essentially ruined that old woman's life."

A sound not unlike a growl rumbled through the studio.

"Our chief was troubled by this, and that's why we came up with the RAT program. We could have simply followed old folks around until they were attacked, but that would have subjected them to abuse and could have taken months. So we decided that the only sure way was to put ourselves out there in their place. And that's what we did."

"You were followed countless times during this operation, weren't you?" McGowan said. "Describe for us what that was like, that feeling of being followed all those times."

"It does give you a rush. It's definitely a different experience," I said. The audience laughed. "The big difference is that these people don't know that I'm a police officer, a victim officer. That realization comes later, when I walk into court."

"Have you had that happen?" asked Fraser. "What's that like?"

"Christmas in July."

That got another appreciative laugh.

Fraser and McGowan then opened the show up to questions, running a microphone over to a gentleman who wanted to know if the problem was confined to San Francisco or existed elsewhere as well. Finally, I thought, we're on the right track. I framed my answer carefully.

"By this coming Sunday there will be another 295 Americans who will reach the age of one hundred." There are over ten thousand Americans living in this country who are over that age right now. These people make tempting targets for criminals who seem to be getting younger and younger. This problem is not going to go away, sir, and it's nationwide."

Someone else asked whether or not we were entrapping these criminals. Craig Woods jumped at the chance to answer that one.

"Entrapment is when you instill the idea in a person's mind to commit a crime and then offer them the opportunity," he said. "That's not what we do. We simply offer them the opportunity. It's up to them if they want to take it any further than that."

Ann Fraser was standing next to an elderly gentleman she introduced as John, a wonderful old guy who, in a straightforward manner that hushed the audience, described in detail how he had been beaten and robbed at knife point in his apartment the year before. The angry growl I had heard before rifled through the studio once again. John, it turned out, was ninety-nine years old.

A member of the audience asked what it had been like, walking the streets *knowing* I was going to be beaten and robbed, and whether the experience had left any emotional scars as well as the obvious physical ones. It was odd, but it was the first time that I can remember anyone asking about the mental strain of my chosen profession.

"In the film clip," I said, "you saw me become emotional. What you have to realize is that we're not robots covered in dark blue Teflon. We're human beings. We see this going on out there and, all things being equal, we know it could happen to us because we're all going to get old. What people twenty-five or even twenty years old don't realize is that, if we don't stop this abuse right now, we're all going to be in a lot of trouble."

Ann Fraser jumped in. "Do you think people caught preying on the elderly should get stiffer sentences?" she asked.

It was exactly the sort of question I was hoping someone would pose.

"Absolutely," I said, grateful for the opportunity to offer what I consider a practical suggestion for inhibiting those who carry out this most cowardly of crimes. "I think the legislature of this state should immediately bring into law a provision whereby anyone caught preying on someone over sixty years of age and causing them any harm whatsoever should have an additional five years automatically tacked onto their sentence. Then these people would have to evaluate the price they stand to pay if they are caught."

This was greeted with apparent approval as the audience applauded vigorously. One person wanted to know if these crimes were a recent phenomenon or if we were simply hearing more about them now because of the attention being paid to the so-called "Graying of America," a growing number of older people in this country.

"Is it a growing phenomenon?" he asked. "And why haven't we been made more aware of it?"

"We're trying to make you aware of it," I said. "More often than not these crimes are being committed against people who have no one to speak for them. They've often outlived the relatives who would normally be there to protest their abuse, and most of them are on their own. As for the criminals, ninety-nine percent of the time they are convicts. They've talked among themselves and have come to the conclusion that to roll an old person on the street is bad for two reasons: because they know people are not carrying any more money than they need, and because on the street they stand a chance of being seen by a concerned citizen or by passing police.

"That leaves doing the crime indoors, in the victim's own home, where the criminal feels nice and safe behind closed doors, sure that they've got all the time in the world."

More questions were directed at the show's other guests, who included Vince Reyes, director of the city's Senior Escort Service. He explained that the seven offices under his direction were handling four to five-hundred escorts each month and that, while the number of crimes against senior citizens were down dramatically, funding was getting short and the worry was that they would not be able to continue with the level of service they had provided in the past.

I was hoping at that point I would get a chance to develop my ideas about SOS, but Ann and Ross moved through the audience again, talking to Lee Tyler and Vanetta Pollett about their part in the RAT program, before the show finally broke up to hearty applause. As people were drifting out of the studio I walked up to John, the mugging victim, and we shared a few words. I told him I was glad he had survived his ordeal, that I hoped he lived well beyond his one hundredth birthday and that he would never again be the victim of crime. He smiled and shook my hand warmly, and we parted. Craig and I then retreated to a quiet corner of the building where I shed my Old Man disguise and walked out in my street clothes.

Within the next week, between times on the job as Bill

Taggart, I was interviewed by Fleet Street West, attended a Rotary Club luncheon with Chief Jordan, and stood by as the day was declared mine by mayoral proclamation. To round out the week I found out the department's Awards Commission had voted to grant me the Gold Medal of Valor—the department's highest award for bravery—for my part in the 1986 RAT operation.

But the wear and tear of my undercover life, combined with the television appearances and other interviews, was beginning to take its toll. Looking back at the videotape of those early interviews, I could see the weariness in my face. I looked absolutely horrible. When the camera was on me and I was talking, everything was all right. But in those instances when I was caught in passing it didn't take much to see that there was a lot going on behind the makeup. Much is made of the effects of delayed stress, and I would have to say that the weeks following the end of the RAT program were in many ways much tougher mentally than the time we actually spent on the street.

All the signs were there: the jerky movements, the way I held my head, the downcast turn of my eyes. For the first time I realized that I was becoming the very person I had portrayed as a victim officer. It was a frightening realization, because I still regarded myself as a relatively young man. But every time the camera swung past me I found myself thinking: that guy's in trouble.

In April of 1988, with Mission Stamp and Coin in full swing and the burglars lining up to do business with us, I was notified by mail that I had been nominated for a very special award. It seemed the Veterans of Foreign Wars had forwarded my name to their national headquarters as a candidate for their Law Enforcement Officer of the Year award. They had already accorded me statewide honors. It was an astounding privilege to be chosen. Later, I learned that only two other men had ever been selected from my department—and both of them had been chiefs. The nomination was pretty heady territory for a lowly patrolman.

With statewide honors came a mandatory appearance at the VFW's annual awards dinner in Southern California on June 22. I trotted off, undercover beard and all, to attend the banquet and receive my award. There were four hundred people in attendance, and that number seemed to grow by exponents of ten as I was called on to accept my award and then to say a few words at the end of the evening. I thanked my hosts, too panicked to even raise the subject of SOS. When I realized they were expecting a little more from me, I launched into the story of "Taps."

This was the tale of the union corporal who was called on by his commanding general one evening in 1864 to compose a bugle call to herald the general's arrival in camp. This corporal, as it turned out, was not only a good bugler but he was something of a composer as well. When he returned to the general's tent with his bugle call days later, both armies, North and South, were settling down at opposite ends of the valley they had fought for all day. The general asked him to play his tune and he did, the notes lingering over the valley as the camp smoke drifted into the darkening sky. An hour went by and there was a commotion at the outskirts of camp as a confederate officer was brought in, riding under a flag of truce and escorted by two Union cavalrymen.

Bowing with formality, the rebel officer told the commander of the Union camp that his men had heard the unfamiliar bugle call and thought so much of it they wondered if they could borrow the bugler to play the tune while they buried their dead. It was such a magnanimous gesture that the Union officer couldn't refuse. He sent the bugler and the rebel officer back to the Southern camp under escort and once again that mournful tune wafted across the valley. Over the years the tune proved so popular, so pure in form, that no one dared try to improve on it. That was how "Taps" was born.

When I was done with the story I looked around. There had been a table full of slightly intoxicated former Marines in the front row and they were dead silent by the time I finished. A couple of them smiled at me and I stepped down.

After the dinner, between the free drinks and handshakes which went on long into the night, I was informed by VFW officials that no plain patrolman had ever won their national award unless it was posthumously. Enrique Camarena, the DEA agent tortured to death by drug traffickers, had been one of the last recipients. And most of the other honorees had all been ranking officers who had done something in an administrative line. Given this information I flew back to San Francisco the next day, slightly hung over and with little hope of ever receiving the national honor, competing against forty-nine other candidates.

But six weeks later, during mail call away from the sting site, I met with one of our guys who handed over a letter bearing the seal of the national VFW headquarters. The letter inside said I had been unanimously chosen by the national board to receive Law Enforcement Officer of the Year honors and gave me the names of people to call to make the necessary arrangements for attendance at the awards ceremony. It was very rare, the letter went on to say, for the board's choice to be a unanimous one.

Things were finally winding down at Mission Stamp and Coin. We had built up a number of cases against the local criminal element and had almost exhausted our "buy back" funds, even though we were at times paying only cents on the dollar for everything from Cadillacs to diamond rings. Time was getting difficult to find but I hustled to make the VFW's national awards dinner in Chicago, with my father giving Kitty and me a ride to the airport but declining to come with us because of a prior commitment.

The VFW treated us like royalty from the moment we got off the plane. I told Kitty to take note of everything that happened to us during the next few days because it was unlikely we would be treated as well again for the rest of our lives. We had a day to rest and see a few of the sights before they sent for us around nine-thirty the next morning, our liaison making sure we were comfortable in a small office outside the auditorium while we waited to be announced.

When the time came, someone tapped on the door and we were taken inside a cavernous auditorium, filled to capacity with about thirty-five hundred VFW delegates from all across the country. Placards at each set of tables identified which states were represented. As we stood there, with Kitty wondering what she had gotten herself into, the Master of Arms whispered something to the speaker stationed at a rostrum at the head of the auditorium.

"I understand we have a distinguished visitor in the hall," the speaker called out. An honor guard materialized out of nowhere, all spic and span, and fell in alongside us as we were led to the stage. The speaker started the introduction, reading from a citation detailing my exploits with RAT, but before he got to the official presentation he stopped suddenly.

"Officer Langlois," he said, "we have a small surprise for you."

I mumbled something, off guard and unsure what lay in store for me. I had never been in front of so many people before and I was feeling a case of nervousness coming on. At that point the speaker introduced my father and brought him onstage. I was dumbfounded. It turned out he had contacted the VFW and they had flown him out the same day we left San Francisco. They had even put him up in our hotel, arranging for him to see a few things and careful not to let our paths cross until the awards ceremony. They brought him out on the stage and I can't remember ever seeing him look so proud. He stood by as they read the presentation for my award and draped a medal around my neck. My father threw his arms around me when it was over and we hugged. "I'm so proud of you," he whispered, and I felt as if my heart would burst.

They dragged me to the microphone, too full of emotion to really express myself adequately in front of a room full of strangers. So I thanked them for their recognition and acknowledgment of our team and promised that as soon as I got back I would throw a dinner for all the Rat unit members with the thousand-dollar honorarium which came with the award.

And I did. As soon as we got back from Chicago, I made up invitations and sent them out to every member of the RAT unit, promising dinner and drinks at a local restaurant and fun until the thousand dollars ran out.

Almost everyone showed up and we had a grand time. I gave every member of the team a personalized identification bracelet with their RAT names engraved on it and people took turns wearing the VFW medal so pictures could be taken. It was, after all, theirs as much as mine.

Lee Tyler made the entire evening for me when he told the story of the knucklehead who had tried to rob the entire RAT unit during a luncheon we had held on the last day of the operation. It appeared that I, the professional victim officer, had been inside Original Joe's restaurant working off the stress and sprained muscles of the past weeks with a cocktail when one of the most flagrant robberies anyone had seen to that time was going down just feet away.

"We were all standing there in the doorway, twelve of us, just waiting to be seated," Tyler said with obvious delight. "You were already inside, Rug. One of the guys from the TAC Squad, Jeremiah Morgan, went off down Taylor Street to get the afternoon *Examiner*. We were still standing there, not thinking anything of it, when, with a bang and a crash, these two bodies come flying through the door there at Original Joe's. One of them is Jeremiah and the other guy is a Kronk, a big one, that's trying to rob him.

"There was a moment when we all kind of looked at each other, of course, after all those weeks on the street and with lunch waiting and all, and then it was if someone said, What the hell? and we all piled on. It was crazy, just minutes after we had decided to shut down the operation, this idiot tries to knock over a cop in broad daylight. We got him laid out on the sidewalk and he was mumbling to himself. I kneeled down and asked him if he'd been having a particularly bad week and he says, 'Why do you ask?' That's when I told him he had just tried to rob a cop with eleven other cops standing nearby. He just sort of put his head down there on the cold cement and said, 'Oh my God!'"

We were both laughing like crazy. Lee said someone summoned a black and white to fetch the suspect but that no one wanted to go downtown with him after doing the same thing day in and day out. Besides, everyone was off duty and a terrific lunch was waiting. So the Street Rats just told the beat cop to take Jeremiah's Kronk down to the TAC Squad and chain him to a bench, and they'd be along presently. Nothing was going to stop them from having their goodbye feast. I was at the bar nursing my wounds when they came in, laughing and talking the way they always did when they were together. But not one of them said a word about the catch of the day. I guess the whole thing had become old hat to them.

We wrapped up the sting operation at Mission Stamp and Coin in August 1988. Together, Dom and "Tiger" Taggart took in nearly two million dollars worth of stolen property—including five brand new Cadillacs and, in one case, a fully loaded roofing truck which had been stolen from a job site and brought to us with its tar pot still bubbling. I think we paid sixty dollars for the roofing truck, thirty-four thousand total for everything else. It was amazing. During our thirteen months at the store we bought jewelry, tape machines, hospital equipment and guns from 153 suspects, all of whom were coaxed into recounting their exploits as the video cameras rolled and the tape-recording equipment logged their every word. Every one of them was rounded up and jailed minutes after Mission Stamp and Coin closed down for the last time. The burglary rate subsequently dipped by ten percent.

One of those we helped jail was a former police officer who had been mustered out of the department after falling into the downward spiral of heroin abuse. In one of the most dangerous moments of the sting, this former officer—who had commented before that I resembled someone he knew—met me away from the store at a raised, dead-end parking lot. He had brought a bare-chested, tattooed, and unknown companion with him. I greatly feared an ambush. Our cars were parked side by side, the trunks open. I was looking at the weapons they were selling when I heard the distinct sound of the mechanism of a shotgun being closed. The move was so unexpected that my hand went immediately to the revolver in my waistband under my shirt. In split seconds I realized I had not been discovered, that my former cohort was merely trying to demonstrate that his wares were in good working order and he was not trying to pepper me with buckshot! Only then did I relax, thinking about how close those men came to not making jail at all.

Working undercover out of Mission Stamp and Coin had been satisfying. But as I had anticipated, public awareness of the RAT unit's good deeds and interest in the SOS program diminished with time. Someone once said that America is a nation of amnesiacs, whose people are quick to forget their own history and unwilling to confront current problems, preferring instead to move on via the remote control to the latest atrocity or passing fad.

A year after RAT left the streets and the story dropped off the front pages, crimes against the elderly began to pick up yet again, this time outside of the Tenderloin, as edgy criminals moved further afield to search for their prey.

Despite the grim indicators of what lies in store for all of us unless we come to grips with the insidious problem of crimes against the elderly, the San Francisco Police Department, beset by the budgetary and manpower shortages faced by big cities across the country, has not been able to field a team to help right this terrible wrong since the last RAT unit left the Tenderloin in 1987.

Cops are frustrated and would like to help, but there just aren't enough of them. It is up to the citizenry in these fearful times to learn how to help themselves and how to help each other to keep from being victimized. Knowledge, as we shall see, can be the best weapon of all.

Chapter 7

THE PROBLEM

Her name was Madeline Mackenzie. She was ninety-three years old, living alone in a walk-up apartment on Hermann Street in San Francisco, in an area of the city known as the Duboce Triangle. Her neighbors said she was a quiet woman, who left her apartment at about the same time each day for a walk down to the corner market to buy her groceries.

When she first came to the attention of police, Madeline Mackenzie was lying in the hallway of her looted apartment, only just alive and bleeding from a severe head wound. Not only had she been bludgeoned, the doctors said, but the thief or thieves who had followed her home from the store that day in July 1986, had also strangled her for good measure, leaving only when they believed she was dead. Although her vital signs still registered as tiny blips on the monitoring equipment, hospital officials held out little hope for her recovery.

When contacted by police investigators who came around to ask the pertinent questions, Madeline Mackenzie's neighbors could shed little light on what had happened to the quiet old woman. Few knew anything at all about her. It was some time, I believe, before a relative could be contacted. Everyone, police officers and the residents who seemed to know her only in passing, tried to piece together the details of her life as she lay comatose in San Francisco General Hospital.

"She lived alone. She liked it that way," one neighbor told our detectives. "She was an independent woman all of her life and she saw no reason to change her lifestyle just because she was ninety-three."

Although she clung to life for three weeks after the

assault, I believe Madeline Mackenzie was murdered the afternoon her attacker followed her home, made his way into her flat, and struck her before ransacking her few belongings. And while she may have technically been considered alive during those lingering weeks in the hospital, surrounded by strangers and breathing with the help of a machine, for all intents and purposes Madeline Mackenzie's life was taken from her during a few moments of terror on July 23.

She must have made a tempting target. Walking with difficulty, clutching her social security money tightly, she negotiated the street to her market at her usual slow but determined pace. The man on duty in the store at the time remembered seeing her come in, buying a few odds and ends, and then setting out for home, possibly intending to make her lunch and spend the afternoon watching television. We'll never really know for sure. Somewhere along the way Madeline Mackenzie attracted someone's attention. A pair of eyes shifted her way and footsteps fell in behind hers. On that day she would fall victim to a thoughtless brand of criminal other neighbors suspected had been stalking elderly people in that area for some time.

"I'm always nervous. There's so much crime out there these days," seventy-year-old Mary Williams told a newspaper reporter who had been sent out to do a follow-up on the assault. "I don't go out much at night anymore."

Reports of crime against the elderly have added to the already-high anxiety level of senior citizens, according to the head of the geriatric outreach program for the city's Senior Friendship Hotline.

"Attacks like the one on Madeline Mackenzie are shocking, but unfortunately not uncommon," he said. "It adds to the anxiety many of these people already are feeling and keeps many seniors inside, prisoners in their own apartments."

I read that comment the next morning while sitting in the squad room at TAC. It floored me. I could feel my knuckles going white with anger at the sense of hopelessness it contained, the acceptance of what should be unacceptable.

An entire level of our society, the fastest growing single age group in our country, had given up hope of walking down the street because a younger element was preying on them. Madeline Mackenzie's neighbors had told the investigators who came to survey her looted apartment that they were frequently the victim of assaults by young thieves but failed to report it because they felt it would do no good.

"What are you going to do?" asked an eighty-two-year old named Anne Marie who still bore the scars left by her encounter with a purse snatcher not far from where Madeline Mackenzie had been killed. "I told him there was no cash in the purse and he took it anyway, dumped it out on the street right in front of me. I had a few pictures of my grandchildren and a few stamps for the mail. He took the stamps and left the pictures there on the sidewalk for me to pick up. I'm over eighty. He's eighteen, strong, and he's got a knife. Tell me what I could have done."

News of the assault on Madeline Mackenzie shook the members of the RAT unit. The newspaper account of her beating was passed from team member to team member the next morning, a curious mix of anger and disbelief spreading across our faces, most of us unwilling to accept that our society could turn on itself in this way. We took to the streets of the Tenderloin that afternoon with a renewed sense of purpose. And every time we threw the net over a culprit as he or she banged away on the Old Man in the following weeks, it was as if we were capturing the person responsible for the murder of Madeline Mackenzie. At the very least, I think we all believed, we were in a position to do *something*.

As it turned out, Madeline Mackenzie was not the first to die at the hands of an uncaring thug, nor would she be the last. But when she finally did slip away shortly after noon on August 14, it was as if a member of the family had passed on. To us she became the classic example of a dastardly new pattern of crime and the quiet, systematic abuse of the elderly which is currently sweeping this country.

Before Operation Dismantle began in earnest that summer of 1986, police in Sacramento also found themselves faced with a rash of assaults on elderly people, both in the state capital as well as in outlying areas of Sacramento County. In most cases, the assaults were similar in method to the ones we were seeing over a hundred miles away in San Francisco: young thieves entering the homes of elderly people and terrorizing them until they were given money or other forms of loot.

It was more than mere coincidence, I felt, that we should be seeing exactly the same crimes committed in such numbers in such widely divergent communities at roughly the same time. As far as we could determine there was no apparent link between the persons responsible for the crimes in both cities. Our crooks did not appear to be striking in the city and then driving north to the capital to do the same crimes there. There was only one conclusion which could be drawn from this information: the problem we thought had been largely confined to one neighborhood in San Francisco was actually taking place in other, more rural, areas of the state as well.

It also did not take long to see that the same atmosphere of fear and dread that prevailed among elderly residents of the Tenderloin was also being felt in the state capital. During a six-week period from late December 1985 to early January 1986, officers reported forty-six attacks on elderly people in the city of Sacramento alone, and nine more in other, more isolated parts of the county.

Two men were ultimately arrested and charged with some of the crimes. But their work and the deeds of other criminals believed responsible for the rest of the assaults left a permanent scar on the psyches of senior citizens who had moved to Sacramento for its warm summer evenings, rural atmosphere, and a housing market friendly to the pocketbook.

In an interview with a local paper shortly after the crime wave broke out, the director of geriatric programs at a Sacramento hospital said how important it was to point out "that potential trauma is a critical issue with the older generation."

Director Marsha Vacca said that seniors were haunted by the "whole sense of fear of being victimized," because they realized that advancing age had deprived them of their physical strength and diminished their senses.

"No person can live for very long with that sort of fear hanging over them," Vacca said. "The threat of harm *has* to have physical and emotional repercussions. It might be ulcers, a level of paranoia, anxiety attacks, depression, or pure anger about the way society is."

Having talked at length on several occasions with those who have fallen victim to this new breed of vicious predator, I have to say I couldn't have agreed more with Vacca's assessment of the impact of crime on these poor people. The vulnerability factor alone was enough to have an adverse effect on an otherwise healthy man or woman who was used to leading an independent lifestyle and suddenly, out of fear, felt forced to curtail their normal activities.

"For those who have been victimized," Vacca went on, "there is also the fear of retaliation if they report the crime, and being scared to go outside their own home. It's like self-imprisonment."

There was no "like" about it. It *was* self-imprisonment. As we began to learn more and more about how the elderly lived in our city, our state, and across the country, we found cases of seniors who rarely, if ever, set foot outside their apartments, opening their doors only to members of benevolent organizations or church groups who brought them food or medicine. In San Francisco, one woman had spent the last six years of her life in an apartment on Eddy Street, staying to herself, sending a neighbor boy out for her necessities. When she finally collapsed and died in her room, a week had gone by before anyone noticed.

Just recently, a Tenderloin resident named Marcella "Granny" Brooks was knocked down by four young toughs who then pushed her wheelchair out into traffic on Market Street. Not only was her wheelchair destroyed, but Granny Brooks had a rib broken in the process. In pain and with her sole source of mobility gone, Marcella crawled from doorway to doorway for four days until she was found and taken to the hospital.

In Sacramento, as in San Francisco, the common denominator of all the victims, battered and abused for their few possessions or for the thrill of hurting someone less powerful, was their age. They came from different communities, with varied backgrounds, some being better off than others. But in each case the ones who survived told police they felt they had been singled out for attack because their assailants knew they could not possibly fight back, and because they were less likely to identify them in court.

After the two suspects were arrested in Sacramento, the number of assaults on elderly residents dwindled, although police continued to report a steady number of "copycat" crimes perpetrated by those who had heard of the vulnerability of the elderly and decided to try the tactic out for themselves. Older people, it was easy to see, had become the criminal element's new target of opportunity. While the intruders were able to get away with hundreds of dollars' worth of booty in some isolated cases, the average take appeared to be in the neighborhood of fifty dollars. Not much money when compared to the amount of physical damage the perpetrators inflicted, or when measured against the incalculable loss of a single human life.

Police in both cities were beginning to see a common thread interwoven among those who had been caught and charged with committing crimes against the elderly. Most were young, under thirty, with prior criminal records for burglary or drug abuse. Driven by the need to ease the persistent itch of cocaine or heroin addiction, they tended to steal in cycles—dormant when in the grip of their drug, jumpy and dangerous when they went out to score the money or goods required to buy their narcotics. Nearly all of them said they would do anything to get the money for their narcotics of choice, up to and including using violence.

Eager to learn more about the criminal type who preyed on the elderly, Inspector Tom Vigo prepared a breakdown of information gleaned from the arrests of forty-three suspects in the 1986 and 1987 RAT programs. He learned that, of the forty-three, five had previously served time in the state prison system. Thirty-two had previously been arrested on narcotics charges, although only eight of them had actually been convicted.

Vigo took the exercise a step further, tracking the criminal careers of those we had arrested to see if their experience with the RAT unit had been some sort of fluke or was actually telltale evidence of an ongoing pattern of criminality. He found that most of those arrested tended to keep within the same range of crimes for which they had initially been arrested, with the most common crimes listed as assault, burglary, robbery, and possession of stolen goods.

Since the forty-three men were caught and convicted during the decoy program, seventeen were arrested again within a short time of their release from prison. All of their most recent crimes were narcotics violations. Four men were returned to prison because they were still on parole from arrests made during RAT. The remaining thirteen crimes were either dismissed outright or were pending at the time Vigo examined them. Within the seventeen drug offense arrests were four arrests for burglary, two for petty theft, and two for battery.

Although it appeared the majority of those caught during the victim officer program tended to stay within their chosen area of criminality, we began to learn of yet another, more violent type of individual. In San Francisco it was the type who sought out older people to victimize because of the sense of power it gave him to have them under his control. People like Whispers. This type of predator, we soon found, became increasingly violent after each successful hunt.

In Oakland, California, just a few miles east of the city across the Oakland-San Francisco Bay Bridge, Whispers' counterpart was a muscled thug named Franklin Lynch. A parole violator with a history of violence and heavy drug use, he waged a one-man campaign of terror against elderly women throughout the East Bay communities of Oakland, San Leandro, and Newark.

In late July and early August of 1987, at precisely the same time the RAT unit was at work in the Tenderloin, this thirty-two-year-old ex-convict was busy as well. Lynch, who was also known as Robert Walker, had been released earlier that year from state prison, where he had been serving time for a burglary conviction. Investigators in Alameda County—an area best known for the winning ways of its sports teams and the heroic manner in which its citizens rose to the challenge of the 1989 earthquake in northern California—said Lynch began using crack cocaine shortly after his release from prison and quickly became addicted. Needing more and more money to feed the persistent craving for more and more crack—the potent pebbles of hybrid cocaine that has held whole neighborhoods in its grip—Lynch struck out to get his drug money the only way he knew how, by taking it from others weaker than himself.

In a few short weeks from July to August 1987, he was believed responsible for a series of random attacks on elderly women throughout Alameda and—it was suspected—Contra Costa County to the north.

Up until the moment he was caught, Franklin Lynch hunted with almost clockwork regularity. Despite an intense manhunt and regular broadcasts which named Lynch as a suspect in the crimes and brought his mug shot into the living rooms of an increasingly edgy populace, he continued to evade police.

In late July, before Lynch was fingered by police and people were told to be wary of him, five elderly women ranging in age from their late sixties to their early eighties were confronted just days apart by an intruder in their homes. Entering through unlocked doors or windows, the muscular suspect seemed to attack with impunity. Some of his victims were bound and gagged, all were relentlessly beaten and terrorized.

A seventy-three-year-old named Anna Constantine was beaten and robbed for all of seventy-five dollars. Two days later Ruth Durham, eighty-eight, was clubbed from behind and assaulted in her own home. Two days after that, Bessie Herrick, seventy-four, was hit in the head and face by a man who walked in through her front door and attacked her without warning.

By this time Lynch was already the prime suspect in the deaths of two San Leandro women: Pearl Larson, seventy-six, who was found dead in her home July 24, and Adeline Figurido, eighty-nine, who was attacked in her home July 29 and later died after failing to respond to treatment at a local hospital. When news of the additional assaults began to spread, police in neighboring Contra Costa County noted similarities between the San Leandro murders and the fatal assault of a ninety-two-year-old retired schoolteacher named Laura Atwood, who had been found dead in her Vallejo home July 1.

When yet another woman was killed in San Leandro, the search for Lynch—who had a record of similar assaults going back to 1973—intensified as a panicky citizenry screamed for his capture. The crimes, which had come at regular intervals up to that point, slacked off in the face of heightened media attention, and then ceased altogether.

Alameda County investigators assigned to the case surmised that the killer had moved on to more fertile hunting grounds and they were quickly proved right. In October, just weeks after the East Bay crime wave had subsided, Lynch was arrested by a heavily armed FBI SWAT team in Los Angeles.

Tried on three charges of first-degree murder with special circumstances because he killed during the course of a robbery, Lynch was convicted on each count.

In handing down the sentence, Alameda County

Superior Court Judge Philip Sarkisian said the unrepentant suspect "showed a high degree of viciousness and cruelty," while Senior Deputy District Attorney James Anderson, in arguing for the death penalty, referred to Lynch as a "human reptile and murder machine."

The jury agreed. They wasted little time in returning with a death penalty verdict, coming back with that weightiest of all decisions in a little over three and a half hours.

Lynch is currently on California's death row, awaiting execution of his sentence.

At five feet ten inches and 175 pounds, the powerfully built ex-convict appeared to have had little trouble controlling his victims. Often, the initial blow he delivered upon entering the home was enough to stun the women for the duration of the robbery. Additional beatings were delivered if his victims proved reluctant to divulge the location of their money or other valuables. Those who survived the attacks told police the suspect was on them so suddenly and overwhelmed them so quickly that they had little time to react. In what turned out to be a common theme, survivors said their attacker often picked them up and then threw them to the floor in order to stun them and to discourage resistance, a tactic the Old Man had experienced firsthand as well.

If Lynch's victims had been able to fight back at all, things may have ended differently. All but the most committed burglar will choose to run if met by any form of recalcitrance on the part of his intended victim.

While the decision to resist has an equal number of arguments against it and should be weighed carefully by those who find themselves in the position at the time, it proved an effective deterrent for one quick-witted grandmother who found herself face to face with an armed intruder at the time Franklin Lynch was still at large.

News of the RAT unit's work in the Tenderloin was just reaching the airwaves and Lynch's arrest photo was being flashed nightly on the evening news as his list of victims lengthened and the hunt for him grew in the summer of 1987. A seventy-seven-year-old San Francisco woman had heard about RAT and also the televised warnings about Lynch. Later, she said both things were very much on her mind when an armed intruder suddenly materialized inside her garage as she was tending her plants late one afternoon in the city's Ingleside District.

"He was suddenly just standing there, leaning on a workbench inside the garage, and I was standing there watering my shrubs," she said. "We were maybe ten feet apart. I asked him what he was doing and he said he was just resting. I knew that wasn't true. I turned around and saw he had a gun in his hand. He was pointing it at me. Then he beckoned me with his finger, motioning for me to come to him and telling me he would not hurt me."

It did not take long for the woman to make up her mind about the man's intentions. She reacted swiftly and, in this case, correctly, fighting back with the only weapon at hand—her garden hose.

"I let him have it with the hose and started screaming at the same time," she said, still too afraid to let the newspapers use her name. "I gave him a good soaking, too. He looked confused at first, as if he was trying to make up his mind what to do, and then he cursed and ran off. He ran right past me and disappeared up the street."

Getting wet, being yelled at, and having attention drawn to him was precisely what this formidable woman's would-be attacker did not want at that moment. As it turned out, our investigators learned he had taken refuge in the woman's garage after attempting to assault yet another victim a short distance away.

There is no way to know what that man wanted or how far he would have gone if given the opportunity. Suffice it to say that if the woman had done what the man wanted, gone to him, and entered her own home with him, the incident might have ended much less happily than it did. What is known is that similar incidents are occurring with ever-more-frightening regularity.

Shortly after the end of my time as a victim officer, I

began to collect newspaper clippings of incidents where elderly people were set upon and robbed. Sometimes the clippings were sent to me with no return address by people who had heard about our work with RAT and who wanted someone to keep some sort of unofficial record of what was happening out there.

After awhile, the accounts in the clippings began to blur into one horrible story, the only differences often being the age of the victims and the brutalities he or she happened to have suffered. In New York, an eighty-nine-year-old grandmother was followed home, bound with electrical cord, and terrorized for several hours until she revealed the location of her late husband's coin collection—the only thing of value in the home. Her assailants were never caught.

In Detroit, an elderly woman who used to bake cookies for the poorer children in her neighborhood was confronted and robbed by two girls, both seventeen, after she had invited them into her home. The girls knocked the old woman down, tied her up, and then, unhappy that she had no money, stabbed her to death with a pair of scissors and a kitchen knife.

No one seems to be immune from this horrific trend. Rich or poor, black or white, it can happen at any time. San Francisco Giants pitcher Trevor Wilson was notified in August of 1992 that his eighty-six-year-old grandmother, Loubenia Wilson, had been robbed and horribly beaten by two men who pushed their way inside her Houston home.

"Some guys came up to her porch, shoved her in the house, and beat her up," Wilson said in a tearful clubhouse interview before leaving the team to be at his grandmother's side. "They taped her mouth and tied her legs with the telephone cord, and she lay there for three days until somebody found her."

Three *days*. It was unbelievable. Two neighborhood girls who knew the old woman as "Lola" stopped by to visit her, saw that her mailbox was full and that three UPS notices had been taped to the front door. When the girls knocked, they found the front door unlocked. When they pushed it open and entered the home they saw the frail woman lying motionless on the living room floor, bound and gagged and with heavy duct tape wound tightly around her head. She was barely breathing and in extreme shock.

Sergeant. A. J. Toepoel of the Houston Police Department's homicide division told reporters that Loubenia Wilson was severely dehydrated when she was found, having gone without food or water for the entire three-day period. The duct tape her assailants had used to stifle her screams had been wrapped a total of fifteen times around her head.

"She was a very small woman," Toepoel said. "They [the suspects] really did a lot of damage."

Doctors gave Trevor Wilson the bad news when he arrived in Houston. His grandmother, they said, was not going to live. Pneumonia had set in. Because she had been tightly bound for so long, the circulation to her legs had been cut off. The doctors were considering amputation of the old woman's legs but then delayed surgery and finally called it off altogether when they decided such a major operation would probably be enough to kill her.

"She's conceded," a shaken and tearful Wilson said after he returned from visiting his grandmother's bedside for the last time. "She's just ready to go to Heaven."

Houston police quickly developed leads on two suspects who, they said, lived in the same neighborhood as the old woman and who had gone to her home with the express purpose of robbing her. Once they had forced their way inside, detectives said, this ruthless pair picked the woman up several times and threw her to the floor while demanding to know where she kept her money. In the end, the two men made off with about two hundred dollars.

"We have quite a few crimes perpetrated against the elderly," Toepoel said as Loubenia Wilson hovered near death. "They are easy pickings for these folks, almost totally defenseless. It just makes me sick to think that it takes two big old boys to do something like that to an old woman.

"And they will have their day of reckoning," he said with the hard-earned wisdom which comes to cops who have seen too much. "If we don't get them, they'll have a higher authority to reckon with one day."

Loubenia Wilson, "Lola" to the neighborhood kids who came to her home, died two weeks later of heart disease and a blood clot in her leg that her doctors said had been exacerbated by her beating.

How can this sort of tragedy be allowed to happen? Here, in a land where mothers and fathers were once revered, lauded in song, and supported by younger members of the family even after they were no longer able to take care of themselves. What does it say about a society that turns on itself this way, where people who lived through the two world wars and saw the realization of some of the world's most amazing accomplishments are merely tossed aside? We put them into warehouses with workers who feed them intravenously and turn them over in their beds every few days and, if we're lucky, they prove not to be too much of a bother.

Our respect for the elderly, which marked our character during the early part of this century, seems to have been replaced with a cruel, almost Darwinian approach to growing old. If you're young and fit, have all your hair and hearing, you're on your way, son, with your material needs being catered to and medical science prepared to help you fend off what the young of this generation have come to fear as a fate worse than death—Old Age.

If you move slowly, have white hair and are vaguely aware that the eyesight and reflexes you were once so proud of are no longer functioning as they once did, you had better beware. The prevailing premise of the 90s, it seems, is survival of the fittest. If you're young and strong, here's to you. If not, get out of the way.

Elderly people are no longer regarded as living history books, a term I've used for them over the years, but as barriers—barely moving, obstreperous old characters who impede our progress on the freeways or keep us waiting in grocery store checkout lines while they fumble for change. In an increasingly youth-oriented society, where the latest fourteen-year-old tennis sensation is lionized and people talk of giving up entirely if they have not made their first million dollars by age thirty, we are beginning to turn on a generation of elderly citizens who are growing in number every day.

One place where the dichotomy between the young and old in America was dramatically driven home recently is Minneapolis, where elderly Americans who settled into a public housing high-rise for seniors moved in with thoughts of afternoon tea, dances, and card games with friends. What they didn't expect was that their idyllic retirement complex would also be opened to formerly "homeless" young people as well as to those addicted to drugs or alcohol. In a few short months, all thoughts of leisurely afternoons in the parlors of longtime friends evaporated in the face of drug deals, assaults, and even murder.

"We have people who have lived here for twenty years or more, fully expecting to retire here and live in peace and comfort for the rest of their lives," said Bear Stradtmann, a sixty-five-year-old who lives in one complex with his wife Jeanne. "Now there are [older] people in the building who won't go out after three in the afternoon."

Since the forty-two public housing high-rises in Minneapolis opened their doors to younger people, elderly residents tired of verbal assaults and beatings and even worse, began moving out in record numbers—if they were financially able. Just forty-six percent of the high-rise residents were elderly while an overwhelming ninety-three percent of the applications for future housing were from younger people, according to the Minneapolis Public Housing Authority.

Elderly residents who grew tired of seeing their young neighbors' apartments used as drug emporiums and centers for acts of prostitution have tried to take control of their homes, forming groups to patrol the halls of their high-rises and reporting suspicious activity to police. But, as the elderly volunteers soon found out, actually going out on patrol can be dicey.

"People are afraid to death," Bear Stradtmann said. "They're afraid if they document something, someone will get them. The fear is a legitimate one... No one wants someone coming to your door and putting a gun in your face."

One seventy-eight-year-old man, Vern Schlief, had been robbed three times, twice at gunpoint, either in the St. Paul apartment he has lived in for twelve years or out in the increasingly dangerous hallways. The former engineer told a Minneapolis wire service reporter that, since the attacks began, he has installed a steel chain on his door and keeps a gun sitting by his door at night.

Ellen Kartak said she refused to use the elevator of her St. Paul building after a young male resident assaulted her twice inside. Evelyne Morrell said her new neighbors play their music too loudly, and that one came begging for a box of baking soda so he could finish mixing his latest batch of rock cocaine. Taxicabs and Cadillacs stop routinely just outside the complex, she said, so that a passenger can run into the building, locate the proper apartment, and get either the sex or drugs they came to find.

This conflict between the lifestyles of the young and old in Minneapolis and in other cities and housing complexes around the country prompted Congress to pass legislation allowing public housing agencies to designate part or all of their buildings as elderly-only. Signed into law by President George Bush in October 1992, the law promptly touched off a new debate and other equally adamant protests of discrimination.

Supporters of people with mental illness and the disabled argued that the bill would only further limit the number of available housing units open to people with those disabilities.

Elderly people said the federal law enacted by Congress was welcome but overdue. People like Bear Stradtmann said they don't want to discriminate against anyone and that they're not trying to clear the building of young people, but that as the average age of building residents goes up, the number of burglaries and shootouts will go down.

"My only preference," Stradtmann said, "is to live in a building free of criminals."

Similar conflicts are expected to occur more and more frequently as a rapidly graying America comes to terms with what many consider to be an increasingly violent youth, weaned on macho movies and raised in family units where respect for one's elders was a lesson that no one felt the need to impart.

The odds of living out a century are getting better in America, where for the only time in history, the average citizen has more living parents than children. In 1974, there were only eight thousand three hundred and seventeen centenarians living in this country. By 1980, census takers noted that the number had jumped to fifteen thousand and to fifty-four thousand by 1990. At this rate there will be one hundred thousand Americans reaching the age of one hundred or better by the year 2000. Besides keeping television weatherman Willard Scott busy with those early morning birthday greetings to the country's growing population of centenarians, that sort of data presents some other serious problems.

In California, where the state's population of residents aged sixty-five and older has climbed by thirty-one percent since the 1980s, the number of elderly people holding down jobs increased even more—by thirty-eight percent, according to information compiled by the U.S. Census Bureau.

By 1990 over 393,000 older Californians were holding down jobs, according to census figures, compared to the nearly 286,000 elders listed on company payrolls in 1980. This significant increase amounted to a clear-cut reversal of what had been to that point a national trend. It also pointed out that, in a state like California, where the cost of living is higher than in most other parts of the country, more older folks may be staying on the job—or returning to work after retirement—out of sheer economic necessity.

"I think there is a great fear among older workers that, when they retire, things are not going to be the same as they have been in the past," said Sef Torres, a work analyst for the American Association of Retired Persons. "As a result, they are staying on the job longer, or seeking out jobs when normally they would be well into retirement."

Hard economic times have also had their impact on elderly Americans. Not only do they face the increased risk of illness, reduced income after retirement, and across-the-board cuts in state, federal, and local funding for services and programs once geared to their needs, but today's seniors are also being confronted by a legion of legal worries.

The intricacies of Medicare and Medicaid, Social Security claims, and problems with individual health insurance companies, daunting to even the most cognizant, have made the prospect of old age less than appealing. Where elderly people once had only to worry about whether their grandchildren would come visit them at Christmas, today they find themselves confronted with a series of legal questions that could mean poverty and ruin if any one is not adequately addressed.

Planning for the preservation of assets in the event they or their spouse are forced to enter a nursing home is only one area of concern for the elderly. With the high costs of hospital care, relatively brief stays in understaffed and under-funded facilities could wipe out a lifetime of savings within months. The average cost of a bed in a nursing home today is about thirty-two thousand dollars a year, with some running as high as eighty thousand. As more older people are out there seeking work to buttress their savings, more and more older people have found themselves engaged in age-discrimination cases.

Just to round out their lives, there are questions of assigning power of attorney, fashioning living trusts and living wills, and other forms of estate planning that would make even the most punctilious bureaucrat blanch with dismay.

Add to this the prospect of life alone after the premature death of a spouse, the growing perception by the young of the elderly as "greedy" for attempting to hang on to their rapidly diminishing assets, as well as the possibility of continued victimization at the hands of a younger, tougher generation—and things do not look at all rosy for those about to enter old age.

With this in mind, it is no small wonder that an increasing number of elderly Americans are choosing to put an end to their lives prematurely. In a survey of 802 Americans age sixty and over, the Gallup Organization found that one percent of all Americans thought of committing suicide at some point in the last six months of 1992. Projected over the entire year, the study, conducted among elderly people living at home and not in health care facilities, found that 627,000 older people had considered killing themselves in the previous year.

As might be expected, loneliness was the most common reason given by those who said they had considered ending their lives. The suicide rate for the elderly, according to official figures, is sixty-five percent higher than for the nation as a whole. Not only do they consider ending their lives more frequently, studies show, but the elderly are far more likely to carry out their intentions than younger people. While the elderly make up twenty-six percent of the population, they account for thirty-nine percent of all suicides.

There is, however, some hope in the face of so much gloom. According to a recently released study by the Bureau of Justice Statistics (BJS), crimes against the elderly dropped sixty-one percent from 1974—when nine out of every one thousand people sixty-five and older could count on being the victim of crime—to 1990, when only three people in every thousand over sixty-five years of age found themselves on the wrong end of a gun or knife.

Using data compiled from the National Crime Victimization Survey and the Comparative Homicide File, the BJS, a statistical arm of the Department of Justice, found that elderly people are the age group least likely to experience crime in society today—if only for one very significant reason.

The BJS report found that people seventy-five or older experienced lower victimization rates than people sixty-five to seventy-four, a factor which may have more to do with lifestyle than luck, according to researchers.

"The lifestyle of a group may affect its vulnerability to certain crimes. In general, compared to younger persons, the elderly are more likely to live alone and stay at home because they are less likely to work full-time or regularly participate in activities after dark."

Essentially, older Americans are not victimized as often as other age groups because they are locked behind closed doors at night. While I cannot fault the logic of the findings, it seems ironic that we should claim a victory in the war on crime if the sole reason the elderly in this country are not being as readily victimized as they once were is because they are shutting themselves in more than ever before.

Still, a drop in the crime rate is reassuring. According to the BJS report, less than two percent of the fourteen percent of older Americans living in this country today have been the victims of crime.

But there is a dark side. Among homicide victims, the elderly are more likely to be killed by strangers during the commission of a felony than those in any other age group—who are more likely to die at the hands of someone they know.

As the Old Man can testify, those elderly people who do fall victim to crime are more likely to face more than one robber during their encounter than are younger victims.

There are other disturbing findings. Oddly enough, given the prevalence of a jungle mentality among teen gangs and other youthful criminals today, it seems that older Americans are, for some unexplained reason, more likely to find themselves looking down the barrel of a gun than younger people caught in a similar situation. It appears that those who assault and rob the elderly are more apt to do the deed with a gun in hand. Statistics give no legitimate reason for this phenomenon and I have no explanation for it. Most of the people who decided to take on the Old Man used their fists first, then a knife if necessary. But there is little doubt that the danger level for elderly Americans who find themselves caught up in a similar situation heightens considerably when guns are involved.

This I knew from firsthand experience. Blows which shook the Old Man to his socks during his walking tours through the Tenderloin would undoubtedly have had a far greater impact on a genuinely older person. On several occasions—as I was being picked up off the floor as a precursor to a headfirst slam dunk into the carpet of our decoy apartment—I remember thinking that a similar blow could easily have killed an older person. The thought of brittle old bones cracking and giving way to such an onslaught was with me every day, especially when my considerably younger bones began to complain after a particularly brutal assault.

It came as no surprise to find that, while about the same percentage of violent crime victims aged sixty-five or older (thirty-three percent) and those under sixty-five (thirty-one percent) were injured during the commission of a crime, government data indicated that the older victims received more serious and longer—lasting injuries.

Of those both young and old who were injured in crime—related incidents, nine percent of the elderly suffered serious injuries such as broken bones and internal damage as compared to five percent of those under sixty-five. Fourteen percent of the elderly victims who were injured required hospital care, according to the BJS report, compared to only eight percent of younger victims.

Another lesson derived from the government's research had also been learned the hard way years earlier, during our time in the Tenderloin. Elderly violent crime victims are almost twice as likely to be victimized in or near their homes as are younger victims. This, it is believed, is due to the stay-at-home habits of elderly Americans. But as we found during our time with RAT, I also believe it is because criminals have learned that the crime is a relatively safe, easy one if perpetrated in the victim's own home, with no one to see and few people willing to get involved should the attack be overheard.

I believe criminals know that elderly people are less likely to protect themselves than younger, more able-bodied victims. Violent crime victims under the age of sixty-five took self-protective action of one form or another in seventy-three percent of the cases recorded by BJS statisticians. People over sixty-five, on the other hand, fought back only fifty-eight percent of the time.

"Moreover," the report states. "Of those crime victims who took self-protective measures, the elderly were less likely than their younger counterparts to use physical action such as attacking or chasing the offender or physically resisting in some other way."

That, I believe, is a known quantity and one of the primary reasons why older people have become the target of opportunity for criminals today.

Females, African-Americans, divorced or separated people, city dwellers, and renters were generally more likely than other older people to experience crime, according to the report.

For many people across the nation, the downward trend in crime reported by the U.S. Department of Justice seems to have come from another, more perfect world. In their world gangs of young men take over entire sections of their neighborhoods, block by block, corner by corner, until the elderly are unwilling to walk the very streets where they grew up. In their world even the slightest noise is regarded as a potential threat and a strange knock at the door is seldom answered. Instead of enjoying their twilight years wrapped in the protective comfort of a warm and caring family, many are simply being disposed of, rolled into hospital emergency rooms, and left there for someone else to take care of in a practice which hospital workers have dubbed "granny dumping."

The technique varies but the stories are pretty much the same. A family or relative will bring a grandparent into a hospital emergency room and tell the staff that their grandmother or grandfather won't eat anything they put in front of them. Or they might say the person's memory has evaporated, that he or she wanders off, sometimes for days. Doctors checking the person can find nothing physically wrong with the elder and judge that he or she does not present a danger to themselves, but by then the family member has gone. A check of the admittance information the family member has given reveals that the home address and phone numbers do not exist.

Caught in the grip of skyrocketing health care costs and a grinding recession, many young people who normally would have attempted to care for a mother, father, or grandparent, have also resorted to a primitive form of euthanasia. Stripping a member of the family group who has lost the capacity to care for themselves of any identifying tags or marks, people have driven their relatives far from their homes and abandoned them in a public place. Those seemingly uncaring souls who are traced, tracked down, and questioned about their motives have said they were no longer able to maintain the level of care needed to keep the senior member of the household at home.

Sometimes, the frustration that comes from maintaining an elderly person in the grip of Alzheimer's Disease or some other comparable ailment manifests itself in other ways. Then, people who once loved each other dearly find themselves locked in mortal combat.

One in every twenty-five older Americans is abused in one form or another, often by members of his or her own family, according to an investigation completed in 1981 by the House Select Committee on Aging. As the graying of America continues at a relentless pace, more and more incidents are being reported of senior citizens being forced—under threats by a family member of beatings or other forms of intimidation—to sign over control of their savings. As difficult as it may be to comprehend, studies show that inter-family, inter-generational rape is not an uncommon occurrence.

It has also been found that the increase in the number of elder-abuse cases can be directly attributable to the increase in the number of Americans over sixty-five years of age. Studies show that a woman over seventy-five is the most likely victim, and that the abuse cuts across every stratum of society, rich and poor alike.

In Orlando, Florida, an elderly woman's screams for help were dismissed by neighbors who thought she was suffering from dementia. When an anonymous caller finally summoned police to the scene, the first officers to arrive found Dorothy Kinney, a sixty-six-year-old woman who lived in the home with her thirty-three-year-old son. The cause of the woman's torment and the reason for her screams were easy to see. Lying naked and neglected in her own waste on a pile of discarded pizza boxes, Dorothy Kinney was covered by maggots and roaches, her legs rotted by gangrene and her body covered in bedsores.

Her son, Steven, was arrested on felony elderly-neglect charges and held without bond. Kinney said little about his mother's condition but allegedly told officers who arrested him that he had been too busy to take her to the doctor when her condition worsened.

As horrifying as this sort of story is, it is made worse when you consider how easily it might have been prevented. A neighbor who lived next door to the Kinney home told police and the inevitable reporters who came to cover the story that she often heard Dorothy Kinney screaming, "Get me out of here!" throughout the early morning.

"I would pace my bedroom at night and worry, wondering if there was really something going on over there," the woman was quoted as saying. "But we thought she had Alzheimer's disease or something."

While there are several lessons which could be derived from Dorothy Kinney's weeks of torment, let me start with the most obvious: when in doubt about someone's well-being, call the police. It never ceases to amaze me how many people pretend not to hear a person's cry for help or their screams. Why pace your bedroom? Why take the kids out for a drive and hope the noise will have died down by the time you get back? It's a simple matter of picking up the phone.

Our history shows us to be a nation slow to accept change and even more reluctant to accept new ideas. Our comprehension of the world around us appears to dictate that all unpleasantries be put on a psychological "back-burner," left alone to fester as we strive to convince ourselves that everything will be all right if we simply ignore the problem long enough.

This is what is happening with the elderly in this country. Only when we join their ranks will the full ramifications of what it means to be old and cut off from a society obsessed by youth be brought home. By then, of course, it will be too late.

We must recall the example set by native Americans, a people who revered and exalted the dignity of their elders and geared the movements of their tribal groups around the ancient ones.

In an age of budgetary cutbacks and recession, there appears to be little federal funding and little energy to devote to the problem. Familial and community participation must exceed the financial and moral limitations we have set for ourselves. We can no longer ignore that which we consider repulsive or impossible to cure. We cannot let this steadily escalating problem continue to remain a smothered moan, for we will never be able to ease the pain and suffering of those who deserve more if we don't take a chance.

There are really three absolutes. Death and taxes, to be sure, as we've been taught. But the longer we manage to avoid the former, the more we are sure to encounter the third absolute—the inescapable grip of old age, and all that goes with it.

And should we not take great pains now to ease the

prospect of a life marked by neglect, abuse, and the fear of crime, then the first absolute—death—will begin to appear as a much more alluring alternative than continued existence in the type of world we are building for ourselves at this moment.

All of this was brought home to me during one of many visits to the apartment on Eddy Street where an elderly gentleman had been murdered by thugs. Images of the room in which he died—the threadbare rug with its tangled, knotted fringe, the off-white walls turned a filmy yellow by the former tenant's cigarette habit—remain with me still. During my display of emotion at the press conference marking the end of the 1987 RAT operation, it was the memory of the chalk outline of his body on the worn Persian carpet that rattled my composure and reduced me to tears.

Maybe it was because I had spent so much of my time in that dark, dingy little hole of an apartment, and had walked among the old gent's things, that I believed we had somehow come to terms with one another, that a bond had been reached between us.

An apartment manager had ushered me into the room the first time, clearly unhappy about having to clean up the mess. It was still in some disarray when I walked in, left as it had been at the time the old man was found. The painting behind which he had hidden his money had been taken down from the wall, revealing the patch of original paint beneath. The victim's murderers—we believed there were two of them—had left the painting on the back of a lumpy sofa during their search for his money.

The sofa padding—visible on the arms and back cushions—had been soiled by hair oil from the countless times the old man had slumped into its springs, his head falling back while an ancient television flickered in the darkened room. On the other side of the room was an inexpensive oak desk, probably made about the turn of the century. Already cluttered, it had been left in total disarray after the old man's killers had rummaged through its drawers looking for valuables.

Boxes containing the personal records, memories, and photos of a once-proud soldier—who had marched off with a million others to defend the rights of Americans—lay where they had been tossed aside. Most of the pertinent personal papers had already been removed by our homicide investigators for release to the man's next of kin—if there were any. But among the boxes I found a barely discernible copy of his discharge papers from World War I, and I marveled at how a man could live through a global conflagration only to meet his end violently, in his own country, defenseless and alone.

As I stood in the center of the apartment, careful to avoid stepping on the chalked outline which marked the place where this old man had fallen, I felt as an archaeologist must have felt when he entered the tomb of the ancient pharaohs for the first time. There was a sense that I was committing some form of sacrilege, that by disturbing the dust of that lightless place, I was disturbing the memory of a very long life. But at almost the same time I felt a sense of communion with his spirit and, while there was no picture of him there, my mind was filled with a vision of the man, young and proud in the uniform of his country.

I tried not to think about how terrible his last thoughts must have been as death came for him on stealthy footsteps and with angry voices. I wondered if he had fought in the Argonne, had known Sergeant York or seen General "Blackjack" Pershing. What history had passed before his eyes? What could I have learned from him if we had had the chance to sit and talk about all the experiences of a lifetime?

But all public memory of the grand old man who lived and died in that dingy apartment had been erased. The only thing I can do is share what I know of him now and confess that it was his memory and the diabolical manner of his death that ultimately caused my on-camera breakdown that day in 1987. Disguised as an old man in the white light of the television cameras, I wept for him as well as for all the others like him.

Chapter 8

SOLUTIONS

Between RAT operations, walking the streets as the Old Man and waiting for the cauldron to boil, the idea, born on a page of my journal, began to form that I thought could be brought to bear against the problem which faces our elderly today.

It was a simple plan, falling in line with the belief that all good things are based on simple ideas executed well, and it could be considered a communal approach to solving the problem. In the past, before the days of insurance companies and lawyers, very direct means were used to help cure a public problem. If someone's house burned down, everyone in the neighborhood chipped in a little bit until the person who had lost his house had enough to rebuild. That's the basis behind the idea I tentatively labeled SOS—for Save Our Seniors.

With city, state, and federal government either incapable or uninterested in tackling the situation, the burden falls on the ordinary citizen to shoulder just a bit of the load. As we have seen time and time again in the wake of calamities, Americans have big hearts and ready pocketbooks, particularly when they know the money is going to a good cause. But with the scandals which have recently plagued some of the larger relief organizations, ordinary citizens are holding back, unwilling to give money to a bureaucracy instead of the people it was designed to help.

It has become clear that if a simple, workable solution can be devised with the lion's share of a citizen's donated dollar being put directly to good use and not toward administrative costs, Americans will respond with the generosity for which they are known worldwide.

Some may call the plan simplistic, and so it may be. I now stand ready to amend it in any way that would increase the flow of funding and ensure that the moneys donated to the program make their way to the people SOS is designed to help. But in the meantime it seems a viable alternative to a growing problem and I have yet to be told why it could not be implemented.

In order to account for all the money raised, the office of controller would have to be established. Working from a secure office at the local Hall of Justice or civic center, the controller would answer to either the chief of police or board of supervisors. Equipped with a phone bank, a computer, and a safe, the controller would account for the revenue netted after each designated SOS event.

Then the supervisors or city fathers could contact the controller, determine the amount of money available, and earmark a set amount for the Senior Escort Service or any other agency equipped to handle the problems of the elderly. If the controller was situated in a secure city building, there would be no need for rent or any of the normal operational costs that eat up a large part of each dollar. Money could be used to deliver meals or medicine, or provide a few additional creature comforts for people in their waning years. The new infusion of cash would also enable the city to hire people willing to work for something better than minimum wage and put them to work as escorts.

Each prospective escort would need to be at least eighteen years old, of good moral character, and willing to help those less fortunate. People on the welfare rolls who want work but are unable to find it, or who are unqualified for higher-paying jobs, would be good candidates. Former service people would also be good choices, providing veterans with gainful employment and a sense of accomplishment. So many men and women fresh out of the service and unable to find work have stated that they want a hand, not a handout. This would be a terrific way of reintroducing them to society as well as providing the elderly with skilled protection.

Although the SOS controller would have his or her office in the Hall of Justice or local town hall, it must be made clear that the revenue generated by SOS is not to be made part of that city's or town's general fund. To do so would turn the fund and the SOS program itself into a political football.

As I have said, SOS is a simple plan, but one I think would work well if correctly implemented. Shortly after the end of the 1987 RAT program, while the team was still locked in the glare of media scrutiny and the letters were pouring in about the treatment of the elderly in our society, I realized that a nerve had been struck. It wasn't just the Old Man! Other people were as frustrated by what was happening as I was.

When I gave an outline of the plan to a local television reporter, her station aired a brief synopsis of what SOS could do if given the chance. Even more favorable responses filtered in to the station, to me, and then to the mayor's office. Nothing happened. Although I was convinced I was on to something and buttonholed every city official I could find in the weeks to come, pestering them unceasingly about the proposal, it became clear that not one of the city's elected officials was interested in taking it on.

It did not take long for me to realize we were just beating our heads against a wall. In many ways I feel the simplicity of the idea worked against it. I don't know that the powers that be realized the potential of SOS because it was so simple. Save Our Seniors did not fit their perception of what a program of this type should look like. And for this reason more than any other, I believe it was allowed to die a quiet death in the weeks following.

The only solid objection to the plan that I heard in all the time we were trying to make it a reality came from a city official who pointed out that not everyone in town went to the symphony or to a baseball game and that a large portion of potential revenues would remain untapped. He wondered how a person who was unlikely to use the entertainment resources of the city could see that their money reached SOS. I explained that there were already existing channels for donations to civic agencies and that, of course, if someone wanted to mail in their donation rather than have it built into the price of an opera ticket, they were more than welcome to do so. But it was easy to see the simplicity of the plan was confusing to some people, and others were just looking for a reason not to go ahead with it.

While I had geared our plan to fit San Francisco's needs and city officials here proved unwilling or unable to carry it out, I believe the principles of SOS could be applied anywhere. Take a small town in the South, with one theater and a four-man police department and you could implement an SOS program as easily as you could, say, in Atlanta or Boston. Any town with a sizable population of elderly people and a modest budget could stand to benefit. And even though they would account for a smaller amount of money, the principle of accountability would remain the same: A similar percentage of money gets to its citizens in that community. That's the important thing.

What I liked most about the plan, aside from its simplicity, was the fact that SOS didn't depend on the federal government for money and that it did something for the good of the community almost immediately. Truly, of the people, by the people, for the people. I reasoned that, if every donor continued to live in the town or city where they had been giving, they too would one day end up a recipient of these good works and public generosity.

It's a form of self-taxation that I think would work, especially now, when people are seeing the infrastructure of our inner cities deteriorating in leaps and bounds. The proof of the pudding can be found when you see the outpouring of affection and care when hordes of citizens bring cash or canned foods to the annual Christmas collection centers, or to those who have just had their homes leveled by a hurricane. The American people are very generous, but they want to make sure they are doing the most good with their donations, and SOS would make that a top priority. If the organization is aboveboard and truthful, and an official could show a donor that his or her dollar is here today but by tomorrow afternoon eighty-five percent of that dollar will be put directly toward helping an elderly person, I believe the money would be given gladly.

But as SOS appears to have no immediate future, at least in my city, we were left only with an opportunity to offer a few words of wisdom to those older people among us who find themselves confronted by the likes of those who battered the Old Man during those long weeks in the Tenderloin. It would be nice to think that our efforts in one of the city's toughest neighborhoods effectively stopped this type of brutal crime. However, while the efforts of the RAT program effectively knocked down the number of assaults on the elderly long after we left the area in 1986 and 1987, these crimes are creeping back into my city and others across the country yet again.

Looking for "easy marks," packs of young toughs are returning to hospital waiting zones, automatic teller machines, and isolated parking lots to ply their trade of crime and ill will against the elderly.

Now in retirement and eyeing the looming approach of old age himself, the Old Man can only chafe at the latest report of a carjacking or assault on an elderly woman by young thieves, and offer a few hard-earned words of advice. Having been on the receiving end dozens of times, I know what many people feel when fate, the odds and circumstance combine to make them the target of the day for a young hunter who is faster and stronger. There are a few simple things people can do to keep both fate and the odds, at bay a little longer and I hope that people will try to keep them in mind.

AWARENESS
A person's own senses—especially that vital "sixth sense"—are the best weapon—they can have on the street today.

Walk with your head up and constantly moving from side to side. Watch for things and people that look out of place, those who react to you when you pass. Listen for the sudden chirp of sneakers on concrete when a young man takes an interest in the way you're carrying your purse and abruptly changes course to fall in behind you. Be aware of people who get too close to you, who actually "get in your face," to use the jargon of the day. They may bump into you, say things to see if you are listening, move up to you in a crowd and run their hands over your pockets while looking for the telltale bulge of a wallet or coin purse. This shows that they have no respect for your personal space and are testing your hearing and awareness.

If a total stranger invades your privacy without warning and for no apparent reason, beware, because the next step can be much more drastic. They may ask for the time or an opportunity to use the phone or bathroom in your home or apartment, but what they're really doing is testing your ability to fight off that intrusion. If you acquiesce, they know you will be an easy mark. They'll think, Good, I'm superior, he's inferior, and proceed with their attack.

If you turn to confront them or tell them off, they know you may fight them and chances are they will back away.

The same principle can be applied when you're out for the evening trip to the grocery store. Once you step out of familiar surroundings, the way you act and how aware you are will determine whether or not you're going to attract an unwanted admirer who wants to do more than just strike up an idle conversation.

Perhaps the best example of just how one's awareness can be enhanced came to me courtesy of Lee Tyler, a very fine investigator who served with us in 1987 as "Cab Rat."

Not long after the RAT unit disbanded, Lee found himself driving through the Tenderloin with a new partner. The new man was also an experienced investigator, but after a month spent running down and catching bad guys who tried to take on the Old Man, Lee was seeing the Tenderloin with an enhanced vision his partner could not possibly be expected to share.

"As we were driving along, I looked over and saw this old woman walking down the street," Lee said when he told me the story. "And at the same time I saw this guy standing on the sidewalk, looking very jumpy and excited. I turned to my partner and said, 'Doug, that guy is going to rob that old lady.'

"Doug turned to me and said, 'What are you talking about? What old lady?' but I was already out of the car and starting to parallel the guy as he started his stalk. It was incredible. It was just the way it had always started when we were working RAT. I told Doug to trust me and back me up from across the street if I got into trouble. I knew the two of us were in no position to get into a chase with the suspect, so I moved up behind him and hauled him into a doorway as he closed in on the old lady.

"I said, 'I know exactly what's on your mind and you're lucky I'm stopping you now.' He was really stunned, with this look on his face that told me he knew exactly what I was talking about. But even so he kept saying, 'What do you mean? I don't know what you're talking about.'

"We kept him in that doorway for about five minutes, long enough for the old lady to get far enough up the street that the Kronk couldn't catch her. Then we sent him off in the other direction. Doug and I walked back to the car and once inside he looked at me and said, 'Can you please tell me what the hell just happened?' It would have been comical except that, in another five minutes, that old woman would probably have been on the ground with a broken hip and her purse gone.

"It's amazing what you see out there once you take the time to look."

CARRYING A WEAPON

Older people whc have either been victimized already or who fear their declining neighborhoods will soon make their victimization inevitable frequently ask me whether or not they should carry a gun or some other weapon while walking the streets. My unequivocal answer is: absolutely not! The problem with arming oneself is that unless you have the weapon—gun, knife, or sap—readily at hand during an encounter and are practiced in its use, it will serve no purpose other than to give you a sense of security that you most assuredly should not have.

If you take to walking to your local market with one hand in your pocket and your fingers wrapped around the butt of a gun, then you've become paranoid and are just as dangerous as some of the people out there with actual criminal intent. Innocents who arm themselves are more likely to suffer an injury due to mishap or from the criminal wrestling the weapon away from their intended victim and shooting them with their own gun. Then we have a victim down with gunshot wounds and a previously unarmed miscreant who has acquired a weapon.

As for keeping a defensive weapon in the home, I have less of a problem with that, as long as the owner submits to extensive testing procedures to prove that he or she is capable of using that firearm in a responsible manner.

Guns have always been a part of the fabric of American society, probably because of our pioneering past. But today they are not viewed as a tool to be used only when absolutely necessary, but rather as an extension of yourself, to be used when someone steps in line ahead of you at the movie theater, or when a disoriented stranger who doesn't speak a word of English seemingly ignores an order to "freeze" and takes another, fatal step forward.

Our priorities have gone askew in this country when it comes to firearms. In some states it's easier to buy an assault rifle than a container of non-lethal tear gas.

Large-bore weapons have become a part of our pop culture, with movies featuring slow-motion shots of Rambo flexing his muscles and firing the latest in automatic hardware. Schoolchildren casually repeat the lines from the latest Dirty Harry film word for word—seemingly unaware they're talking about shooting someone with "the biggest, most powerful handgun in the world..."

We've entered a dream state when it comes to guns in this country. Owning a weapon should be governed on the basis of it being taken from you if you cannot prove that you can handle it responsibly. And if you are found in possession of a weapon without a license then you should spend five years in jail. It's the only way to stop the senseless slaughter. Extreme evils require extreme remedies.

THE WATER-HOLE SYNDROME

The importance of being aware of your surroundings comes even more to the fore as we approach old age. Officers from the old Street Crime Unit recall the duo who told them shortly after their arrest for assault that their favorite hunting ground was the square block area around a hospital. Disbelieving officers asked one of them why.

"'Cause that's where the old people go when they're hurt," the thug said without blinking. "And everybody knows they're easier pickin's when they're already hurt."

As hard as it may be for the great majority of people to understand, the principle of the weak becoming the target of choice for the strong in this so-called civilized society of ours has become even more true as the gap between generations broadens. The cruel truth is: big fish eat little fish.

Difficult economic times and the plethora of narcotics available today also lend themselves to this primitive interaction. As modern science gradually lengthens the life expectancy of the average member of the herd, the watering hole becomes filled with weaker, more tempting targets for the ever-circling pride of lions.

If you have difficulty walking, fall down every once in awhile, and have a pronounced limp, chances are that the lions in that particular area will come for you. They will key on you and they will bring others with them to make sure they can make their kill and get away without endangering themselves.

During the time I walked in the Old Man's shoes, I learned that there are three types of "lions" to contend with out on the street. The first one is the Opportunist, essentially a coward who will come in and strike only if the odds are heavily weighted in his favor and the right opportunity presents itself. A perfect example of this type would be Craig William Hill, who became docile upon his arrest in 1986 and apologized profusely for attacking Leanna Dawydiak. This type is most likely to seek out another lion with whom they can pump up their courage prior to carrying out an attack.

Then there is the Stalker, the type of urban lion who enjoys the hunt but could be dissuaded if confronted by a sufficient show of force. For most of them, the thrill is in the chase, they play with their intended victim, convincing themselves that they are more clever than their intended target.

And finally we come to the True Predator, a proven hunter who has developed a keen sense for the hunt and the kill because of the sense of power and the thrill it gives him. An example of this type would be Franklin Lynch, or Whispers. While the Opportunist may rationalize the evil he is about to commit by saying, "Normally, I wouldn't be doing this, but I really need this old guy's money and he's got so much he won't miss whatever I take from him," the True Predators among us do it for the sheer pleasure it gives them.

True Predators will not let an opportunity pass them by. To do so would diminish their reputation as hunters in the eyes of their fellows. And a True Predator does not care a whit about his victims. At no time was this point driven home more soundly than during the frequent occasions the Old Man was taken from behind, straightened up, and taken headfirst to the ground.

The True Predator knows a blow from behind will cripple an older person and reduce the risk of the victim crying out or fighting back during the initial stages of the assault. The final crushing blow, the power slam into the carpet, is meant to stun their victim.

Once a person is helpless at his feet, the True Predator succumbs to a murderous rage which is quite beyond the capacity of a real lion. The human predator will drag his victim further into the apartment, tie him up to reassure themselves that he is in control, and then begin a barbaric game of cat and mouse aimed at extracting the pass code to a bank card machine or the whereabouts of any hidden valuables.

Anyone unfortunate enough to find themselves in this situation cannot afford to compromise with these people. The only thing you can do is keep your wits about you, try to remember a peculiar feature of your attacker—a tattoo or distinctive scar—that will help police track them down and arrest them later. Take their anger away from them if you can and attempt to disarm them with an air of calm. These people feed on fear—it excites them—and if their intended victim shows no fear, the sense of superiority they feel when the target is helpless and begging begins to ebb.

Ultimately, the key here is to survive the experience, doing whatever it takes to stay alive. That's the critical thing. You have to live through the horror of the assault, no matter how brutal. But the ultimate goal of the potential victim is not to be selected as someone's target of choice in the first place.

VICTIM AURA

There is a certain look the Opportunist and the True Predator will key on before they make their decision to strike. As a victim officer I used to spend long hours perfecting the image of a victim, working hard to project what I came to call the Victim Aura.

It is a perception each one of us gives off and sends to others. Some of us exude confidence, bravura. Others, either through a hesitation in their step or the furtive manner in which they choose to avoid eye contact with others on the street, send out the message: I am weak. I am trying not to be seen. I can be taken.

There are telltale signals—as alluring to a mugger

looking for an old person to rob as blood in the water is for a shark—a misbuttoned sweater, a hospital release band, a limp. I used them all.

A mugger is also looking for evidence of disorientation in a person: a lack of purpose in their walk, head down and mouth agape, concentrating on making it from point A to point B, and eager to avoid the slightest confrontation. All of these things taken together make this person stand out as a victim. A True Predator wants to win, and is looking for someone who will not be able to put up much of a fight.

If you are unaware or just plain foolish enough to walk around with your wallet exposed or counting off bills as you leave the ATM machine, sooner or later the odds are going to catch up with you. The stronger the Victim Aura you project, the higher your chances are of being targeted.

DISRUPTING THE STALK

One of the worst things an older person can do is to stick to a daily routine. This, I believe, is what helped contribute to the death of Madeline Mackenzie.

If you walk by the same place at the same time every day, people will not remember ever having seen you. After a while you will blend into the background until you become invisible. And unless you make a point of talking to the store owner or postman on a particular corner at a given time, you are soon lost against the background of the city. This is why we hear a witness say so often: "I don't know what happened to the old lady, one minute she was nowhere to be seen and the next minute she was just *there*."

Truth be told, the old woman was there all along, it's just that no one noticed her. And this can be dangerous for a person who, while they may feel they *want* to blend in to the background, actually needs to be seen by others who may be able to come to their aid.

There are many ways to throw off a potential stalker, but the easiest, most effective method is simply to keep changing your life's routines. Take the same route to the bank or grocery store every day and you've unconsciously programmed your life. Any predator in the neighborhood will think, There's that old lady. It's the first of the month, she's just gotten her social security check and it's three-forty in the afternoon, so she must be on her way home. And bingo, that's it for that person. She's become an automaton and the True Predator can set his watch by her movements. A uniform and routine life is not the best thing for your safety, although many older people feel more secure in the regularity of their day-to-day routines.

What the good people of the Tenderloin did, which I thought was an exceptionally brilliant plan, was to establish safe houses in the neighborhood. These refuges, usually a place of business or residence easily accessible from the street, were marked with a placard which sent out the message to anyone in trouble that they needed only to run there in order to get help.

This was a brilliant move in many ways. First, it eliminated the need for any long-winded explanation of the problem faced by a stalking victim who is attempting to seek help from a stranger. Instead of attempting to explain that someone was following them and that they feared for their safety, a person under the safe-house system needed only to run in and say, "I need help," and the store owner or resident would call the emergency 911 number right there, no questions asked. It has worked countless times and has probably saved lives.

When you are able to gather more people around you who are willing to lend whatever assistance you may need, all but the most determined criminal will skulk away. They have come to learn that the police or an ambulance have been sent for, and that the attention of the good neighbors in the particular block will soon be focused on them. No lion will continue the stalk when every other herd in the area is on the alert and gathering themselves for a defense.

Perhaps the most important thing to remember is that, should an older person—or anyone else for that matter—

find themselves the object of a stalker's attention is to never, NEVER lead them back to where you live. Although it is human nature to try and return to the place where you feel safest, it is absolutely the wrong thing to do in this case. As the Old Man learned only too well, many stalkers will not commit themselves to an actual attack the first time they fall in behind you. Many simply want to pin down where you live, determine the apartment number, and assess the difficulty they would have in following you inside the next time—when they are ready to follow through with the assault.

Often, the farther a person is caught away from home, the more panicky and scrambled the thought processes become as they try to make their way back to home or apartment, sinking ever lower into their Victim Aura and giving their stalker an even greater sense of power. Try to think. Head for an area where there are people, lights. Look for a policeman. Do not allow yourself to get trapped in a confined space alone with the person you think is behind you. Above all, don't show them where you live.

The awareness of being stalked reaches down through the psyche and tickles the most primitive responses. The sensation of being hunted by one, two, or even six other human beings can be almost paralyzing in its intensity. When that sixth sense kicks in and the hair on the back of your head bristles and stands straight up, it's time to look behind you. And if the same two fellows who followed you out of the bank or the grocery store are still there, pretending not to look at you but always staying within striking distance, know that their intent is not to strike up a conversation about the weather.

Change your route. It will not only make it more difficult for someone to plot your daily routine, but it makes life a little more exciting. If you change your route, you will see new people along the way, new things. It will become a challenge, an adventure, and you may find yourself walking a little taller, head up and alert for anything unexpected. This new attitude may in itself be enough to significantly diminish an older person's chances of being targeted.

A little common sense also goes a long way to heading off a possible attack. Time and again in the roughest areas of the city, the Old Man would see women carrying oversized purses on their shoulders, often with money, credit cards, and expensive sunglasses in plain view. I'll never forget the old woman who carried her shopping money in a clear plastic purse. She may as well have hung a sign around her neck saying, "Rob me, please."

After being followed by a determined group of predators for three, four, or five blocks, with my backup team telling me over the radio that they were closing in and completely oblivious to traffic or anything else, I soon learned that once the stalk had progressed to that point these people were not to be denied. They were locked in on their target. For a genuinely old person to try and resist True Predators then and there would have been futile, if not fatal.

The time to fight back, psychologically, is before the predators get set on their stalk. You should be sufficiently aware of their presence that you are able to cut off the attack on your own terms before they have a chance to settle on you as the target of the day.

But if you do find yourself being followed, there are a couple of tricks you can use to give your pursuers second thoughts about carrying out the attack.

When walking, at least on city streets, it is best to walk in the middle of the sidewalk to prevent an attacker from running ahead and then pulling his victim into an empty doorway or alley as they pass. It is also wise to avoid walking behind large parked vehicles—trucks, buses, or trams—that would obscure you from sight. There may be hundreds of people on the sidewalk that day but not one of them will ever see what happens to you once you are pulled down behind a bus.

Should you be confronted on the sidewalk, it might be a good idea to put your back up against a wall as soon as possible, swing around to at least visually confront your assailant, and verbally draw attention to yourself in as loud a manner as you are able to muster. Often, this will be enough to dissuade an attacker, and your position of advantage against the wall will prevent anyone from getting around behind you. Seeing what they believe to be a helpless old man or woman "circling the wagons" and readying themselves in a defensive posture may plant enough doubt in a mugger's mind to make him think twice about taking that person on. In addition, a prospective victim's awareness factor has just increased one hundred percent and the victim aura has been diminished, as well.

Another strategy to use is to check who is behind you by looking at reflections in store windows. Stopping every so often to look over the window display of a store is a good way to catch your breath and have a quick look to see if the man in the baseball cap and windbreaker who left the grocery store when you did is still behind you.

If he stops when you do, it may be confirmation that he is tailing you for a reason and that you should be alert to a threat from his direction. After you have ascertained that the man is indeed following you for no apparent reason, a long, deliberate look in his direction may be enough to signal him that you know he is there.

To win any possible conflict, you must have a genuine belief in yourself. You cannot run scared. However, a truly dedicated criminal intent on robbing an older person at any cost will doubtless carry out his assault, confronting that person on the street or on the threshold of their home and leaving them with only a split second in which to prepare a defense. How a person uses this second, the fraction of time between an idle inquiry for the apartment number of a non-existent neighbor or a request to use the telephone, can determine whether the victim is actually robbed or, in more drastic cases—whether that person lives or dies.

THE GOLDEN SECOND

In 1986, during Operation Dismantle, I first became aware of the existence of the split second in time when an attacker hesitates just before starting his assault.

The Old Man had returned to his apartment on Eddy Street when the miscreant who had slipped into the building with him came up from behind and asked the time. That instant between the moment the question was posed and when he started pushing me inside the apartment could have been used by an older person, who had their wits sufficiently about them, to try and cut off the violence that was surely to come.

While I was being driven to the floor, my earphone popping out of my ear like a cork out of a bottle from the impact, I wondered how an elderly victim should have played out the scene. I came up with a few ideas I think may prove successful.

1. Devise a plan of action for a variety of scenarios. Think, What do I do right now if someone comes out of this store and makes a grab for my purse? What do I do if I'm hit from behind? You're confronting the problem with a solution and now it will depend on reflex. I can guarantee that with a plan already in mind, that "Golden Second" can be used to your advantage instead of to the advantage of the predator.

Even in police work I have found officers who were woefully unprepared for the unexpected. During informal lectures on officer safety I would tell them that, instead of sitting in the coffee shop talking about the kids or golf, they should come up with a plan of action they could rely on if the pair of them were to walk into an ambush. I would ask them to devise a scenario and to come up with a way to react to it. You're driving down an alley at two in the morning and someone fires at your patrol car. What do you do? Nine times out of ten I found that officers had perfectly logical and sound plans of action, but they were *independent* plans which did not include the other. The same maxim should apply to the elderly.

2. Make plans with your companion. For example, if you're walking down the street and a man grabs your wife's purse, you should have already planned what you're going to do with that split second of time. How a person

reacts can mean the difference between severe injury and death. If you no longer have a spouse or close friend you can rely on, there is a very specific plan of action I can recommend you take if you are confronted by an attacker.

3. In that split second when your eyes lock and you know that something very bad is going to happen, grab your chest area and fall to the floor or sidewalk, yelling loudly that you are having a heart attack. Now, it may be that by falling down an older person has made themselves more vulnerable to attack. But I believe the advantages of this approach far outweigh the drawbacks. Because elderly people are not able to engage in a physical battle with an assailant, their one and only hope is to launch a psychological counteroffensive of their own. It is almost certain that a person who stalks you, follows you into your apartment, and demands money is no criminal novice. Most have done this type of crime before. This isn't the apologetic opportunist who saw you flash some money on the street, ran up to you and took it out of your hand. This is somebody who is criminally bent and more than likely has some knowledge of the law.

If you fall to the ground, chances are good that this person will flee. Why? Because he knows that if there's a death in the commission of a felony then he's going to be put away for murder. By clutching your chest and feigning a potentially fatal heart attack, you've left the realm of simple burglary and entered another plane where the penalties are much higher. Also, if you're on the ground, he's less likely to bend down and expose himself to a possible kicking attack while attempting to strike you with his fists. He may try to kick you with his feet (if he gets that far), but to challenge that, you can swing around on your back or your buttocks and kick at him with your feet.

Chances are that people will say, I don't want to fall down and expose myself to attack like that, but the chances are high that this predator, having gotten to this point in his hunt, is going to knock you down anyway. When you go down this time however, it will be on his terms—disoriented and possibly severely injured—and at that moment you're at the mercy of a man who is now electrified by the thrill of his lopsided victory and the hatred he has for his victims.

And you should realize that it is a hatred, that a criminal is often blaming the victim at his feet for the perceived injustices of his life, and that once you become the focus of that sort of hatred, anything can happen.

4. Watch their eyes and listen carefully to their voices. If an attacker is highly strung to begin with, chances are good that if you say something completely off the wall, something to the effect that you are suffering from infectious impetigo, the time he spends trying to figure out exactly what that is will give you an opportunity to get away or to summon help. Many women have successfully dissuaded prospective rapists by telling them they are suffering from a particularly active sexually transmitted disease. This may sound extreme, but it could be argued that people who make themselves disgusting in the predator's eyes may not become his victim.

Look at the alternative. If you're seventy-seven years old and you decide to fight two eighteen-year-olds, and you do make a show of it, but in the process they've broken your hip, your wrist, and your jaw as well as gotten your wallet or purse, who's really won? You've got your pride, but in the long run you've also sacrificed your health and maybe even your sanity because once it happens to you, you are never the same again. Think it over. The object of the exercise is to hear the click-click of the handcuffs going on them, not to hear the click-click of the ambulance door closing on you.

There is another reason why I caution older people against striking back physically. That is because, while Charles Bronson may make it look easy in the movies, it seldom works. It also *hurts* to hit someone, something the movies rarely show. As people seek effective methods of dealing with increased crime, I hear recommendations made by so-called self-defense experts such as poking at your attacker's eyes or kneeing him in the groin—all the things that sound nice and effective in theory. But in reality it takes some time and no small amount of practice to get good at that sort of thing, and I just don't know if any older person is capable of hitting a human being who is trying just as hard to protect himself as he is trying to rob you. Any attempt at physical resistance is probably going to fail.

Now you're going to make them mad because, if you are lucky, you may have succeeded in hurting them slightly—something they did not take into consideration when they initiated their attack. But even though a successfully landed blow may be a tremendous boost for the ego, only the worst will come of it, because your assailant will most assuredly try to reestablish his superiority and then it will be pay-back time. At the end of your attack will you have now won? And if you haven't, now you're going to lose in a bad way. To make matters worse, there's always the very high chance that your mugger has got a confederate and, as the Old Man quickly saw, these people are not hesitant about jumping on their victims in tandem.

5. Confronted in your own home I think you have to draw the line somewhere. It's either Fight, Flight, or Feign. Either you hurt him and make him afraid, which is the unlikely scenario, you run away, or you do something so completely off the wall that it stops him in his tracks and makes him think. Looking down at you writhing in pain on the floor, a grimace on your face, and your hands clutching your heart, he's got to wonder if you're worth a murder conviction. He's got to stop and think about what he's going to do and that's when you've managed to turn the Golden Second to your advantage.

Each person has to make their own decision about when they will fight and what they are willing to fight for. Some human beings can stand by and watch their parents killed or their sister assaulted and live to give the police an accurate description of the assailants. Some can do that but not live with themselves successfully afterward.

Our reaction to a given situation is predicated on what we have on hand at the time, our state of mind at a given moment. All kinds of factors must be taken into consideration—whether there's one attacker or two, whether the person is armed. The trick is to turn the element of surprise around and come up with a surprise of your own. Ask the woman who drove off a gunman with the garden hose if she would have done the same thing if she had been walking home with her groceries and the garden hose had just been lying there. I think not. She was defending her home. Caught off of her own property I think the result would have been much different.

6. An important thing to remember is that most criminals are, when it comes down to it, essentially cowards. Many are simply not capable of carrying out a crime unless they bring a henchman along to help them. Why? Because they like the guy and they want to share the loot they're going to get in this robbery? No. It's because they're afraid and they want to make sure they can win. Their sense of bravado is heightened when they have a confederate with them.

If, in the worst-case scenario, you are confronted by assailants wielding guns, I don't know what you can do beyond adopting the strategy I've already mentioned. Should that fail to drive them off, there is little else you can do except to acquiesce, keep calm, and give them what they want. That Golden Second when one well-planned move might be enough to confuse and frighten an unarmed opponent has now been heightened considerably, because if you fail, you're staring death in the face. Whether you are to live or die depends on how you react and on that unknown quantity—how your attacker is going to react.

Remember that there are a good many armed robbers out there these days who would be perfectly happy to shoot you dead, even if you comply with their demands. Pumping hard on alcohol or drugs, many feel they have nothing to lose and everything to gain by taking your life. It's a difficult spot to be in. I've been there and I have to say there are no tried and true methods for disarming the situation. When that instinctive drive for survival inherent in each of us comes out, I hope the action you take is the right one. But the object of the exercise is to prevent the situation getting to that point.

7. One thing you can do if confronted by a man with a gun is to try to not stare at the weapon, something everyone—even police officers—do when they find themselves at the wrong end of a firearm. Try to look at the person's face. Look for a mole, a facial tic, or a tattoo, so that when that man is brought before you after the robbery, you can look at him and in all certainty say, "That's the man." Go for some detail and key on it. One robber was recently caught and convicted after his latest victim described the Mickey Mouse shoelaces he was wearing.

8. Beware of women offenders, who often use their wits instead of a weapon. Be careful of young women who come up close and run their hands over your clothes, as "Barbara" used to do, talking about how she is going to cook your dinner and whispering sweetly in your ear at the same time her hand is going for your wallet.

9. Remember that anyone can be assaulted, even the youngest, bravest among us. Recently a female officer from my department went to a public housing project in plain clothes to follow up on an investigation she was conducting. She boarded an elevator in the building. She was standing there when the elevator stopped, the door slid back, and two men got on, one taking position to her left, the other to her right. After descending a few floors they put her up against the wall and decided to see what she had in her purse. They took her gun and her money and for one frightening moment taunted her until the elevator stopped again and they got off. Fortunately, they didn't see her badge. When those two guys got on the elevator, she should have gotten off on the next floor or maneuvered into a corner, keeping one hand in her pocket and her head up.

When your fear sensor goes off and you've been bracketed by two men, try using a little psychology. Once they focus on you, try to break their train of thought right away. So you say, "Excuse me, I'm very sick. I just learned I have meningitis," or something else to make them stop and think.

Every day of our lives we either learn or teach something. You get something from that acquired knowledge. You take it with you and, if applied correctly, it can help make you a winner. There's an attitude you have to develop about winning. The battle of winning versus losing can be won or lost in the trenches of your mind.

Chapter 9

END OF WATCH

During a career in which I had been called on countless times to notify a family of a death, my own life was suddenly turned upside down when I received word that my youngest son, Jeffry, had been killed in a car accident.

It was Memorial Day weekend 1990. When the call came, I could not help but think about all the times I had given the awful news, standing on a front porch with my hat in hand while the keening wail of human suffering spread throughout the household.

Only this time it was my turn—someone calling to notify *me*, and I found myself suddenly unable to function. It felt as if a light switch had been flicked off somewhere deep within me, and nothing—not my job, not my wife— could reach in and turn it back on again.

This wasn't the way it was supposed to happen, I told myself over and over again during those first cold days. I was fifty-five years old, a beat cop who smoked far too many cigarettes, and who was paid to carry a gun and take his chances. I'd survived the wilds of Alaska and the Marine Corps, embassy duty in Taiwan, a burning building that collapsed around my ears, and a shootout with a desperate stickup man in a North Beach housing project.

Jeffry was just nineteen, fresh out of high school and bound for the Navy. His life hadn't even started before it was over. It should have been me, I reasoned, not someone so young and with so much yet in store for him. But it *was* him and my mental picture of my son ran around and around in my head until the image became a blur.

In the three years since RAT had been disbanded for the last time, I had left undercover work for a beat patrol back at my old station in the city's Sunset District.

Pounding the pavement up and down Irving Street all day, ticketing cars and directing traffic was not nearly as exciting as having some miscreant pound on me in the Tenderloin, but it was still satisfying, fulfilling work—at least it had been up to the point when I lost my son. With his death I found myself forced into a plane of existence known only to those parents who are called upon to bury children. I began an acute reexamination of my priorities.

Looking back, I would have to say that I probably made the decision to leave police work while the phone was still in my hand and a somber voice informed me in very polite terms that Jeffry had just been killed. I began to wonder if there wasn't something *else* waiting for me out there, something that would fulfill some broader, as yet indefinable, inner need.

Thankfully, the rituals of death kept me busy during those first cataclysmic days. Even though my world had been brought down around me, there were still the calming duties to perform—the notification of distant relatives and the making of funeral arrangements. My fellow officers, big men who could be counted on in life-and-death situations but who could not find the right words to say at times like this one, honored me by providing a police escort for my son to the funeral home, I watched them, bull-necked and tough looking in their dress blues, wearing the scars of a dozen ancient fights and trying to hold back the tears they felt for me. Numb, I watched them pass through the reception line and thought about how unjust it all was as I stood there, shaking their hands and nodding at their mumbled words of condolence.

We buried Jeffry in his Navy uniform, a kindness granted us by the Navy even though my son had yet to serve, and I returned home with my wife Kitty after the funeral. My thoughts were muddled and without form. Soon after, however, it became clear to me that I should leave law enforcement as soon as possible. Only two years shy of a full thirty-year pension, I knew there were other things I had to do in life. My son's death had made that point clear. But since I couldn't participate in anything as worthwhile as RAT anymore—even if the department had had the wherewithal to mount such a program again (which it did not)—I felt that just plain walking a beat every day and being a good police officer would not really be of any benefit either to society or to me.

A lot of time had run its course. I'd worn a gun and a badge for twenty-eight years, and since I'd been in one uniform or another since the age of eighteen, I reasoned that the time was right to take the uniform off and move into civilian life.

It was a big decision, but when the moment came I marveled at how easily I made it. Kitty and I worked out a plan to clear up all my debts so that we could live comfortably on my pension and I set about getting all my affairs in order. From there on it would be a new day, and I hoped I could use the time to its best advantage.

I have learned from grief counselors that people who lose someone dear to them, a son or daughter or close family member, often try to lose themselves—and ultimately the horrible pain they feel—by trying to help others through some positive act. It became more and more apparent as time went by that I could do more good telling the older people of my neighborhood how they could ensure their safety in their later years than I could by remaining in uniform. After so many weeks of walking in the Old Man's shoes, it seemed a logical extension of my abilities.

Public speaking had always been sort of fun for me, a chance to loosen the tie and talk to people about what policemen were about and, more importantly, ways they could protect themselves. On one occasion while I was still attached to the Canine Unit, I had been dispatched to a local school with my second dog, Judge, to talk to a group of about seven hundred older people who were having some crime problems in their neighborhood.

It was a very informal thing (though I was still in uniform) and I let Judge off his leash so he could paddle out into the audience and show them he wasn't trained to attack on sight. He charmed the socks off these old people—some slipping him their pieces of cake when I wasn't looking, and I had one sick dog on my hands afterwards. But all in all it was a very pleasant evening.

But this group wanted answers. So I told them how we often hear of people who regret having been too careless or too trusting but that we almost never hear of anyone who regrets being too cautious. We talked about being properly apprehensive without being paranoid and they started to loosen up and actually talk back to me.

We chatted for some time about various tricks and methods for survival on the street. Then I told them about the Golden Second and how to make the most of it and offered a little advice about what to look for when they were outside and walking to the local market. Since we were talking frankly, I told them that for the most part, if they were ever unlucky enough to find themselves victimized, at least for those first few vital seconds *they were on their own.* And I watched the consternation spread through the audience like ripples across a pond.

"That's right, ladies and gentlemen," I said before the murmur had died away. "Let's face up to reality. Our cities no longer have the number of police officers they once did. Crime is up and budgets have been slashed so low some departments are using automated telephone response systems to handle incoming calls. Can you imagine it? Press One if you're being robbed... Press Two if your attacker has a gun... Stay on the line if you are injured and an attendant will get to you as quickly as possible." They were chuckling at the premise, but nervously, because some of them knew it was true.

"People are not self-sufficient anymore. We have been trained to believe that someone will *always* be coming to our rescue. And while that is true in most cases, it is not *always* the case. Today, people think all they have to do is call a magic number and they will be saved. But the average response time to an emergency call these days is just over five minutes—that's if you are able to make it to a phone. A lot can happen in those five minutes, with most crimes taking only seconds to carry out."

An old gentleman who had to be in his eighties stood up, and with a perplexed look on his face asked what they, as old and infirm as they were, could be expected to do. As usual, I gave it to them straight.

"Get involved in your community," I said. "Don't shut yourself off behind closed doors because you can't be bothered with people anymore. If you're in trouble one day, a friend living next door to you is going to come running a lot faster than some disembodied voice on the telephone. Find yourself a companion through some community house or sewing center or YMCA and make it a practice to keep in touch with them. Ask these people to go shopping with you. You're much less likely to be attacked walking with a friend than you would be if you were alone. Why put yourself in jeopardy?

"If you go out on a regular basis, set up a schedule with your friend so that you never go alone. Just say, I'll go out with you every Tuesday, Thursday, and Saturday if you'll go with me every Monday, Wednesday and Friday. Then the two of you—more if you can work it out—can go to church together Sunday. That way you never lose your awareness because there's always another set of eyes there. Then, the prospective mugger watching you come down the street thinks, this old lady (or this old man) is looking pretty good but she's got a friend with her who may or may not come to her aid so, I'll wait and try to trap someone who's alone. That's when you've won."

They seemed to like that. A feisty little cheer went up.

"Unfortunately," I went on. "We as a society have gotten to the point where we've lost our intuitiveness, our sense of self-sufficiency. We've become too comfortable. Where are the people who had the gumption to hook up six oxen to a wagon and walk with them from St. Louis to California? Those were the days when the prevailing attitude was 'Kill your own snakes.' But now, modern technology has overwhelmed that spirit. And when you live in a dream world and you've been lulled into thinking that everything is utopian, that's when it's likely you'll get a reality check you may not be able to live through."

There was a stunned silence and, for a moment, I thought I had gone too far, painted too dismal a picture, but then a smattering of applause started out in the middle of the audience and spread until all these wonderful old people were clapping and yelling.

"You know," I said then, waiting for them to calm down. "I feel that I have to tell you all something. I have to tell you that I am deeply envious of you. You could not have picked a better time to have lived than during the years you have been on this earth. You're part of the generation that saw the birth of the electric light, airplanes, jet power, and then manned spaceflight to the moon. You've seen civilization at its best and at its worst. And while you may think that things have gone to hell in a handbasket and while you may feel threatened by a new generation, just remember there are some among that new generation who would gladly pay to have seen the things you people have seen in your lifetimes."

It was an off-the-cuff statement but it brought the house down. And I meant every word of it.

In the days and weeks which followed Jeffry's funeral I gave many similar talks, usually to small groups or to civic organizations eager for practical advice about survival in today's society, with its soaring crime rate.

These talks have always been enjoyable experiences for me. I enjoy the give and take and the thought that perhaps I had helped someone that afternoon. But at the same time I frequently catch myself looking back on my life, appraising its successes and inwardly bemoaning its many failures.

A series of images, running through my mind with varying degrees of clarity and at different speeds, comes back to me again and again. There are pleasant images of Grandma Alice sending me off to buy some bread, of the pet eagle I kept as a young Marine in Alaska, and of my first years as a police officer.

There were also a fair share of not-so-pleasant images, chief among them the moment when I was called upon to take the life of a young man who raised his gun to shoot me in the dirty stairwell of a graffiti-scarred housing project, firing at me just as I fired at him.

This image proved more lasting than most: the exact moment, when in a burst of noise and orange muzzle flash, I traded shots with a man not much older than my son Jeffry. His name was Juan B. Moore. He was twenty-two when we met that night, guns drawn in the heart of the Bay Street housing project. And although he had chosen a very different life's path than that of my son he, too, ended up dying far too young.

I know now that it was probably because they were both so young when they died that their images somehow became intertwined in my mind—the two of them haunting me still.

The events of that cool, crystal-clear night of September 25, 1967, are as clear to me now as the night they happened. I was assigned to a Canine Unit, riding in Patrol Car Three with my dog Bourbon. We'd just gone back into service after a meal period when Officer Troy Dangerfield's voice came over the police radio, crackling with nervous excitement.

It was 4:20 a.m., well beyond the witching hour when a policeman normally expects to find trouble somewhere along his watch. But Dangerfield and his partner, George Labrash, had been responding to a call to an armed robbery at the Travelodge at Fisherman's Wharf when they encountered a speeding car running west on Bay Street with its lights turned out. It passed them at a high rate of speed, going in the opposite direction. George and Troy made a U-turn and pulled up behind the car, activating their red lights in an attempt to stop it. As they approached Columbus, the vehicle suddenly angled across the opposing lanes, drove between parked cars, and crashed to a stop on the sidewalk.

Troy and George pulled up behind the wreck, left their car, and approached the suspect vehicle as it sat there, hissing and clicking from its high-speed run. Without warning, the driver's-side door suddenly flew open and a man leapt out, dropped to one knee, and fired his revolver at them, the bullets going wide but leaving two web-like holes in the glass window of a drive-in across the street. While both Troy and George sought to recover their composure and make the call for help, the driver darted from the car into the dark confines of a public housing project across Bay Street.

"This man is shooting at us, Headquarters," George said, very deliberately, into his car radio. "This man is shooting at us." Anyone with so little to lose he was willing to fire on armed police officers spelled trouble for those called on to subdue him. But everyone in the area, me included, converged on the location Labrash gave over his radio.

It was a large complex, easy to get lost in. Several stories high and built around two interior courtyards, the project was ringed by chest-high, open balconies—any one of which would have provided a gunman the perfect perch for shooting a pursuer below. The suspect had run into the westernmost square and was somewhere in the interior courtyard when eight police cars pulled up in an attempt to contain him.

A sergeant used a bullhorn to hail the occupants of the building: "Remain in your apartments and turn out your lights," he called out. Then the night was filled with the sound of additional gunshots as Moore encountered and exchanged fire with four different police officers at less than 10 yards range, everyone missing in the confusion of the firefight. Unhurt and reloading as he ran, Moore was loose in the project again, running along the darkened balconies in a frantic attempt to break out of the cordon of police officers rapidly closing in around him.

I arrived at Bay and Mason Streets at about that time, parking quietly at the easternmost section at the end of the housing unit. It was an odd scene, nothing like that normally portrayed in the movies. There were no sirens, no lights, no squealing brakes—just car after car sliding quietly into the area with their lights out, and officers jumping out to take up positions around the project—a nocturnal ballet of silence and stealth.

Bourbon, as usual, had picked up the excited tone of the voices on the police radio and was prancing madly in the back of my patrol car when we arrived. I elected not to take him along, much as I would have liked to, because the thought of an excited ninety-five-pound police dog running around amongst all the other officers and perhaps hundreds of residents who might be called out of their apartments at any moment was untenable.

Every officer I encountered on my way into the interior courtyard of the easternmost complex seemed unnaturally quiet, every man filled with a strange sense of foreboding. Chasing an armed suspect through a dark and crowded housing structure is the realization of every cop's worst nightmare.

Then I ran into Ray West and Charlie Brewster, two old friends of mine who were partners working out of Central Station at the time. Ray went west to check the southernmost area of the project while Charlie and I began a methodical search under and around the many cars parked in the structure's main lot.

The silence was deafening as we searched. Just the scraping of our shoes as we crabbed along carefully watching each other's back. Our leather belts creaked, our equipment got heavier by the second. Each of us fully expected to run into a lethal fusillade of gunfire at any moment.

As all this was going on, someone had the presence of mind to run the license plate numbers on the car Moore had abandoned. We learned then that it had been reported stolen and fit the description of one used in a hotel robbery hours earlier in Daly City, during which a lone gunman had made off with about forty dollars.

Apparently not satisfied with the haul in that robbery, the occupant of the car had then driven to the North Beach area of San Francisco and had once again used a gun to rob two men in the lobby of the Travelodge-at-the-Wharf at Beach and Powell Streets. This time, however, he had netted $641.

But his luck ran out on him when Dangerfield and Labrash spotted his car trying to leave the scene.

The additional information helped. For the first time that night the officers at the scene knew more or less what sort of person they were dealing with. It was up to us to track down and capture an armed man who had stolen a car, robbed two businesses at gunpoint, and fired his weapon at at least six policemen at close range and who was now lurking somewhere deep in the heart of a large, blacked-out housing project. It has often been said that police work is comprised of long hours of boredom interjected with moments of sheer terror, and this night surely qualified.

It was pitch black with only the street lamps to cast even darker shadows on all that we saw. Monsters, gargoyles, and armed robbers seemed to loom from every unknown shape and from under every parked car.

Since Charlie and I were both former Marines, we realized we had to take the high ground if we were to be successful that night. Charlie said, "Bill, get up on the third floor interior balcony and keep an eye on the courtyard while I check out these cars."

Rather than have a guy look under a car and take a bullet in the face from a gunman hiding there, we worked it out that I would get higher and use my angle to cover Charlie while he peered under the parked cars from a safer distance away. But as I made the third floor landing, I saw a dark shape on the balcony just above Charlie, a mere silhouette of a man running with a gun in his hand. The first thing I remember thinking was, what's he doing over here? because he had been last seen running into the other building two blocks away.

"Charlie," I yelled. "He's right above you! He's right above you and opposite me!" Charlie stepped back under the protective cover of the landing to stop the suspect from firing down at him while I measured my chances for a successful shot and eventually gave it up. Even though the suspect was only one hundred feet away and directly across the interior courtyard from me, I knew I had no shot at him at all. He was moving fast, crouched down and running past apartment doors which opened out onto the landing. I was armed with a .357 Magnum revolver. To fire at the man from that range and miss would have endangered the lives of any residents unlucky enough to be on the other side of the wall.

I was yelling and pointing. We didn't have the portable radios officers are blessed with today, and Charlie yelled back that he was coming up. He sprinted to the Bay Street staircase and started taking the stairs two at a time but went too high, climbing past the third floor and heading straight for the roof. In the meantime the bad guy had run back underneath him and out onto an outer balcony overlooking Bay Street, firing at a motorcycle officer who was just pulling up, the shot going wide and cracking into a telephone pole on a level with the officer's head.

Although I couldn't see what was happening, I heard the shot and wondered if our man had just gotten Charlie. I was running in their direction when a dark shape came around the corner from the direction of Bay Street and headed straight for me. I couldn't believe it. The only cop around who is yelling and announcing his presence and the bad guy makes a beeline straight for him—for *me*.

It was really dark on that landing, no lights at all. I heard the suspect's footsteps and presumed he was going to go up another level, up to where Brewster was searching for him. I didn't want that so I yelled to him, "Hold it, police!" I had my gun drawn and was ready to fire and, as it turned out, so was he.

We ended up firing simultaneously. I saw the orange light of his muzzle flash and my training kicked in, telling me that if I had lived to see that, the man's bullet was already past me.

He was not as lucky. My bullet pierced his face, just under the right eye, and he went down solidly into the staircase. I approached him, flashlight in my left hand and gun in my right. It was completely, totally dark. He lay crumpled on the bottom stairs. As I watched, his body appeared to turn and when his gun started to come up again, I fired twice more at him until he was still.

My ears were ringing. The report of two guns going off in the enclosed space of a concrete stairwell had been like a bomb detonating just inches away. I have problems with the hearing in my left ear to this day as a result. When the coroner rolled him over I looked hard at this man I had just killed. Although I had no recollection of the incident, a check of his lengthy police record showed that I had arrested him a year earlier for auto theft and that he had been given five years' probation for that offense.

Moore's gun was empty when the coroner turned him over and found it underneath him. He had fired his last shot at me. After everyone had settled down enough for us to think things through, we deduced that in the course of the gunfight Moore had fired a total of eighteen shots at police officers. The whole action had taken twenty-five minutes, a veritable battle when compared to the brief flurries of violence police officers usually experience.

I still remember looking down at Juan B. Moore as he lay there on the stairwell, the bond between two human beings forced by fate to confront each other in combat already beginning to develop. A sergeant from Northern Station came up to me, saw the darkening look on my face, and said, "Don't let this bother you. Just look down and imagine a police officer lying there. One of your friends. That's how these things usually end up. In this case the good guy won and the bad guy lost."

I remember that very clearly, standing there with my ears ringing, looking down at this man—*my* man now because I had taken his life.

Three weeks later I met Moore's mother at the coroner's inquest. I wondered how she would react to me, the policeman who had killed her boy. But she came up to me with a soft light in her eyes and touched me briefly on my sleeve.

"You know," she said. "It's a shame that two men have to confront each other like that, with guns on some balcony in the middle of the night, one on the side of good and one on the side of bad."

A parent's wisdom. I resisted the embittered urge I had to tell her that, if a judge had put her boy in jail for a year instead of granting him probation, he might not have graduated to armed robbery. If he had been put in jail after I arrested him the first time, I might not have had to be the one to take his life the second time around. But she seemed satisfied just to make contact and I, too, took comfort in the meeting. I read a world of understanding in her eyes. Eventually she walked away, knowing I had been left with a ghost that would come back to haunt me the rest of my life.

Those thoughts were very much on my mind when I submitted my resignation in January of 1991. There was very little ceremony at the time, no fuss. Some handshakes and up to the fifth floor of the Hall of Justice for a picture of me shaking hands with the chief of police. The entire procedure had sort of a muted, other-worldly quality to it and, except for some very personal and private moments with a small cadre of old friends—some of whom were actually angry I was leaving—I remember hoping it would end quickly.

Police reporters for the two major San Francisco papers each did a story on my retirement, as did a couple of the Bay Area television stations. It was nice to be remembered at all, but it was even nicer a few weeks later when a letter from someone who had seen one of the stories was forwarded to my home by a colleague at the Hall of Justice. It turned out the letter was from a young woman who had written me in 1987 when RAT was broken up for the last time. She wrote:

"Recently my mother sent me an article stating that you had retired after many years on the force. The last time I wrote, it was because you said that you hadn't received one letter of thanks. My reason for writing now is to thank you once again and to share a story with you that makes me think of the work you've done each time I read it:

"A man was walking along the beach during the late morning. The sun's rays were beating down, scorching everything they touched. Thousands of starfish were strewn along the sand, having been washed ashore by the tide earlier that morning. As the man walked, he bent down and picked up each starfish he came across, throwing it back into the ocean and saving it from the deadly sun. Soon he approached another man who asked him what he was doing. 'I'm saving this starfish from the harsh sun... the tide will never come in soon enough to wash them back out to sea and if I just let them lie here, they will die,' replied the man. 'Well, what does it really matter?' asked the other man. 'There are thousands of starfish on this beach... there's no way you can save them all!' But the first man just picked up another starfish, looked out to sea and said, 'It matters... to this one.'

"Thank you, Mr. Langlois. We need a lot more people like you in the world. Have a very peaceful retirement and enjoy your time away. You deserve it!"

That one letter helped remove any doubts I may have had about retiring. I had wondered if I would miss the fellowship that comes with being a policeman, of knowing that if I called for help at a given time on a given night, every officer within the sound of my voice would break down walls to reach me.

But I was luckier than most. Living only three hundred feet away from my usual beat on Irving Street, nothing changed for me at all. After I retired I saw the same people, went to the same stores. I just wasn't their neighborhood cop anymore. All the older people that I used to see at a local bakery for a cup of coffee each afternoon are still there. In fact, after I retired I made our afternoon meetings a more formal affair dubbing them the "Fourteen Hundred Club,"—fourteen hundred being military time for 2:00 p.m.—and we began to look forward to these regular afternoon meetings where we could continue to talk to each other and stay involved with each others' lives.

Older people are a lot of fun to talk to because they've seen so much more than most of us. I've learned a lot listening to members of the Fourteen Hundred Club talk about their past. Oddly enough, everybody is quite diligent about keeping that 2:00 p.m. appointment. The oldest of the gals is ninety-six. She takes me to a different century and provides me with an unusual perspective when she talks. She is, in fact, a walking history book. How many people get a chance to talk to someone who is ninety-six years old and is still lucid, can remember all that has happened to her in the course of those many years? Elders give you a sense of what your own life might be like.

Unlike a lot of other police officers I have known, I had no great expectations about my life when I finally left the department. In my case, I was able to depart with a solid record of achievement, a fair share of medals and commendations, and the knowledge that, in my career, I had done my job to the best of my ability, and I had survived.

During my early years as a police officer, one of my greatest heroes had been a wizened old sergeant named Richard Reed. In 1963, while I wallowed in an ocean of wonderment and rookie confusion, Dick took me aside and handed me a pearl of his hard-earned wisdom. I heeded it during my twenty-eight years of law enforcement.

With that tough-but-fair manner of his, Dick told me, "Never report off, even if it makes you a little late, without first doing something positive for a citizen." That was it—an extension of what I had already sworn to do, I suppose, but coming from a man the caliber of Dick Reed, this pearl suddenly took on a new dimension.

His admonition has stayed with me—more and more as the mirror continues to confirm what I already know: that I am headed straight for the Old Man's shoes and, this time around, there will be no need for makeup.

Do something *positive*. The more I think about it, the more I appreciate the beauty in that simple wisdom. I have been fortunate—probably more fortunate than I deserved. I managed to cheat death literally dozens of times. Working with RAT gave me an ability to project ahead to what I could expect later in my life, and it was interesting for me to walk for awhile in the Old Man's shoes.

I learned that life is tough if you are older, maybe even deadly. I also learned that older people can get away with a lot of things a younger person cannot. When I used to walk out into traffic, smacking cars with my cane as a crotchety old person would, when they came too close, I knew the Old Man could get away with it, whereas a forty-year-old probably would have ended up getting punched out in the middle of the intersection.

Older people can put their sweaters on inside out and misalign the buttons and no one seems to think anything about it. In that sense being old was fun, slipping into that persona for a few hours each day.

A lot of older people I know say if you can hold up one hand and have the same number of friends as fingers, then you are a lucky man. It's true. Many of my friends are civilians, not associated with police work, and I find that has been good for me. Seeing the things a police officer sees day in and day out can tend to make you reclusive and narrow. I don't feel I am that way and I don't want to be. I still like people and I don't have to surround myself with police officers to feel comfortable.

I've heard older people say you start out life with a narrow waist and a broad mind and that when you hit fifty they exchange places. There is truth to that, too. But you beat that by being self-sufficient and going on with your life.

There are a few tricks to learn but no real magic to them. It's an attitude predicated on the value of common sense. I had to laugh when one of the television stations, when airing a piece on my retirement, brought up my past work with the RAT units and went on to call me one of the department's greatest undercover officers. That really got me. Being a former Marine, I remember reading something Admiral William F. "Bull" Halsey told one of his junior officers when the younger officer referred to his admiral as a "great man."

"There are no great men," Halsey said gently. "There are only great challenges which ordinary men are forced by circumstance to meet."

And so it was when it came to our work with RAT. The unit was faced with a great challenge and made a small contribution against evil. We were good, but we were also lucky, taking our lumps but scoring heavily against those of far less noble intentions.

Possibly unrealized by our society is the fact that our police officers are the most powerful of our citizens. We have literally given them the power of life and death, and they are not Teflon-coated robots. During a tour of duty, an officer may be called upon to disregard some mundane task and in just seconds be forced by circumstance to take away someone's liberty or even their life. No other citizen, not even our President, is obliged to make those decisions in that brief time lapse.

This weighty responsibility should ensure, therefore, that our society have the best candidates for their police force that they can afford. We should not consider, even for a minute, the lowering of standards in the selection process. Being a police officer is not just a job, it is a vocation, and if anyone entering into the profession has a different attitude than that, perhaps they shouldn't aspire to be a police officer in the first place.

Since my retirement I have been asked countless times what I regarded as the high point of my twenty-eight years in law enforcement. In all honesty I would be hard pressed to come up with just one. There was the fellowship and camaraderie that can only be shared by people whose very lives depend on one another, the incredible high which comes after you emerge from some particularly dangerous episode and are able to tell about it.

I remember the look of sheer joy on the face of an

eighty-two-year-old woman I managed to retrieve from a burning building an instant before the structure began to collapse around us; the sight of my backup officers dancing around me in celebration of my two-hundredth hit as a decoy; and the look of pride in my father's eyes when he joined me on stage as I received my award as the Veterans of Foreign Wars National Law Enforcement Officer of the Year.

High points all, each indelibly etched in my memory. Looking back, I view my career as one of great contrasts, ranging from the exhilaration of saving a human life to the low I felt after taking one. But I got the most satisfaction out of helping old people. Knowing that in a way I had helped prevent countless injuries and possible death by offering myself up to those who prey on the elderly filled me with a deep sense of accomplishment and gratitude unequaled during my time in uniform. Seeing that one bad guy slap himself on the forehead in self-chastisement after I performed my Old Man act for a skeptical jury, hearing the handcuffs go on a man I know in my heart was responsible for the murder of at least one old woman—that's when the satisfaction was complete and I knew I had done my job.

But now, as I leave police work behind and settle into life as a genuinely retired gentleman, I sometimes look at the faded piece of pink paper I took from a fortune cookie in 1986 and smile at the now familiar message: "Among the lucky, you are the chosen one."

So I was, and so I am.

ACKNOWLEDGMENTS

SENIORS

Plaudits to our senior citizens, who are this nation's "talking history books," our most valuable living resource—those who have contributed so much to our country and who are now mostly treated as cast-offs because of their seniority. Such narrow-mindedness also casts away their wisdom, forgetting that the youthful are destined to fill their depleted ranks, and thus suffer from the same attitude. Truly, what goes around comes around.

We are all part of the human family and we should maintain respect for life and for those of us who have lived it longest. Seniors deserve our gratitude and security, for where would we be without them?

We should pray for them rather than prey upon them.

U.S.M.C.

General Randall M. Victory [retired]
Colonel Charles W. McCoy [retired]

Both extraordinary Marine commissioned officers and gentlemen for whom I personally worked. How could a young sergeant not be inspired by a general named Victory and a colonel who was the real McCoy?

N.Y.P.D. - N.Y. TRANSIT POLICE

I would like to publicly thank the New York Police Department and the New York Transit Police for sharing, with Captain Charles Beene, the decoy tactics they developed in the late seventies. Those tactics were the foundation for the 1977/78 Street Crime Units of the San Francisco Police Department, whose members have not forgotten the cooperation extended by the city of New York.

OTHERS

Marvin E. Cadoza, attorney, former police commissioner, SFPD, since 1972—a mentor and a gentleman to emulate.

Gary R. "Bud" Smith, U.S. Air Force veteran, Vietnam war hero, fellow Civil War student—over twenty years a faithful friend, no more, no less.

Elaine Herscher, *San Francisco Chronicle* reporter, a diligent and compassionate newsperson—owed much that cannot be repaid.

Malcolm Glover, *San Francisco Examiner* reporter, known on the police beat for over twenty-five years—"Scoop" gave everyone a fair shake.

Jack M. Riordan, attorney, friend of eight years—tutored me on how to remain focused, thoughtful, and kept me from being hypocritical.

Alvin Nachman, former Baltimore City Police Officer, Federal sky marshal and spook—a most reliable friend who reeks of common sense. In this vehicle called life he never steered me wrong.

THE STING

Sergeant Eric Olsen, #1128, SFPD
Officer Robert Blazer, #58, Daly City Police Department
My gratitude for their cleverness and steadfastness and for tolerating thirteen months of my bad jokes daily while we shared the tedious operations of this undercover assignment.

SAN FRANCISCO POLICE DEPARTMENT

Fond memories and gratitude to all members, particularly those sections where I served—The Bureau of Identification, the Dog Patrol Unit [fourteen years], the Tactical Squad, Bomb Squad, [E.O.D. Unit], the Crime Specific Task Force, the Street Crime Unit, the Robbery and Fencing details, the Southern and Taraval Police Stations.

STREET CRIME UNIT: 3 TOM 12 B [1977]

Officer Edward L. St. Andre, #60
Officer Joseph W. Carlin, #1674
Officer James McKeever, #857
Faithful and reliable as my backups for over a year, their teamwork was constantly exhibited by their courage, conviction, and determination—good coppers.

FORMER PARTNERS SFPD

Sergeant Donald W. Brewer, #1486, retired
Nineteenth century man true to his word, honor, and conviction—Mr. Reliable, a friend.
Sergeant Gene Powers, #588
One of only two officers who rode with Dog Unit personnel who was not a dog handler—great sense of humor, moral convictions, a friend still.
Officer George Grant, #1285
Well, educated, always gave good advice, asked meaningful questions, and sought viable answers—has a bad back but a good soul.

THE ROBBERY ABATEMENT TEAMS [RAT] 1986–87

Captain Charles F. Beene, #165, retired, "CAPT. RAT"—wife, LeAnne

A commander who never expected actions or sacrifices from his personnel that he himself would not be willing to make—always had a genuine non-biased regard for the law.

Captain John Brunner, #820, retired, "SUPER RAT"—wife, Lesley

A friend of three decades—had a penchant for delectable nastiness, great expectations for, and wholehearted belief in, the RAT Units, and an inspiring leader of Robbery Detail.

Captain Fred Lau, #1967, now Deputy Chief, "CAPT. RAT" II

Always had great confidence in his officers and was a constant wall of support.

Inspector Thomas Vigo, #552, "OFFICE RAT"

Diligently cared for the records of the miscreants, kept the paperwork flowing.

"RAT" STREET PERSONNEL

I will state that money alone could not have purchased better officers than those I worked with in the SFPD with the 1986–87 Robbery Abatement Teams as the victim/officer. They were the best.

Their tenacity, innovative courage, and devotion to our cause demonstrated the highest degree of professionalism. It was my privilege and honor to have placed my life in their very capable hands. They have my unrelenting gratitude and my affection.

Inspector James Bergstrom, #2007, "KING RAT" III

Enjoyed his time out in the slime and grime helping to remove some of society's tumors from our streets.

Inspector Anthony Camilleri, #1081, "OFFICE RAT" II

Did the paperwork, but couldn't resist the temptation to see "the crime in progress."

Sergeant Robert B. McEachern, #83, "KING RAT"

A good leader who thought we were all "nuts"—could never determine why he was assigned to us, not realizing that he really belonged.

Sergeant Charles E. Brewster, #1714 "KING RAT" II

Spent most of his career trying to prove his elevator did go to the top floor—not understood that he was just another former marine—a good member of the team.

OFFICERS

Robert Aitchison, #1382, "VAN RAT"
James L. Batchelor, #1219, "CLOSET RAT" II
John R. Chesnut, #1507, "CLOSET RAT" III
Brian M. D'arcy, #1745, "HALL RAT"
Leanna M. Dawydiak, #626, "MINNIE RAT"
Edward B. Dullea, #669, "CLOSET RAT"
Jeremiah Morgan, #668, "LOBBY RAT"
Gregory J. Randolph, #1734, "STREET RAT WEST"
Reno L. Rapagnani, #1641, "ROOM RAT"
Tony Rockett, #2081, "CURB RAT"
Edward L. St. Andre, #60, "SWAMP RAT"
Craig A. Woods, #685, "STREET RAT WEST"

DISTRICT ATTORNEY INVESTIGATORS

Karen Hibbit, #7022, "HOOKER RAT"
Ron Leon, #7024, "POCKET RAT"
Vanetta Pollett, #7008, "PHOTO RAT"
Lee Tyler, #7051, "CAB RAT"

FRATERNAL

My gratitude to the Fraternity and Brotherhood of my Lodge 169, F & AM, and the San Francisco Bodies, A. & A.S.R. for the southern jurisdiction of the United States, for teaching me pride of patriotism, love of flag and country, respect for law and order, loyalty to the people, citizen control, civil and religious liberty as set forth in our Constitution and Bill of Rights.

For reminding me to remain kindly in my relations with fellow citizens, to be community-minded, public-spirited, charitable, and fair in my behavior and dedication, while remembering the ideals of Freemasonry.

To the American Legion, Post 456. The Veterans of Foreign Wars, the Company of Military Historians, the San Francisco Veteran Police Officers Association—my thanks for their support, that I might remain strong in will, to try and have high standards in life while endeavoring to leave something behind so others might benefit.

Respectfully,

Bill Langlois

— Officer William D. "Bill" Langlois, #1870
San Francisco Police Department, Retired Victim/Officer

ABOUT THE AUTHORS

*O*fficer William D. Langlois (Ret'd.), San Francisco's most honored police officer, has waged an unprecedented undercover war on those who prey on the city's elderly. After his retirement from the department in January 1991, he has continued his efforts on behalf of seniors across the country. Officer Langlois was awarded the San Francisco Police Department's Gold Medal of Valor. He also holds six silver medals and two bronze, as well as the National Veterans of Foreign Wars Award for National Law Enforcement Officer of the Year.

*J*ohn O'Connor has worked as a reporter for the *San Francisco Examiner* for the past eight years, five of those on the police beat. A second-generation San Franciscan, he worked as a longshoreman and fueled fishing boats in Alaska to pay for college, graduating with a degree in journalism from the University of California at Chico. He is a Pulitzer Prize and George Polk Prize nominee, and has received several awards for writing.